Tango Charlie

The Cold War Adventures of
U.S. Navy Submarine Spook
and
Singer–Songwriter

Tommy Cox

TANGO CHARLIE

The Cold War Adventures of
U.S. Navy Submarine Spook
and
Singer–Songwriter

Tommy Cox

A History of Submarine Music Annotated

(Includes Song Lyrics)

**"We drank their water, ate their food, and breathed their air –
But we were never there."**

Riverdale Books
Riverdale, Georgia

Tango Charlie

Riverdale Books

is an imprint of

Riverdale Electronic Books
P.O. Box 962085
Riverdale, Georgia 30296

ISBN-13: 978-1-932606-16-4
ISBN-10: 1-932606-16-5

Library of Congress Control Number: 2006933398

Printed in the United States of America

TABLE OF CONTENTS

Introductions   vii

Acknowledgements   xii

Foreword   xv

Monologue   1

1.   Scorpion   39
2.   Big Black Submarine   45
3.   Gitmo Blues   49
4.   Torpedo in the Water   54
5.   Ballad of Whitey Mack   57
6.   The Sacrifice   62
7.   Boomer Patrol   65
8.   Diesel Boats Forever   68
9.   Long Separation   73
10.   Seawolf   76
11.   Freedom Patrol   83
12.   Sailor's Prayer   88
13.   Bring the Nautilus Home   91
14.   Kursk   95
15.   Blind Man's Bluff   100
16.   Still on Patrol   103
17.   Paybacks are Hell   107
18.   Mighty Mine Dodgers   111
19.   Slade Cutter   118
20.   Frenchie   125
21.   Paybacks   133
22.   The Dives We've Known   140
23.   Run Silent, Run Deep   146
24.   Navy SEALs   150
25.   Tango Charlie   158
    Epilogue   161
    Appendix A   167

Dedication

This book is respectfully dedicated to all qualified submariners, past, present, and future, to the Submarine Veterans of World War Two, and to the United States Submarine Veterans, Inc. Thank you for your service. May all your dives and surfaces come out even. It's been an honor. — Tommy Cox

Introduction
by Bobby Reed

It has been said that a picture is worth a thousand words. In Tommy Cox's case, his songs paint images into memory. These memories evoke our emotions and serve to mark a transition of time honoring our heroes.

But this book is not so much about song as getting to know the man whose character chiseled words into music we've grown to know and love. His tunes capture the inner feelings of the man behind the pen. We slowly get to know that we are not just learning about a submariner but a man with deep experience, thoughtfulness, and sensitivity.

The fabric of Tommy's character synthesizes his competitive spirit, confidence, warrior attributes, caring nature, and intellect. It is the perfect marinade of ingredients for a submarine singer/songwriter. Through these passages we learn the rationale for writing these works and the impact they had upon him. Strangely enough, we feel he is talking to and about us. We are with him—all the way.

Mark Twain once wrote – "Write what you know about." Well, submarines are something Tommy Cox knows about. Join us as we *Take Her Deep* and enter the inner world of the man, the legend, and his music.

Bobby Reed

Introduction
by Steve Corneliussen

Sometimes in life, we find ourselves in the right place at the right time. Many times this is not by our own design. I think everybody who ever served in any branch of the military had, at some point, the same emotions Tommy Cox had when he penned the words "Whatever put me in this circumstance?" in his song "Torpedo in the Water."

So, it came to pass that I, by random chance, found myself in a scrappy little bar, carved into the bank of the Thames River in Groton, CT, listening to the live performances of one George Thomas Cox.

Back in 1981, I was stationed aboard the Submarine Tender U.S.S. *Fulton* (AS-11) at State Pier in New London. One Saturday night, a shipmate of mine, "Red," who was a "recovering alcoholic," asked me to go with him across the river to Groton to some bar, called Norm's Lounge, to hear some singer named Tommy Cox. Red explained to me that even though he couldn't drink, he really wanted to go to this bar and hear Tommy. My "mission" for the night was to keep Red from drinking. When he explained that Tommy sang songs about submarines... well... this was something I just had to hear. It was going to be either really good or really bad. But everybody had told Red that Tommy was great, so what the heck?

Red and I trekked across the rickety little train bridge, across the Thames River to the Groton side to Norm's Lounge. We found a seat and ordered a couple Cokes. Out of courtesy, I joined Red on the no alcohol program.

Back in 1981, the crowd at Norm's was an odd mix of sailors, bikers, Electric Boat shipyard workers, aging hippies, and women who hung around with the aforementioned. Overall, a rough crowd with lots of tattoos!

It didn't really catch our attention when some guy went to the stage and started fiddling around with the equipment. It caught us by surprise when he quietly picked up his guitar and turned to face the audience. Suddenly, out of nowhere, came the diving klaxon:

"Aaaaah oogah!"

"Aaaaah oogah!"

"Dive!"

"Dive!"

Then Tommy rolled into his signature song, "Big Black Submarine," with his booming voice, flawless guitar picking, a passion that nobody could argue with and the unmistakable steely-eyed stare of a veteran submariner.

Hey, this guy is serious.

By the end of that first song, *Big Black Submarine*, Tommy had won a special place in my heart, with his raw musical talent, great voice, and uncanny instincts with the audience. Tommy could have, like most local singers do, played the usual list of other people's songs. But here was Tommy, singing his own songs. Songs about something he had true passion for, the Submarine Service.

And, he played all night.

His own songs!

As the night passed, the crowd got bigger and louder! By the end of the night Tommy had all but blown the roof off of ole Norm's Lounge. Tommy was rocking!

What in the world was *this* guy doing here, in some "dive" singing songs about, of all things, submarines? Who was this Tommy Cox character? (I still don't have a clue.)

And, so it went week after week. Every week, the crowd got bigger. Tommy rocked the doors off Norm's Lounge on Friday and Saturday nights, while the bar staff nervously kept count of the crowd, half of which was outside, standing outside in the cold, rocking along with Tommy. His show included many audience participation songs that simply do not translate into recordings. There was one song, *Tugboat Annie*, which involved the audience making a chain and doing some silly dance around and around the bar. We would even go outside the bar and around the building while Tommy rocked on.

Keep in mind, Tommy was playing his antiterrorist song, *Paybacks are Hell*, just down the street from a major military base, while the United States was still in shock over the Iran Hostage Crisis.

Tommy would also belt out *Bring the Nautilus Home to Groton* to a screaming hometown audience in the middle of Groton's efforts to actually bring the U.S.S. *Nautilus* home to Groton, where she was built.

And there was always that group in the crowd, with a few gray hairs, who would shout the words to *Diesel Boats Forever.*

Tommy could instantly inject the seriousness of submarine life with his songs *Scorpion,* or *Sailor's Prayer.*

And, Tommy could make 'em cry with (one of the few songs he would sing that was not his) *Ghost Riders in the Sky.* There wasn't a dry eye in the house by the end of *Ghost Riders.* (It would be 25 years before I found out why he sang that one.)

Tommy was the master of his audience.

No doubt about it, Tommy's natural habitat is a dim spotlight in a smoky bar, watching his audience, making his little adjustments with rhythm and style to keep the audience involved, and singing about his beloved submarines.

Even the aging hippies, a mostly antiwar group, found themselves singing along with lines like "God, Love and Country, The Freedom Patrol." One by one, Tommy won them over, every weekend. By end of the night, we were always one big happy family of Tommy Cox fans. Me and all those people with tattoos!

And, so every Saturday night, I would venture across that train bridge, and become a face in the crowd, while developing a genuine admiration and respect for Tommy Cox and his music.

I will always consider it my good fortune, in the randomness of life, to have been in the right place at the right time to experience Tommy's incredible live performances, on the banks of the Thames River, down the road from the Submarine Base, upriver from Electric Boat, in a smoky little place called Norm's Lounge.

Thank you, Tommy.

Thank you, Red.

Steve Corneliussen,
IC2, U.S.S. *Fulton* (AS-11)

Introduction
by Mike Hemming

"Play submarine music, Grand Dad," from both my grandkids, a boy of then 6, and a girl of 8. I keep Tommy's CDs in my car, and they would ask for them every time they rode somewhere with me. This proves the timeless quality and good music of Tommy Cox's songs. After all a good story is a good story, sung, written, or chanted. The songs are about a life a group of good men lived, and some of them died doing. All the songs mean something to a submariner. They bring back sweet memories, fun times, bad times and some cold chills times. My cold chills song is *Torpedo in the Water*, I have heard the screaming of the screws of a Mk 16 warshot passing close overhead. Not close enough for the influence warhead to detonate, thank the good Lord.

Submariners remember the men we say are "Still on Patrol," for they are our brothers that we respect for their courage and dedication even though they may have been our enemies in the past. Once the wars, hot or cold, are over, we still respect them. In "*Kursk*" and "*Scorpion*" Tommy tells the sad story of those lost during our dangerous times.

Tommy Cox is our troubadour, his songs are part of our history, our mystic, and what we are and were.

One thing I have learned is that the greatest thing a man can be is a shipmate to other sub sailors. Once said, nothing else is as important.

Mike Hemming,
Boy Throttleman,
Shipmate

Acknowledgements

First and foremost, I must acknowledge my love, respect, and appreciation for my wife of 42 years, Sandra J. Cox, who can attest to the difficulties of life with a submariner who thinks he's an artist; my dearly departed parents, James and Lorraine Cox, who set high hopes and standards I didn't always meet, but their example and encouragement was inspirational; my lovely daughter, Cher Maria Hebert, who converted my original *Take Her Deep* album to CD, which led to three more albums; and my son, James Thomas Cox, who served in *Trident* submarines, and now is a shift supervisor for Exelon, a nuclear power plant in Moline, Illinois. All are highly supportive, and I love them dearly. I also remember my first son, William Louis Cox, who died in 2002. He was my best friend. I miss him tremendously, and I think of him every day. Each of these children has a wonderful family with super grandchildren, which will give me somebody to play with as I reach my second childhood.

I was introduced to J.T. McDaniel of Riverdale Books by Harry Lieberman of The Submarine Store. This was the single contact to bring life to *Tango Charlie*. Harry, thank you for all you have done, and for all the CDs you sold. Hand salute to your partner, Bodega Bob Homme, who assisted with publishing information. Bodega is also an accomplished songwriter, who can contribute greatly to the submarine music genre. J.T., thank you for taking a chance on *Tango Charlie*.

One individual whose artistry knows no bounds is my dear friend Don Ward. Don is the reason the last two CDs exist. He did all the instrumentation and recording on both CDs, and even added some vocals on a few of the cuts. Don is not only a musician; he is an unpublished author, and an abstract artist. I have several of his paintings. Additionally, he is a talented photographer. Don, you have no idea what an inspiration you have been for me. Don Ward is generous to a fault. He spends much time doing charity live performances at Veterans Centers and nursing homes. He started his military service in the U.S. Marine Corps, and subsequently became a submarine Torpedoman. He has my deepest respect and admiration.

There are many individuals who assisted with this project by proofreading, editing, and suggesting changes, and those who advised regarding security. These contributions were invaluable. Without question the two most helpful shipmates were my singing partner and songwriter, Bobby Reed, and a fellow artist and songwriter, Steve Corneliusen. Others were Robert "Dex" Armstrong; T. Michael Bircumshaw, current editor of the *American Submariner*, who authored many books himself; my uncle, Ray Dufour; Mike Hemming; Ken Cadran, the consummate Master Chief Petty Officer; Gus "Pete" Pedersen, the executive director of all the Tommy Cox CDs of Wooden Ships Music; Peter Pira, outstanding submarine spook officer and author; Bill Hollaway, mustang officer and superior submarine operator; Rodney Sirois, U.S. Navy SEAL; Tom Tucker, LCOL, USAF, Retired; and C.J. Vieira and Barbara Webster, two dear classmates, my cousin Frank Magner, retired Senior Chief EOD diver; Sherry Sontag, co-author of *Blind Man's Bluff*, Gladys Shelden, who assisted with the *Mighty Mine Dodgers* chapter; and Cathy Dickey, daughter of "Frenchie," who assisted with that chapter; and Captain Joseph Rodriguez.

My eternal gratitude goes to Charles Heller, of Liberty Watch Radio, KVOI, Tucson, Arizona, for introducing me to published authors who made great suggestions and assisted in the attempts to publish *Tango Charlie*. These were LT Claude Berube, author of *A Call to the Sea*; Captain Charles Stewart, of the U.S.S. *Constitution*, and I.C. Smith, author of *Inside*.

Other published authors who helped were Ken "Pig" Henry and Don Keith, co-authors of *Gallant Lady*, Ron Martini, author of *Hot, Straight, and Normal: a Submarine Bibliography*, and *The Submariner's Dictionary*; Ron "Warshot" Smith, author of *Torpedoman*, and an honored World War II submarine combat veteran, and Robert McManus, Editorial Editor of the New York *Post*.

Two other fine gentlemen who have graciously provided invaluable assistance are Don "Mac" Smith, webmaster of http://donmac.org/submarinesongs.htm, and my former coworker, Justin Healey, who kept my computer, donated to me by Bobby Reed, operational long past its expected utility.

There are musicians who taught me the ropes whom I wish to thank: Harry Anderson, who first showed me how to play a guitar; Gil Morrow, Dave Wheeler, Herb Bettevy, Denney Brown, Olin Barber, Nick Hickie, Vern Denney, Ray Mangrum, Jim Strahan, Lewis Bearden (Tom & Lew, the Country Two); and my dear friends of the Tommy Cox Band and the North Star Band, Jim Corbett, Gerry Rucker, Howard Jones, Hank Schafer, Patty Benjamin and Nate Benjamin, and, of course, Bobby Reed and Don Ward.

There are three Navy submarine commanders I wish to thank for the honor of serving with them: Captain Chester M. "Whitey" Mack, of U.S.S. *Lapon*; Captain Charles MacVean, of U.S.S. *Seawolf*; and Captain Jack Maurer, of U.S.S. *Parche*.

Lastly, I must take personal credit and responsibility for all errors contained herein, such as spelling, grammar, faults of memory and perception, inclusion, and omission.

FOREWORD

My name is George Thomas Cox. I was born, and I now reside, in Caribou, Maine. I am 63 years old. Since infancy I have been called "Tommy." I have essentially had three careers: (1) U.S. Navy, as a submarine "spook" (1960-79), (2) State of Maine Child Support Law Enforcement (1983-2003), and (3) singer-songwriter (1957-2005). This book is about careers 1 and 3.

A submarine "spook" is an intelligence specialist that serves aboard the fast attack submarines. My uncommon ability was speaking, reading, and writing the Russian language, and other acquired, atypical skills. My career as a singer-songwriter was more a hobby and an avocation than a career, but in my lifetime I have merged these two vocations. I have participated in the production and publication of three music albums (See Appendix A) that are mostly songs of the U.S. Submarine Service. This book is a history of the creation of 25 of these patriotic compositions.

The impetus for writing this book comes from being mentioned in the best selling book, *Blind Man's Bluff (The Untold Story of American Submarine Espionage)* by Sherry Sontag and Christopher Drew. I also appeared in the History Channel two-hour special of the same name. It has been suggested, and I have been encouraged by my brothers in the United States Submarine Veterans, Inc., that this book be written for the sake of preserving the history of the music of our Submarine Force.

I guess, at first, I did not suspect the public would be interested in reading about the genesis of the genre of submarine music as created by Tommy Cox. But I do have ten thousand people somewhere in the world with copies of an album of music entitled *Take Her Deep*, about the U.S. Navy and the Submarine Service.

I did this album back in 1977, published it in 1978, and these people may be interested in the circumstances surrounding the creation of those songs and others since then. The Monologue contains highlights of my personal history in the Navy, early music experience, and my service in the attack class submarines of our great country. I have stated privately that in my life I have had more adventure than any three normal people. This collection will reflect some of that adventure. Listening to the music described in this book would do much to assist the reader to experience the full spectrum of the music and prose.

Each of us is the sum total of our genetic structure as modified by our every experience. This is the old nature/nurture controversy. I once shared what I call my "marble theory" with one of my college Ph.D. professors, who agreed with it. It is as simple as this: "Nature determines how many marbles we get; nurture determines how many of those marbles we get to play with." What we do in every instance is the result of these two influences up to that point in time in our lives. The genetic plus environmental influences are certainly finite, but they defy absolute quantification. This is about as philosophical as I care to get. These influences affected my song writing.

In this Foreword, and in the Monologue, I intend to give you a synopsis of my life, intentionally limited to those situations needed to understand this music. You will be presented vignettes from my life experiences, as they pertain to these songs I have written. I will do my best to include what is pertinent to the music. Sometimes the experience or situation I describe may not be apparently relevant to a specific song, but, hopefully, it should explain a situation that had a significant effect on my personal attitude and served to influence the song development. Any commentary I make regarding historical events is based solely on my personal assessment and recollection of the situation and my personal opinion. Omissions and misperceptions are solely my own. It is certainly not necessary that anybody agree with me.

I must also emphasize what is represented here is truth as limited by my own memory, interpretation, and perception. I must admit, like most people, my memory is flawed. My perceptions of events may differ from reality and certainly differ from the perceptions and observations of others. I promise there will be no intentional attempt to alter the truth in any manner, or any intent to deceive. I also admit that if there is something, such as personal information or classified material that should not be included, I will simply omit it. Silence is often misinterpreted, but rarely misquoted. This will be the same where the embarrassment or criticism of others would not be fair to them by including their name. Every name used in this book is of a real person who has had an influence on me, and my life has been enriched for knowing them. I thank each for that.

Another situation, which may require understanding, is the liberal use by the media of the value-laden label of "spy." Two of the interviews I have given resulted in ascribing this term to me. I never called myself a spy except in jest. I never thought of myself as a spy. I have made the tongue-in-cheek comment that I am probably the world's most unsuccessful spy. Everybody knows about it. Most of the characterizations in print regarding my duties in the Navy were obtained from others. This is certainly true of the book *Blind Man's Bluff*, by Sontag and Drew, and the History Channel special of the same name. While personnel of the Naval Security Group (NSG) are certainly involved in matters of national security, there are very few, including me, who ever thought of us as spies. In the beginning days of fleet support by NSG staff in submarines (circa 1950s), the submariners called the embarked teams "spooks," and the appellation stuck. Mostly, this situation arose due to early security procedures, where the crew members were given a briefing and signed non-disclosure statements. Frequently, as part of the briefing, members of the crews were advised not to associate with the "spooks" when ashore. The suggestion: "They were never here" also contributed to the "spook" mystique. These standards and admonitions evolved and modified over the years. If there's one thing that never changes, it is the fact that conditions in the Navy and security rarely remain the same. Some may argue with this. But the whole idea is not to give a potential adversary any knowledge or advantage by what we do or say. It's apparent how the sum total of this knowledge can change from command to command and person to person. See my example regarding the three-star admiral below.

Since May of 1968, and as of March 2005, I have written, recorded, and published these 25 songs, and others, in three albums about the U.S. Submarine Service and other "military associated" subjects. All of these songs are real. They reflect true-life experiences. As I have performed these songs at a variety of venues associated with submarine veteran functions, and, as I incorporated short introductions, the songs would take on a new meaning and significance for listeners. Many times I heard a comment such as, "I understand that song now," or "I wondered what that song was about." This is the purpose of this book, to explain for the sake of posterity what the songs express, and what they are all about, and the circumstances surrounding their creation.

Although I wrote my first songs in 1957, I began writing songs about submarines in 1968 when I was 25-years-old. Since a couple of songs were written in 2005, at the age of 62, there's been a span of 37 years in there. Certainly many changes in international relations and my personal experiences and attitudes have occurred in that period. These changes are reflected in the songs, depending on the time and content. These influences must be considered to understand the expression of the moment, and are significant and affect the hook (main idea) of each composition. Also, please consider that this book is being written at age 62 and 63, and many of my opinions have modified over the years.

Writing about military stuff, especially the Submarine Service, can be problematic from one unique perspective: classified information. One thing I found very early was it depended upon who was doing the disclosing. One of the best examples in my personal experience is the following: I got berated by a three-star admiral at the 39th Anniversary of Submarine Veterans, Inc., at the Port & Starboard Banquet Room, Ocean Beach, New London. This was in May 2002. I was sitting at the entrance to the banquet room when the admiral asked me if I'd seen the Groton Base Vice Commander. I told him I had not, and he then asked me who I was. I told him my name and that I was selling my CDs of submarine music. We shook hands. I told him that Ms. Sherry Sontag was also there to autograph the *Blind Man's Bluff* book, but at the moment she was outside with her son.

He became visibly hostile at the mention of the book and probably associated me with the History Channel production and made a point of stating, "A lot of people violated their security oaths to contribute to that book," clearly implying that included me. I wasn't about to go into my act of explaining all I had done to obtain guidance to appear on the History Channel production and that I hadn't done anything to contribute to the book, nor did I wish to play verbal ping-pong with a three-star admiral. I did not reply. Later, in the banquet hall as the distinguished Vice Admiral rose to give the keynote address regarding the Cold War, the first thing out of his mouth was, "I remember when I was commanding officer of a diesel submarine off the coast of Vladivostok..." Now this paragraph may not be very politically correct, and I have no intent to express anything but total respect for the Admiral, who had a splendid career in submarines, but it did happen this way and exemplifies the issue. I strongly suspect the admiral opted out of any opportunity to participate, as many of his contemporaries appeared by name in the *Blind Man's Bluff* book, and the subsequent History Channel production. A retired three-star, two Captains, and NCIS (Naval Criminal Investigation Service) provided my guidance. Anyway, great care was given in my interviews and writing the songs to make sure no classified information was stated. This was done in the songs through use of the double *entendre*, symbolism, and metaphor. These will be identified in this book. Sometimes these expressions had some unexpected, if not comical, results.

I must state for the record, I was *not* given any official approval from any source to appear on the History Channel program. However, those I spoke with would state, "If you appear, you should..." I was well aware of the media approach for a quid pro quo to speak of submarine operational specifics for the favor of using the submarine songs. This was especially true of the NOVA program, *Submarines, Secrets, and Spies*, which was first broadcast in January of 1999. I refused to work with this program outright. The moderator was a total jerk in my opinion.

The following is pure speculation, with some circumstantial evidence: During the period of time the *Blind Man's Bluff* book was written and published, and the follow-on History Channel special was aired, the Submarine Service was in great fear that the number of fast-attack submarines would be reduced to 50. I'd read where the Navy determined a minimum of 56 attack submarines were required just to keep up with the existing level of assigned submarine missions. Positive publicity for submarine operations was sought for Congress to continue to fund the Submarine Service at the required level. *Blind Man's Bluff* contributed to this effort. The participation of a former Chief of Naval Operations, a former Director of Central Intelligence, and a former Secretary of the Navy, *et al*, certainly suggests interest at some very significant level. If Tommy Cox could assist by singing a song and making a few guarded comments, I am indeed honored.

For those of us who have been totally away from the Navy and the security of classified information since retirement from active naval service, as I have, our education regarding the evolution of standards of care for security ended. Many of us joined organizations that could give us some level of knowledge of these matters. I belong to the Naval Cryptologic Veterans Association (NCVA). As I read the articles, and evaluated the level of security, I have observed many items that were totally protected during my active service that are now openly discussed in the organization's periodical, called the *Cryptolog*. I am told the security office for the former Naval Security Group reviews and approves each issue. Therefore, one could logically conclude these subjects expressed in the *Cryptolog* could now be openly discussed. In my opinion, much more than I believed should be disclosed is made public in the *Cryptolog*. Well, I do not intend to go that far. My intention is to use an uncommon standard called "common sense."

When I was first contacted by one of Christopher Drew's staff writers for the *Chicago Tribune*, Bob Becker, in 1990, I called my friend Lewis R. Bearden, also a retired Navy submariner. Lew was still in the security business. I knew he would know who to contact. I requested guidance regarding the interview Mr. Becker wanted. Other than obtaining confirmation from Lew that he had passed on my request to the security people, nobody came or called. Mr. Becker came to Caribou, Maine, and we met on Thanksgiving Day. I told him up front I would talk to him solely about the music and nothing else. Mr. Becker had no knowledge of my personal background. His interview with me was quite uneventful. I did give him the last copy I had of my album, *Take Her Deep*, on vinyl. He promised to send me a copy of the articles being written for the *Chicago Tribune*. When I read the articles, which were published in 1991, I could see I had not impressed him with much, as the only reference to me was as a "*Lapon* crewman who wrote a song about Captain Whitey Mack." Two months later an agent from NCIS showed up to interview me about the incident, two months late in my view. My impression of the meeting with NCIS was adversarial. The agent wasn't there to assist me with my security question; he was there to investigate if he could bring an action against me. I'm sure glad I put myself on report.

I don't exactly remember when Sherry Sontag called me for information ('95 or '96). Once again, I advised I would not speak to submarine operations, but I would talk about the songs. Sherry tried to suggest that the Cold War was over, we won it, and now the story remains to be told. Although our acquaintance presently is amicable, in the three phone conversations Sherry had with me prior to the publication of the book, our discussions were confrontational. The same limitation regarding my participation was expressed to Tower Productions when they called to interview me on videotape for the History Channel, two-hour documentary.

Well, when the book came out and the History Channel started airing the special, I received word through the grapevine that certain people believed I'd violated my security oath, and I was literally treated as a traitor. The part that really hurt was many of these detractors had been my friends, shipmates, and coworkers many years ago. One shipmate, Bill Hollaway, had the courtesy to ask, and I explained to him what I am explaining here. This is what a friend would do. So, to all of you who think I did a bad deed, I deeply regret that you were neither involved nor consulted in the preparation process. Suffice it to say, I was comfortable with my guidance, and I would never do anything to endanger anybody or compromise our nation through poor judgment.

Robert Gates, who was a former Director of Central Intelligence, made the comment in his address at the reunion for the USS *Parche* a few years ago words to the effect that, "We know, the Russians know, the only people who don't know are the American public who paid for it." He was speaking of a high-level special project regarding a few of our nation's submarines.

In discussing Whitey Mack's trail of a Soviet *Yankee* class submarine in 1969 with a three-star, prior to the History Channel taping, the Vice Admiral advised the U.S. had no more 637 class submarines, and the Soviets had no more *Yankee* class boomers. He suggested this could be talked about. Curiously, with much care and concern on my part, the program missed two important points that distorted the truth. I'd demonstrated how the *Yankee* traveled relatively shallow, while *Lapon* ran deep. They missed the point that the range between *Lapon* and *Yankee* was usually around one mile. Secondly, I stated the *Yankee*'s patrol area was further out in the Atlantic than we would have expected. We believed her to patrol closer to the U.S. if we were the primary target. They concluded that meant the Russian missile could be fired at a greater distance than anticipated. Well, the *Yankee* was also in a position to respond to hostilities in two hemispheres. The success of the *Yankee* trail by the *Lapon* was leaked to the press during the course of the mission, before *Lapon* returned to port. It would have been difficult to blame that leak on a crew member. I understand the Joint Chiefs of Staff were in their perennial conflict over funding for their respective services, and as the specter of a Soviet ballistic submarine presence became a reality, each service was competing for resources to neutralize this potential threat. The success of Whitey Mack in proving the ability of the U.S. Submarine Service to deal with this issue threw heavy consideration for allowing the submarine Navy to resolve a submarine Navy problem.

Of course, there are some things that are just unknown, and writers, authors, and songwriters exercise what is called literary license. Many misuse the privilege to the extent that the result is pure fictional manure. Some of these individuals should begin their historical treatises with "Once upon a time…" Well, my uses of literary license are well known and understood to the submariners. Most are jokes, and could begin with, "This is no s—!" Essentially, that's the difference between a fairy tale and a sea story. These, too, will be explained in this book.

Surprisingly, these songs were not written originally for the purpose of making money. I simply converted some intense experiences into lyrics and music. I had no methodology that was consistent from one composition to the next with my approach to song writing. I get asked about this from time to time, as in: "How do you go about writing a song?" In fact, my personal sense of discipline has its peaks and troughs and, at times, is simply nonexistent. Even with songs I have been singing for years, I can honestly say I rarely sing them exactly the same way every time.

This reality creates problems when recording, especially if the music is recorded separately from the vocals. I also strive to sing with feeling and emotion, and the way I feel on any given day certainly varies. Well, it's a good thing that money wasn't paramount, as it took more than 27 years to move approximately 10,000 copies of *Take Her Deep*. Notice I did not say, "sell." While I paid to obtain 10,000 copies from the producers, I certainly didn't sell that many. The first 3,500 units were 33-1/3 rpm vinyl records, and the balance of 6,500 units was compact discs (CDs). A significant number of these were donated for such things as the Dolphin Scholarship Foundation, families of sick and terminal submariners, and to some close friends and family and to others who were just at the right place at the right time. Mike Hemming, noted submarine scribe, was sitting with me at the 38th SUBVETS anniversary when a young Seaman Apprentice, who was part of the Honor Guard, asked about the CD *Take Her Deep*. When I heard him say he was going to go borrow the money to buy the CD, I refused to be paid for it and made it a gift. I told him I remembered the days when I was a Seaman Deuce, and the fact that he wanted the CD was a real compliment. Generosity? Maybe, but I suspect it's more a reflection of the reason I will never be a successful businessman. The experience with *Brothers of the Dolphin* with Bobby Reed is similar. We bought 2,000 CDs early in 2001, and between us we still have approximately 500 to 600 left as of January 2006. A lot of these got donated. We will count our blessings if we ever break even.

Cost effectiveness was a consideration for quite awhile. Until I met Bobby, I hadn't really considered different options for recording further music other than renting a studio and paying musicians. There is no way that could be cost effective, given my track record of CD sales. Bobby Reed, and his gracious and generous offer to donate his time, equipment, and expertise, is instrumental in resurrecting the urge in me to do more submarine songs. Additionally, a dear lady from Florida, Gladys Shelden, whose husband was aboard the U.S.S. *Tinosa* when they entered the Sea of Japan in 1945 with eight other boats in Operation Barney, urged me to continue singing and honoring submariners in music (See Chapter 18). So the new goal with Bobby, and ever since, was to make the music available for our shipmates for the sake of posterity. If the music becomes institutionalized, that is wonderful. If it does not, so what? The expressed purpose of the United States Submarine Veterans, Inc., is as follows: "To perpetuate the memory of our shipmates who gave their lives in the pursuit of their duties while serving their country. That their dedication, deeds and supreme sacrifice be a constant source of motivation toward greater accomplishments. Pledge loyalty and patriotism to the United States government." This creed is the purpose for going forward with the third of my CDs, entitled *In Honor of...* The songs on this album, both old and new, each represents an honor significant to submariners and military veterans. Bobby Reed also put out a single CD of his own called *Proud to Be an American Veteran.* There are some great songs on that CD.

I have a bumper sticker on my truck that reads: "Silent Service—our nation's unsung heroes." I wanted to change that and give our Submarine Service a collection of songs to recall our history and support our future.

The CD of *Spirituals*, a fourth CD, was one of the last requests of my mother, who passed away in December of 2002. On occasion I would sing a spiritual for her. She loved the music and always wanted me to do a spiritual collection. I regret that she passed away before I made the recordings.

MONOLOGUE

Early Background

After I'd written several songs about submarines, the idea of doing an album became self-evident. Barry Sadler had his very successful album about the Green Berets during the Vietnam War. Could an album about submarines do just as well? Gordon Lightfoot had done a very successful album with just guitar and bass for backup. Maybe I could do likewise. This notion became a serious goal around 1971–72 when I was attending Tidewater Community College under the Navy's ADCOP (Associate Degree Completion Program) in Portsmouth, Virginia.

In 1956–57 I was a freshman at Caribou High School in Maine. Through junior high and my freshman year I'd been a baseball and basketball player. I think the real motivating factor was the opportunity to meet girls through sports. Most of the popular guys were athletes. During this school year I met a new friend from New Sweden, Maine. Harry Anderson had a new talent. He knew how to chord the guitar. Also at this point in time, the teens, including me, were taking an interest in music, and Elvis Presley was becoming a star. The interest the girls had in Elvis suggested to me that I could meet more girls playing a guitar and singing than I could playing sports, so Harry showed me my first chords on the guitar. I would do the rest.

I did my first talent show in 1957 on the Gene Hooper Country Music Show at the Caribou High School auditorium. Harry had showed me how to play *Blue Suede Shoes* in the key of G. When the band leader asked me in what key I was going to do my song, I looked at him like he was crazy and responded, "Why the key of G, of course." Little did I know there were other keys to learn. Pretty funny now! But I won the talent show and first prize was five dollars.

So I was fifteen years old when I first started singing and playing guitar. I also wrote my first song called *Heartbreaker's Desire*. I cut an acetate demo of this song for WNVY Radio, in Pensacola, Florida, when I was stationed there for class "A" school in 1961. I would caterwaul a verse of the song much the way Elvis did on his early recording of *Blue Moon*. I haven't been able to do that song in that manner since I got through puberty. No more caterwauling! A deal was worked out by WNVY radio and our command at Corry Field for a group of us to be allowed to have liberty each weekend to play music on Friday and Saturday evenings, so we could play at a live dance sponsored by the radio station. This included an hour each night of live broadcast, so we became fairly well known in Pensacola. Radio advertising for the gig referred to me as, "Pensacola's answer to Elvis Presley."

In addition to being a fan of Elvis, I greatly admired Johnny Cash, Roy Orbison (nobody could do his stuff), and the great Hank Williams. In later years I added Waylon Jennings and Willie Nelson to this list. I not only like their music, I believe their personal conflicts with the Nashville establishment had something to do with it. Besides, Waylon and I sang in the same keys. I firmly believe Kris Kristofferson is one of the most talented songwriters in the country along with Willie. To this list I must add Alan Jackson for his great song *Where Were You When the World Stopped Turning*, and Toby Keith who succeeded in the big time with his "in-your-face," pro-military songs where I did not. Fans of the Tommy Cox Band, who joined us at Norm's Lounge 1980 – 83, can attest to the fact that our performances supported our country, our military, and our beloved Submarine Service, as we rode out the Iranian Hostage Crisis. Charlie Daniels is another whom I admire with his songs of a patriotic nature. And Lee Greenwood's *God Bless the USA* is a classic.

Some have concluded my voice sounds like a cross between Elvis and Johnny Cash. Personally, at this stage, I would hope my voice sounds uniquely like Tommy Cox, but the comparison is done in a spirit of good faith and intended to be complimentary. I'll live with it. I'd been listening to country music since I was a child. I remember listening to mother's 78 rpm records and announcing that I was going to be a singer.

Along these lines I have a recent e-mail to share with you with you. A submariner named Dan Meyers sent me the following on 10/25/05:

"Tommy,

"My son is 8 now and occasionally asks me about what I did during the cold war. I shared with him bedtime stories that ranged from riding in boats to the pole, to colliding with underwater mountains and icebergs, to an occasional Crazy Ivan and high speed screws in the water. He always listened politely and intently, but I had the impression he thought I was making it up.

"Then about six weeks ago we received your CD's in the mail.

"Dad is a lot cooler now than he used to be. And when the kid saw a TV ad for that new movie, *Walk The Line*, he asked me who it was about. When I told him, he didn't have a clue who Johnny Cash was, but he said that whoever he is, he sounds a lot like Tommy Cox :)

"Thanks again and may God richly bless you, as you have blessed me.

"Dan"

It's things like this that are priceless for me.

At age 16 I was hired to sing in a country band with young fellows from the U.S. Air Force stationed at Loring AFB, Maine. While we started as a country band, it didn't take long to transition into a rock and roll group doing hits of the era. I was singing six nights a week, making $10.00 a night, and I was beginning to pay my dues in experience. This was a lot of money to a 16 and 17-year-old boy. In fact, I even wanted to quit high school. But mother wouldn't hear of it, bless her heart.

As a young singer I had something of a following. At that young age I had a full beard and looked older than I was. I don't think the waiters or waitresses knew how old I was, because they didn't hesitate to serve me beer with the rest of the band with the law requiring drinkers to be 21. Man, this music business was fun!

You can take the boy out of the country, but you can't take the country out of the boy. One winter evening in 1959 we had a small crowd in the bar, and this "old" lady, probably about 30 years old, came in dressed rather conservatively. She was quite attractive. She really looked out of place in that bar, and she was alone. I danced with her when I was not on the bandstand, and she bought me a beer. As we were ending the evening, she asked me where I lived. I told her Caribou, and she asked how I was getting home and did I have I car. I told her the boys in the band usually drop me off. Then she spoke real low, and even I could tell she was a bit embarrassed. She said, "My husband's gone TDY (I didn't know what that meant then); would you like to spend the night with me?"

Without even batting an eye, I answered, "I can't, I have to go to school tomorrow." The look on her face told me I'd just made a big boo-boo. But she wasted her evening on me, and I went to school the next morning. Perhaps it was Divine intervention to help her through a crisis. I hope it worked out for her.

In May of 1960 my high school best buddy and I decided we should join the U.S. Army together under the buddy system. These were the days of the draft, and it was just something young men had to do. So we went to Presque Isle and took the screening test at the Army Recruiting Office. The screening test was 100 questions, and I completed 97 correctly. I must have had a good "guess quotient" on that day. The Sergeant was willing to give me anything I wanted except instant promotion to Brigadier General. My friend and I were scheduled to go to Bangor early in June to take the basic battery of tests for enlistment. We were going to go Regular Army. I returned to Caribou with my announcement.

Sometimes things happen to us that are unexplainable that affects our lives significantly. Just before graduation my Mom was scheduled to receive a community citation from the American Legion in Caribou at the same time I was to be in Bangor for the Army tests. I dearly wanted to go to Bangor with my buddy, but mother was adamant that I would appear at the reception for her and sing *I Want a Girl Just Like the Girl that Married Dear Old Dad*. I was ready to go over the hill on this gig, but Dad convinced me this was the right thing to do to honor mother. Dad was very persuasive. I did not go to Bangor.

In the meantime I graduated from Caribou High School in the class of 1960. My guitar playing friend, Harry Anderson, had quit school a year or so earlier and was living in East Meadow, Long Island, New York. He and his wife arranged for me to get an audition for the *Ted Mack Original Amateur Hour* in New York City. I got a bus ticket, packed a suitcase, took my Harmony guitar, and went to New York. The audition went very poorly. I didn't know what to expect. I sang an Elvis song badly. And I didn't get selected for the show. I returned to Caribou with the intention of resurrecting my intention to join the Army.

On the day I hitchhiked to Presque Isle the Army Recruiting Office was closed. So I crossed the Street to see how things might be in the Navy. I did well on the Navy screening test and enlisted under a program called Electronics Field Seaman Recruit (EFSR). So much for careful planning! It was off to boot camp in Great Lakes on a path that would eventually lead me to a Navy "spook" rating and submarines.

Naval Career 1960-79

On every submarine mission I made, I either brought my own Gibson, or I would borrow a guitar that belonged to another shipmate. I often joked that my guitar had a Top Secret clearance. I bought that guitar in 1963, when I transferred from Guantanamo Bay, Cuba, to the U.S.S. *Oxford* (AGTR-1), home ported in Norfolk. The Gibson even has "time-in-grade" on my wife. I've had the guitar longer than I've been married.

It was not uncommon for friends to suggest "going to Nashville." My response to that was, "There are singers and songwriters in Nashville who are so much better than me who are literally starving. Why would I want to go to Nashville?" It was a compliment though. The other reality was, who in Nashville would have an interest in songs about submarines? I once met Yodelin' Slim Clark, who was a Maine recording artist throughout his lifetime, who was famous for his yodeling and bluegrass music. I told him I was an admirer, and I told him I wrote and sang songs about submarines. He just said, in his slow talking drawl, "Well, Son, (I was nearly 60 and he was much older) I don't believe I've ever heard a song about a submarine." Mr. Clark is now deceased, but his statement certainly summarized the attitude of the conventional music industry about submarine songs.

The *Take Her Deep* album was recorded in the Omega Studios of Bob Yezbek in Kensington, Maryland. I'd met Bob at the Holiday Inn on Route 198 in Laurel, Maryland. Bob played organ, and sang at the Holiday Inn with a drummer Wednesday through Saturday, and I played Sunday and Monday as a single act. There is a little more than thirty minutes of music in thirteen selections on the album. It was recorded in about two and a half hours. I didn't waste time, as I rented the studio and engineers by the hour. I had to obtain a loan, using our family van as collateral, to finance the project. It was recorded on quarter-inch reel-to-reel tape at fifteen inches per second using DBX noise reduction. The album was produced at 33 $\frac{1}{3}$ rpm as a vinyl, long-play album, and I sold them for $7.00 each. I began selling them in February of 1978. The records were pressed by Sontec of Northwest Baltimore. There were 3,500 record albums produced. I'm not sure if I sold more or gave away more.

The album cover was created by my father, James F. Cox. He had a picture of *Bergal* that was on a postcard to go by, but he had no idea what the submarine looked like below the waterline. I didn't do anything to assist him, so, when he did the submarine silhouette, he drew the bottom part of the submarine as he thought a ship hull would look. I got such a kick out of it that I kept his original design. Nobody ever commented on it.

On my first hitch (1962 -63), I joined a rock band in Gitmo. We played at a couple of the clubs and a few private parties. When I transferred to the U.S.S. *Oxford* I sang on TV in Curacao, Dutch West Indies, at a military gin mill at the Rodman piers near Balboa, Canal Zone, on radio in Valparaiso, Chile, and at the North American Cultural Institute in Lima, Peru. Whether it was planned or not, I and two other sailors, one was named David Atkins but we called him Chet, wound up being the ship representatives in a *de facto* People-to-People program. I'll never forget Valpo! We had been given a radio spot that belonged to a group of school children. They'd all showed up ready to do whatever they'd rehearsed, but here were these three Americans taking their spot. They were invited to become our audience, and we went on. They were very enthusiastic about the music chanting "*Otra, otra*," which was the Spanish version of "Encore." It occurred to me what the situation was, and I asked the Cultural Institute representative to translate for me to thank them for their courtesy for allowing us to have their radio spot and that it was our honor to play our music for them. Apparently this made quite a hit with the kids, their parents, and the radio audience as a write-up in the paper the next day mentioned something to the effect that the American sailors were very gracious. This was in 1964, on April 30. Later that year Allende was assassinated, and there was a revolution. Our last night of liberty in Valpo was that evening. Our liberty was secured early, as the communists were planning a rally against the ship at midnight, which would have been the beginning of May 1st, May Day, the communist holiday. I left the Navy at the end of July 1964 and returned to my home in Caribou, Maine, my military obligation completed.

I'd been writing to Sandra McNeal, who I met on my last leave at home during the Christmas and New Year's holiday 1963-64. Sandra was 18 and I was 21.

Perfect! She was, and still is, absolutely gorgeous. I returned to my hometown, because this is where Sandra lived.

I'd taken a job for two weeks as a taxi driver. The second week, as I remember, I worked 83 hours and made $43.00 plus $2.00 in tips. I bailed out of that job. I obtained an entry-level position at Northern Sales, Inc., a General Motors dealership in Caribou. They wanted somebody who could type (I learned to type taking Morse code) who could do the warranty work submissions and be the service department cashier. The owner offered me $60.00 a week for two weeks to "learn the job." I took the office over after one week and asked for my raise after the second week. The following week I was informed I would receive my pay raise to $65.00 per week. These were 45 and 50-hour weeks. Every other week I would get Saturday morning off. This was an obvious dead end. It was time to reevaluate the situation and my future.

When I left the Navy in July of 1964, I'd applied for a government position in the Central Intelligence Agency. Here I was, 21 years old, no college at the time, but I knew Morse code and I could speak, read, and write Russian, thanks to two years of Navy schooling. The CIA must have had something I could be trained for. I was in good physical condition, and, it seemed, there wasn't anything I wouldn't do (within reason). Maybe I could be a real spy? As I moved from place to place, I kept informing them of my new address. I'd submitted passport photos. I was just waiting to hear. None of their replies to me could be traced to the CIA, no letterhead, no telltale return address. Then on August 28, I married Sandra. I sent an addendum to my security information. Within two weeks I got an answer back, on letterhead this time, advising me there were no jobs available "in my field." And what field would that be? So that opportunity disappeared.

I also spoke to the resident FBI agent who had an office in Fort Fairfield, Maine, at the time. I later learned he was the one who did the background investigation on me for my Navy clearance. He knew more about me than I thought. I inquired about an FBI job. He found something in the book where my skills could be utilized, but the annual pay was about $3,600. Special Agents either had to have a law degree, or be a CPA, at that time.

In the meantime I joined up with a local group to play music in the area. We didn't play much, but I met some real good musicians. The guitar player was Arnold Cochran. He was an outstanding guitar player. He backed some really big stars in his career. But he died broke at age 70 in a car accident. He always reminded me of Tom T. Hall's song, *I Remember the Year Clayton Delaney Died*. I think every country singer or musician has one or more Clayton Delaneys in their life. I had several.

Early in our marriage Sandra and I couldn't seem to decide which roles we should adopt respectively, and we parted company after three whole weeks of marriage. I never knew a relationship could change so quickly. After getting served annulment papers, I decided to leave town and seek my fortune in the music world again. There were no jobs for Russian speaking guys in Caribou, and I couldn't get a job as a teenage singing idol, so I wound up in California. I really didn't want to go back in the Navy, so I tried the Marines first. It was January 1965. A high school buddy, Ritchie Bubar, had been killed in Vietnam the previous September, and at 22 years old, I wanted to make that right. However, the Marine Gunny Recruiter was an honest person, and he advised me it would be most likely that I would be assigned to the Naval Security Group as a Marine given my schools and skills. In thinking this over I concluded if that's what was going to happen, I might as well avoid Marine boot camp, keep my Navy rank, and go back on active naval service. I called the Navy recruiter and asked, "Do you guys still have chow cards?" He answered, "Yes!" very hesitatingly.

I said, "Make me up one and tell me where to find you. I'm coming over." He got quite a kick out of that. I rejoined the Navy, got my Third Class (E-4) crow back, and went to Treasure Island, California, to await orders. I volunteered for Vietnam. I got sent to Kamiseya, Japan. Actually, I needed a soft place to fall, a job, and some meaningful direction to my life. I'd reenlisted for four years to pay my debts (car), but my goal was still music. I just didn't have a military mind!

Now those of you who don't know us may wonder how Sandra and I wound up. The Lord gave us a gift in the form of our first son, William Louis Cox, who brought us back together in September of 1965 in Japan. Billy filled that role in our lives up to August 2002 when he passed away due to a careless medical accident while undergoing surgery. His memory continues to hold the family together. Did we live happily ever after? Hell, no! But we wouldn't quit on each other, and we're still working on being together every day of our lives. And we worked out those role issues. I've been retired for two years now, and Sandy and I have spent two Maine winters together without killing each other. I think it's going to work. We married 42 years ago.

I played a lot of music in Japan as a solo performer, a country music singer in a country band, and I was even assigned to represent the Navy in an Armed Forces Variety Show, headed by an Air Force Major at Yokota AFB. I sang *Danny Boy* and claimed to be an Irishman. Actually, there is Irish in my Dad's family, but for this show I had to be Irish. This was the theme of the show. We performed in civilian clothes, and each of us represented different nationalities that made up the American melting pot. Then, for the finale, we appeared in uniform to take our bows. I met some pretty high ranking officers and legislators doing this show. That's who we performed for, dignitaries and royalty. One gentleman I remember fondly for his humor and graciousness was L. Mendel Rivers, the namesake of one of our 637 class fast attack submarines. I could have continued this duty for as long as I wanted, but all the free time to me was a waste. So I went back to work at Kamiseya.

It was at Kamiseya where I met Senior Chief Denney Brown, who helped me get established in the music community there in Japan. We've been good friends ever since. It was also here that I met a guitar player like no other, Herb Bettevy. Herb was another "Clayton Delaney" for me. Herb was a Second Class CT on his second Navy hitch. At first I thought he was a lifer, but he got out around ten years. He was playing lead guitar in one of the better established country bands in Japan. They played at a lot of the Air Force clubs at Johnson, Yokota, and Tachikawa. Herb played a double-neck guitar. He was the best guitar player I'd ever heard. Until I got established with a group, I would go with Herb to his gigs. Herb finally moved back to Louisiana, where he joined the National Guard. He kept playing music his whole life. He retired from the Army as a CWO-4. His lovely wife, Deloris, passed away a couple years ago. I think of Herb often. I learned a lot from him. Herb was another Clayton Delaney to me.

My old Division Chief, Robert I. Bowie, had been transferred to Kamiseya during 1966. Many of my old buddies from language school were going to sea on submarines. I wanted to do that, too. So, with Chief Bowie's assistance, I got myself transferred into the Fleet Support Division and started riding submarines early in 1967.

The Boats

My first boat was the diesel submarine *Barbel*. This was one of the last three diesel boats built for the Navy. It had an *Albacore* hull (teardrop), which gave it better underwater speed and maneuverability. There was no After Torpedo Room. It was fairly habitable. I liked it! I got the experience of having my sinuses plugged and my ear vacuumed to a flash cover (an artificial leather mattress cover) due to the pressure changes during snorkeling. I also got the experience of being held down for several days by a foreign nation's anti-submarine warfare units, the air going bad to the point it would not sustain a lit cigarette, and the headache that went with it. I got to ask the question, "Why was the diesel exhaust always upwind from the snorkel intake?" I loved the diesel boat and admired the diesel boat sailors, but tactically the nukes ruled. The one advantage of the diesel was its quietness when submerged on the battery. The *Barbel* was the only diesel boat in which I served.

One of the first things that impressed me about submarines was the professionalism, ability, and dedication of submarine sailors. In 1967 the diesel boat sailors aboard *Barbel* didn't seem to adhere to any consistent regulation uniform. Many, including me, usually wore sweatshirts with the Navy dungaree trousers. It was usually a bit chilly inside the submarine at that time of year. A lot of the crew wore sandals that kept their feet from sweating in regular shoes. It helped the atmosphere. Feet would sweat then get real cold in the temperature in the boat. Quite a few sailors wore beards. Most of us shaved every few days. It occurred to me that for a military group, the crew looked more like pirates, but they were exceptionally competent. I always had a personal disdain for stupid personnel inspections held by power freaks who needed to do this to assure themselves they were still in charge. My personal view is: "What do you want? Form or function?" Then in later years I read somewhere that, "No combat unit could ever pass inspection." Well, I'm entitled to my opinion!

My next boat was out of Ballast Point in San Diego. While in San Diego I visited a band leader with whom I had worked in Japan in a country band called the Top Hands. Olin Barber was a Navy senior First Class Petty Officer in an aviation rating. He was a real good bass player and a good band leader. The master plan was to get together in a couple years, my hitch was to be up in January 1969, and Olin stated he had made an arrangement for the star Tommy Duncan to book our band. If this was true, our path to the big time was clear. Olin had a band in the San Diego area and was playing at a western club out on Imperial Beach Boulevard. Olin also had another singer working with him who was very good. When I left there I had the impression I had been replaced in this dream. I guess I made the right choice in the long run, as the arrangement with Tommy Duncan didn't materialize. Olin became a deputy sheriff somewhere in Oklahoma and never did make his way in the music business.

The U.S.S. *Scamp* (SSN-588) was my first nuke. The white hats on our team lived in makeshift bunks in the Torpedo Room. This was the last class of U.S. fast attack submarines to have the Torpedo Room in the front of the boat. I remember the personal thrill I got when the Torpedoman of the Watch made the announcement after we left port and were making about twelve knots on the surface. "Underway on nuclear power." This was the famous log entry made aboard the U.S.S. *Nautilus* the first time this happened. When a submarine with an *Albacore* hull is on the surface the great majority of the boat is still under water. The *Albacore* hull boats did not run all that great on the surface, like the old style diesel boats did. The trade off was their speed and maneuverability underwater. The diesel boats were faster on the surface and very slow submerged.

I believe it was the second day out in the afternoon, after everybody got everything stowed for sea, it was announced on the 1MC (public address system throughout the submarine) to prepare for "angles and dangles." Now here was a new experience! It was also a great way to test to see if the ship was really rigged for sea. Angles and dangles are done fully submerged. After ensuring we were alone in our little spot in the ocean, the Captain orders up "Flank Speed," then does left and right radical maneuvers including going deeper and shallower. Initially, I was near my rack in the Torpedo Room, witnessing the torpedoes shifting on the skids as the ship would list from side to side. I moved back to where the torpedoman was sitting and marveled at the "speedometer" mounted there in the after part of the Torpedo Room. Yep, I was impressed. I decided to leave the Torpedo Room and I went into the Crews Mess and sat at one of the tables with a few of my other teammates. What a ride! What a submarine!

Many of the "riders" in my division back at Kamiseya, Japan, warned that the submariners didn't like the spooks very much. "Riders" were considered "hazards" and "NUBs," non-useful bodies. Personally, I didn't find this to be the case. But, if I wasn't doing anything when there was work to be done, I would assist the crewmembers in field day (cleaning) and working parties moving stores and stuff like that. I also learned the submariners were very proud of their respective skills and jobs and would willingly share their knowledge with you if you showed an interest. As curious as I was in my early twenties, I was soaking this up like a sponge. I found the more I knew about submarines, the smarter I could be in providing assistance to the submarine's mission. One subtle resentment seemed to be the crew's perception that the submarine special operation was to carry the spooks to special parts of the world, so we could do our job. I started countering with my suggestion that the reason the spooks were aboard was because their submarine received a special mission to operate in a certain part of the world where our skills were needed to support the boat. I guess both perspectives were correct.

Submariners have a unique socialization process. I imagine it has a lot to do with whether or not an individual can "cut the mustard" in a submarine. "Life is simple; you're either qualified or you're not." There is a lot of teasing and playing jokes on each other. Most of it is done in jest, but I've seen some fairly vicious attacks, too. I never saw a fight. Functionally, it serves to weed out those who could not adapt to the rigors of submarine life. Many of our spooks considered themselves as "outsiders" and refused to join in with the crews. Some of our people were elitists and actually thought they were better than the submariners. Many of our officers cast themselves in such a position, and, if they couldn't adapt, they were quite ineffective.

This is a tangent! One of the things I did not learn as a Chief was that I had a responsibility to train the junior officers who were assigned as our Officers-in-Charge (OIC). I didn't realize this until many years after I retired, then I regretted this omission on my part. So, if you're an active duty sailor reading this, learn from my error. There was a very good reason for this poor attitude on my part. By the time I was a Chief, I was committed to doing the best I could to support every submarine in which I served. Many of the officers assigned to Naval Security Group Fleet Support were people who had non-technical college degrees. We sometimes referred to these as "degrees in underwater basket weaving." Many of these prima donnas were actually obstacles to get around while we were at sea doing these missions. Their major function was to act as intermediary between our team and the ship and to write a specific section of the patrol report. Notwithstanding their writing skills, their ability to mediate for us depended upon their interpersonal relationships with the ship's officers in the wardroom. Many who did poorly in this department would rather argue and question the advice of their team than represent that view to those in command. Usually it was because they simply didn't understand the issue. This is where a good Chief could make a difference. There were a lot of screw-ups due to this relationship. Smart Captains, like Whitey Mack, established a personal rapport with the team members to obtain different perspectives to make his decisions. Of course, Whitey Mack was the best. Our most successful OIC's typically were the mustang officers (former enlisted). They understood and conducted themselves very effectively. It was great working with these guys. Some of the college boys learned the trade, too. One gentleman, Peter Pira, was a gem to work with. We had some great successes with him as the "spook boss." Another was Jack O'Neill. I particularly liked working with Donald Fallon. He'd been a Chief and was a Lieutenant when I was on his team in *Lapon*. Fallon had been tipped off (by me) that Whitey distrusted our previous OIC on *Lapon*'s first run. This next situation was reported in *Blind Man's Bluff* (Sontag and Drew). Shortly after getting underway, LT Fallon and Whitey Mack were alone in the Wardroom, and Whitey was checking out Fallon to see what kind of a guy Fallon was. Fallon was ready for this conversation and replied, "Captain, when that brow goes over, you're what's known as the NOMFWIC." Captain Mack asked what that was and Fallon replied, "Sir, that's the Number One Mother F— What's in Charge." Mack and Fallon got along famously. With the exception of the mustangs, you couldn't tell the good guys from the bad guys without a scorecard. The worst kind of OIC was one who would take credit for the work of his team as if he was the genius behind the event. The OIC got the medal, and a deserving operator got forgotten.

My third submarine in 1967 was the U.S.S. *Guardfish* (SSN-612) out of Pearl Harbor, Hawaii. *Guardfish* was the next class of submarine following the *Skipjack* class, to which *Scamp* belongs. *Guardfish* was a *Thresher* class submarine. This name was changed to *Permit* class after *Thresher* was lost with all hands on April 10, 1963. This was also the first class of submarine to have the Torpedo Room amidships, leaving the bow of the ship for a super sonar sphere. This design was a quantum leap in sonar technology. American submarines were getting better all the time.

Guardfish also had a great crew. The Radioman, Chief Robert Farrell, was one of the finest gentlemen I'd ever met. I spent a lot of time working with him and learned a lot about communications. He was a natural leader and very competent.

This vignette has to do with the ship Communications Officer. He was an academy graduate. This is another example of an officer who just didn't understand operations. *Guardfish* had to send a message out in Morse code during this mission. They wanted to send the message as fast as possible, so the Comm Boss decided a speed key must be used. However, there was nobody in the communications department who had a great deal of experience with a speed key. Our team had a ham radio operator who was very good with a speed key. I took the liberty of offering his services. The Comm Boss declined. Chief Farrell had a first class that worked for him who was very good with a standard key. The Chief recommended this man send the message. The Comm Boss declined stating this was a "high priority" message, and it must be sent with a speed key. He also decided the Chief must send the message. The Chief just shook his head and did the best he could to send the message. He got it out.

After my experience in San Diego, and my visit with Olin Barber regarding the Tommy Duncan opportunity, I began giving my future in music a lot more serious consideration. I had a wife and two children at this point. Caring for them was a very important responsibility that could have been very tenuous if I left the Navy to pursue a music dream. I was nearing eight years in the Navy. I was a Second Class Petty Officer (E-5). I was 25 years old and a bit more mature (but not completely). Growing old is obligatory; growing up is optional. I was really enjoying and proud of my contributions to the success of submarine missions. I started receiving recognition and credit for my job performance. My evaluations were good. I gave serious thought to reenlisting for six years and making, at least, a 20-year career in the Navy. Since I had not received any reenlistment bonus when I came back into the Navy in 1965 (I had been out for six months), I qualified to receive a significantly larger reenlistment bonus up to $10,000.00. That was a lot of money in those days. I decided to stay in the Navy, in the submarine program, and make a career. During the *Guardfish* mission my attitude and professionalism changed.

We had been on a very successful mission aboard *Guardfish*, and our return to Pearl Harbor was scheduled for Christmas Eve. Morale was high and *Guardfish* was making "going-home turns." ("Going home turns" is where the Throttleman adds a few turns on the screw to the ordered speed to inch the submarine at the "fastest possible ordered speed" when heading for home.) However, Murphy's Law (whatever can go wrong, will) was about to strike. Just outside of Pearl Harbor, *Guardfish* surfaced. There was a delay getting the Officer-of-the-Deck on the bridge, as the bridge access hatch was difficult to open. During this evolution *Guardfish* was approximately 150 yards to the right of the channel and ran aground on a reef. I was in the Radio Shack when Captain Hines came in with the Chief Radioman to call Pearl on the ship-to-shore circuit. The Chief asked me to keep a log of the radio transmissions. The Captain reported we'd grounded on the reef, he'd blown all ballast in an attempt to back off, and we'd been unsuccessful so far. The word came back on the circuit to flood down to preclude going further up on the reef. I knew at that directive the Captain was in deep trouble. My heart went out to Captain Hines. He was a great guy, and he'd had a very successful mission. Now he was going to lose it all, due to this grounding.

On Christmas Day they sent out a small landing craft to pick up our team and take us over to a torpedo retriever that took us in to the base. They really didn't want us on board when the press arrived. That was fine with us. The next day we flew back to Japan, arriving on December 27, 1967, (a day later) due to the International Date Line.

Upon my return to Japan, we lived in Yokohama, I learned that Sandy had received a phone call while I was away informing her that I had been killed. Needless to say, this was quite a shock for her. This was during the Vietnam War, so it was never out of the question. However, she was astute enough to know this was not the manner in which a death of a service member would be announced. She called Chief Bowie and reported what happened. Within an hour Chief Bowie and his wife, Lu, the Division Officer, and an officer from the Office of Naval Intelligence were visiting Sandy. First, the Chief informed her that there was no information regarding the death of anybody. All they knew for sure was the boat had been extended, at least, twice during the mission. All information was obtained, and the guilty person was found and arrested, and he was no longer stationed at Kamiseya, Japan, when I got home. I think that was a good thing. Among other things he was charged with misuse of classified information, the ship extension messages. These were classified messages to the *Guardfish* that extended the time at sea as a modification to the Operational Order.

I put in my request to reenlist and for my reenlistment bonus. My transfer date was for February 1968, and I put in for the 3rd, so Sandy and I could go with my parents to Quebec, Canada, for their annual Winter Carnival. Then another spook world tragedy occurred when the North Koreans attacked and captured the U.S.S. *Pueblo* on January 23, 1968. Almost immediately everyone in the Fleet Support Division deployed on every kind of ship and aircraft available. I could not be sent out due to my transfer, but I voluntarily shifted my transfer date from February 3 to February 28. There were only half a dozen of us left in the division to do the duties required of the unit. It was during this period I got to work with Chief Donald Perreault, who we all called "Frenchie," (not the one in the song in Chapter 21) who was a superior operator. I learned a lot from his guidance. I was a Second Class then, and in later years he and I made a submarine trip together when I was a Chief. I'd caught up with him. Frenchie was a Communications Technician (CT) legend. I believe he made more submarine patrols than any other CT. Where I ended up with an aggregate of four years underwater, Frenchie exceeded six years. At one point, the Chief of Naval Operations learned that Chief Perreault had made 28 submarine missions at that point in time, and he directed that the Chief be given a personal award for that achievement. Chief Perreault was certainly one of the NSG sailors who went unrecognized for his unique contributions to this special program during the Cold War. Somehow, I don't think Frenchie really cared. He is now deceased. It was a great honor to know such a patriot.

Along with my reenlistment, I also applied for the Navy Associate Degree Completion Program (ADCOP) while at Kamiseya. This was a two-year college program for senior enlisted personnel. The command approved my request with the endorsement: "Forwarded recommending approval." In later years I learned that verbiage was the kiss of death for a Navy request.

Sandy and I returned to CONUS (Continental United States) and were met at Travis AFB by my Uncle Ray Dufour (mother's brother), and we spent a few days with him near Sacramento, California. Uncle Ray was an engineer who worked for Aerojet, and he worked on the propellant for the Polaris missile. Sandy and I flew on to Maine with our two children, William and Cher Maria, to enjoy some time with our families.

In April I was to report to the New London Submarine Base to attend an electronics school for three weeks, which was part of the Submarine School. This was the suite of equipment our teams were to use aboard the 637-class submarines. The first two weeks, Sandy and the kids stayed with my Aunt Flo Spencer (mother's sister) in Everett, Massachusetts. I'd come north on the weekends. The third week of school, we stayed in a motel in New London. We then headed south for a full tour of duty at a Naval Security Activity (NSGA) in Maryland.

At the NSGA I met more guys I knew, some who preceded me from Japan, and others that I knew in the schools I'd attended. It was like old home week. Almost immediately I got assigned to the team that would deploy in U.S.S. *Lapon* on her first mission. There were some great guys assigned to this group. The Chief was Russ Krause, a good teacher and supervisor. The alternate supervisor was Jim Reeb; Jim and I became lifetime friends and have stayed in touch to this day. Another fellow on the team was named Joseph David James, but we all called him "Jesse." This was also the trip where we learned to appreciate what a great leader and submarine skipper Captain Mack was (See Chapter 3). After a work-up period we got delayed for a few days while *Lapon* engaged in the Search and Rescue for the U.S.S. *Scorpion*. (See Chapter 1)

Submarine Qualification

Lapon was "my" boat. I'd done a good job on the first run. Captain Mack asked to have me assigned to his next mission, which would be a few months away. I didn't know the Captain made this request. When I got back to the Division, I made a personal request to the Chief-in-Charge to be assigned to every mission made by *Lapon*. He didn't have a problem with that.

As I had personally contributed significantly to a certain event aboard *Lapon* involving the safety of the ship, Captain Mack asked the team OIC about recommending me for a personal award. The OIC told the Captain my contribution would be reflected in my trip evaluation, and I would be assured of a personal award upon transfer. Russ Krause told me of this situation, after he became the Division Chief some years later. I would like to make clear that in my Navy career I was awarded seven personal awards, two Meritorious Service Medals, two Joint Service Commendation Medals, two Navy Commendation Medals, and one Navy Achievement Medal, and not one of these came from the Naval Security Group. Sadly, not only from my perspective, many NSG enlisted personnel lost valuable points for promotion because of this lack of attention to detail by those responsible for personnel administration in our divisions. The personal awards, and unit awards at this point in time in the Navy, were worth promotion points up to the amount of 15, which is the amount allotted for a Medal of Honor. More to follow regarding promotion below!

Lapon's second trip was to be early in 1969, and I was assigned to the team. LT Don Fallon was the OIC and Bruce Reed the Chief-in-Charge. Bruce was the consummate professional. He was an instructor when I went to language school and at another course of study where Jerry Henley and I did so poorly that we won a tour of duty in Cuba. I had also made the decision to go through the submarine qualification program. *Lapon* had a new XO, LCDR Brickell. I applied to him for a qualification card. He provided me with a booklet that described the qualification process, and it had a Xerox copy of a qual card in the back of the booklet. He told me to use that as a qual card. I didn't think much of it at the time, but I later discovered he didn't believe I was serious about this and I would quit. Fallon told me he'd heard this from discussions in the Wardroom.

The *Lapon* qualification program was designed to be accomplished in thirteen months. My goal was to do it in three months. I told Chief Reed of my plans, and I dedicated every possible minute to learning all I could about submarine systems and having qualified submariners sign off that I knew the system for which they affixed their signature to my qual card. The process was also a check on the person who signed the card, as their professional reputation was on the line if the candidate did not know the system properly. Once again, I found the Lapon crew willing to do everything to assist me to qualify on their submarine. I would literally sit with these guys for hours listening to their instruction, answering their questions to show my understanding, and studying the piping manual that showed diagrams of the submarine systems plus the Ship's SORM (Submarine Operating Regulations Manual). The biggest responsibility was damage control. This had to do with responding to casualties everywhere in the boat. The sailors needed to know where to find the damage control equipment, tool kits, fire extinguishers, pipe patch kits, etc., and how to use each. All emergency systems needed to be understood. I totally dedicated myself to learning all I needed to know to qualify. I do believe I was the first CTI to earn submarine dolphins. I can attest that submariners *earn* their dolphins. This is why there is such a thing as *Brothers of the Dolphin*, as penned by my friend Bobby Reed.

Towards the end of our on-station time, I had completed all the requirements on the qualification card. I approached the XO to apply for a chiefs' board. The XO took my card (sheet) and handed me another card for planesman/helmsman/lookout and topside watch. This floored me. I had not considered that I would be required to do these things, as they were ship requirements not really dolphin requirements as I understood it. I knew other spooks who had qualified in submarines did not do these things. I went to the Crews Mess and coffee to think this over. I considered quitting at that point, but then decided that this man would not get the best of me. An innate stubbornness kicked in. *Lapon* was going to Holy Loch for an ORSE Board (Operational Reactor Systems Exam). This is where a team from Naval Reactors comes aboard the submarine to conduct a series of tests and interviews to ensure the crew is operating according to regulations and standards. LT Fallon arranged to have our team get several days of "basket" leave, leave that didn't count from the member's regular 30 days annual leave. I spoke to Chief Reed for permission to remain aboard to complete my ship qualifications. I did the lookout watches while transiting on the surface on our way in and out of Holy Loch. I did the planesman/helmsman watches under instruction pretty much during the ORSE and in transits. And I did the topside watches while in Holy Loch and Faslane. I noticed something while going through these requirements. Even the ship's officers were assisting me to know all I needed to know. I didn't realize it, but they were rooting for me to get through the program. It seems the XO was clearly against it. But I did enjoy these duties and understood what they were all about. I especially loved the lookout watches while steaming on the surface. Thankfully the weather was warm and nice. I'm sure it would have been different had it been stormy.

I got through my Chiefs' Board, and the XO assigned officers for my forward and after walkthroughs. These walkthroughs generally take from six to eighteen hours. The forward walkthrough was fine and a real good learning experience, as the Lieutenant (can't remember his name) spent a great deal of time explaining running lights and some basic navigation subjects. However, back aft the XO assigned a gentleman who was the most knowledgeable nuke on the ship, CWO-4 Herschel Hobbs, who was waiting for his commission in the Limited Duty Officer program. This gentleman later retired as a full Commander. I was really worried about this guy. My shipmates advised, "Just wing it!" "Yeah, like I'm gonna fool Mr. Hobbs." We did the aft walkthrough and my impression was I wasn't doing so hot. Mr. Hobbs asked me who my division officer was, and I replied, "Mr. Fallon." Then he said, "You're the spook?" I admitted I was. He obviously didn't have a clue as to who I was, so it was clear he was not there to disqualify me. I did feel fine about this, as it was more evidence that I was not getting any special treatment in my qualification process. He signed the qual card. I went back to the XO.

Lieutenant Commander Brickell later advised me he had found an instruction that stated "midshipmen" could not earn their submarine dolphins in less than six months. Apparently, the XO believed I was only aboard for three months. He advised he could not award me submarine dolphins. He congratulated me on my success for completing the process and wished me well. I didn't know if he was jerking my chain or not. Maybe he wanted to see what I would do with this obstacle. Back to the Crews Mess and that mood-adjusting cup of coffee! I never felt more depressed in my life. In my mind and my personal sense of justice, I had completed the submarine qualification program, and I *should* be issued my silver dolphins. Then that stubbornness kicked in again. I went to the ship's yeoman and got a Special Request Chit. I requested an Article 15 Captain's Mast to be held before Captain Whitey Mack before we reached Norfolk. In the chit I pointed out that I had been a *Lapon* crewmember for nine months, since this was my second consecutive mission aboard *Lapon*. I found Chief Reed, who approved my chit, then I cornered LT Fallon. Obviously, he knew what was going on, as he determined to take the chit to the XO himself, as the XO was the next officer in the chain to the Captain. If a problem cannot be otherwise resolved, the Article 15 must be granted, and the Captain must rule on the matter. Mr. Fallon came back to me the next day and advised, "Don't worry about it." I had the kind of faith in Don Fallon that if he gave his word on something, it was the truth.

The night before pulling in to Norfolk I was in the Crew's Mess with my guitar entertaining the crew. I'd been singing for about a half an hour when Captain Mack came out and sat down and listened to the music. I was honored that he did that. After about twenty minutes, he stood up and suggested I take a break. I sat down and the Captain came to the front of the Compartment where I had been singing. Then he started talking about some guy who was working on his qualifications, and it occurred to the crew before me that he was talking about me. I don't remember anything about what he said. Pretty soon somebody said, "Stand up, Dummy!" So I stood up and Captain Whitey Mack pinned silver submarine dolphins on my poopy suit, handed me a qualification certificate signed by Chester M. Mack, not the XO, aboard "U.S.S. Classified." They did not want to divulge the name of the submarine in which I qualified at the time. I was so proud! I couldn't have been happier. The crew gave me a great ovation. This day, I became a submariner. There are two people I wish to thank for their guidance, encouragement, and confidence: the late Billy Burchell, the Senior Chief Radioman, and Howard Jones, a nuclear electrician who retired as a Lieutenant Commander, and who played the best guitar on the boat. Later in 1982 Howard played music with me at Norm's Lounge in Groton, CT, for about a year. I have a picture of Howard and the band with Jeannie C. Reilly from our show at the Brooklyn Fair in 1982. As an aside, Jeannie had a backup band with her called the Red Mountain Boys. Today their band name is Diamond Rio. Yep, I qualified in submariners. I also got promoted to First Class Petty Officer (E-6) on that mission. That didn't matter; I had my dolphins.

There's one more story about LT Fallon. He was quite a joker. He had snow-white hair, and he kept it cropped short in those days, in a crew cut. It seems on one of his earlier trips he had colored his hair brown with something that could be readily washed out in the shower. Then he waited until the first situation occurred that would cause crewmen on the submarine great concern (don't worry; it always happened). Then after expressing his "overwhelming personal fear at the event" in front of a significant number of the crew and wardroom and feigning to be visibly shaken, he took a shower and washed the color out of his hair. Then it appeared that his hair turned white overnight.

Atlantic Operations

When I think of LT Don Fallon there are a few things I remember. First and foremost, LT Fallon is the only spook officer to qualify in submarines aboard a nuclear fast-attack boat that I know of. He started his qualifications aboard *Lapon*, and he finished aboard the U.S.S. *Flying Fish*. LT Walt Pickett, the tall guy in my reenlistment picture with Sandy and I at Kamiseya, qualified on a diesel boat circa 1966–67. LT Steve Wood was an academy graduate who qualified in diesel boats before he became a NSG officer. I did not get the opportunity to make a trip with Mr. Pickett. Mr. Wood had the makings of a great NSG OIC, but he decided to leave the Navy. I later worked for Mr. Wood at A&T Technical Services in New London, Connecticut, where he was General Manager of the company. I remember Mr. Wood for his excellent leadership.

Secondly, when I think of Don Fallon, I'll never forget the story he told me about a post-mission briefing that was given to the Chief of Naval Operations at the Pentagon. I think it was a *Flying Fish* mission, but I'm not certain. Of course, where the CNO is, there are as many officers as the space will allow, and representatives from the Commander, Naval Security Group (CNSG), were present including a Captain (O-6). The submarine commanding officer had been presenting his briefing to CNO, Elmo Zumwalt, on a very successful patrol. The CNO asked the Captain of the boat a very direct question regarding the efficacy of the embarked NSG team. The ship Captain replied to the CNO, "Admiral, my spooks were magnificent." At the use of the term "spook," our NSG Captain addressed the commanding officer saying, "Commander (he was an O-5), don't you mean cryptologic personnel?" The use of the rank "Commander" for the Captain of a ship was the NSG Officer's way of letting the submariner know he was outranked by the NSG O-6, and the remark contained a certain amount of obvious rancor. The submariner simply ignored the obvious barb and repeated, "As I said, Admiral, my spooks were magnificent." This was an example of the kind of people we worked for. Many of us joked frequently that the difference between the Naval Security Group and the Boy Scouts is the Boy Scouts have adult leadership.

Lastly, I have been trying for years to get in touch with Don Fallon without success. I especially tried to find him for the *Lapon* reunion held in Virginia Beach in the year 2000. I do hope and pray he is well.

The third *Lapon* patrol, the second in 1969 and the historic *Yankee* trail, resulted in the song *Ballad of Whitey Mack* (See Chapter 4).

Following *Lapon*, my next three missions were aboard *Sea Devil*, *Greenling*, and *Hammerhead* in that order. This took me to the end of 1970. In *Sea Devil* we had a super team with my buddy, Lew Bearden, making his first submarine patrol. Dick Ousey was the Leading Chief, and I met Frank Courtney for the first time. Ousey and Courtney, and I believe one other, filled their qualification cards for their dolphins on this mission. Bearden began his qual program, and finished on a subsequent trip.

While aboard *Greenling*, LCDR Pete Pira and LT Mark Hinkley assisted me in drafting another letter of application for the ADCOP program. This one was successful. During these intervening years on the Atlantic side of the world I had completed 37 correspondence courses, some in my field, others in subjects that would assist me in my submarine support duties. My command gave me a superb endorsement, written by another mustang officer, much better than "Forwarded recommending approval." That made the difference. I could have left for college in mid-1970, but Mr. Pira was making a run aboard *Hammerhead*, and he asked me to make the run with him. I agreed. Good decision! He and I became good friends, a friendship that continues today. Also my friend Jesse James from *Lapon* was aboard *Greenling*, and Frank Courtney from the *Sea Devil* team was also on the team. I also met a very unique individual on this mission in the person of Mark Rutherford. Mark was a First Class Submarine Radioman at the time, but he and another Radioman, Charl Davidson, worked with our team. Both these gents were very well qualified and operated a special piece of equipment installed in *Greenling*. They were a great help.

Rutherford wanted to become a spook in the worst way. The success of converting from one critical rating to another, specifically from Radioman to Communications Technician, was virtually unheard of. The fact that he was a submariner made the conversion even more difficult. But Rutherford was one tenacious individual; he bucked the system, and obtained his wish. Rutherford, Courtney, and I were to serve together again in later years. These were formative years with a development of appreciation for each other's skills and ability that were to become important later in our careers.

On *Hammerhead* I got to serve with another dear friend, Neil Mantle. We'd met in language school back in 1961. Of course, with the last name of Mantle, he got tagged with the nickname Mick for the famous ball player, Mickey Mantle. I also called him "Montague," as he was from Montague, New York. He called me "Caribou." Mick and I hunted whitetail deer together in Maryland with bow and arrow. I'll never forget one morning at sea he woke me for my watch by saying, "Hey, Tom, there's a fresh two inches of snow on the ground. Let's go get 'em." That was confusing! For a moment I thought I was going deer hunting. Mick and I "hot racked" in *Hammerhead*. He and I worked as opposite section supervisors, twelve hours on and twelve hours off. So we shared the same bed. It was called "hot racking," because the bed was still warm when the off watch guy got in it.

The submarine crewmembers generally worked six hours on and twelve hours off. Typically, three sailors did the same job and rotated their on-watch time accordingly. However, with our teams, we only sent two men to do one job, so we chose to work twelve on and twelve off. If we did six on and six off, chances were we wouldn't get any sleep from time to time between watches. Being up for eighteen hours was not unusual, but remaining alert for that second watch could be very difficult. Twelve and twelve seemed to be the best approach. On my teams the supervisors worked from midnight to noon and noon to midnight. The other watchstanders worked from 0600 to 1800 and 1800 to 0600 Zulu. This overlap of watchstanders with supervisors ensured good continuity from watch to watch. The best and most experienced operators could be assigned to the 0600 to 1800 watch with the new guys and trainees taking the alternate watch. Modifications in watch schedules could be made as the situations dictate.

Personally, I am a nighthawk. When left to my own devices, I will go to bed late and sleep late. My watch period of choice was midnight to noon. When underway, the ship would convert to Zulu time, which was the time in Greenwich, England. For the sake of clarity and consistency, especially for communications schedules, all submarine reports were expressed in Zulu time. This made it easier for analysts to coordinate activities in all the world's time zones. It didn't take me long to figure out that by coming on watch at midnight, Zulu time, I could determine what would be going on for the day as activities began, and I could pass on to my relief suggestions for ship support when he took the watch at noon. If things were hot and heavy, I would remain on watch to assist for as long as I was needed. And if I got off watch at the regular time at noon, I could be available to assist the OIC as necessary, do analysis if required, and write a watch summary to assist with the patrol report. I generally did this in the Crew's Office, as the Yeoman was usually cleared for our operations, as he typed the ship's report. More than one ship's yeoman told me of situations where he was asked to type something but make sure he didn't read it. Duh!

The *Hammerhead* patrol was very successful. I had contributed to a unique method of operating our ship within a margin of safety (that's what the citation reads). Captain P.F. Carter, Commanding Officer of *Hammerhead*, recommended me for a Navy Commendation Medal for this accomplishment. This medal was to become significant in my Navy career.

I left NSGA Maryland just before Christmas in 1970 for transfer to Tidewater Community College, Portsmouth, Virginia, for the ADCOP program. I started college in January 1971.

College

In high school I was very inconsistent depending upon my current interests, girls and music, and distorted sense of priorities. I started high school in the college preparatory curriculum and graduated in the general. I virtually failed my entire sophomore year, passing only driver's education and physical education. However, the administration allowed me to take extra classes the next two years to graduate with my class of 1960. I guess I had a behavior problem, and they wanted to assist me to move on as rapidly as possible. Realistically, I did high school in three years. IQ, intelligence quotient, was a big thing then, and they thought mine was high enough that I could handle the extra courses. My class standing was 136 out of 157. Bad juju!

I believe my poor high school performance was one of the reasons I was not initially selected for the Navy Associate Degree Completion Program (ADCOP). So while I served my tour at NSGA in Maryland, I completed 37 correspondence courses. That helped!

Getting military housing in the Norfolk area was out of the question. We didn't expect to be there more than two years at the most, so we bought a house. It was our first experience with being homeowners. We were close to the college. With the exception of losing my proficiency pay, $75.00 per month, life was good.

I'd been very concerned that I wouldn't be able to do well in college. I had little idea of what to expect. I had a fear my writing skills were seriously deficient. Prior to transferring, I took a high school level English course to brush up, and a Navy math course. That was a bear! All my fears were unfounded. I slid into the college life with unexpected ease and success. When I graduated, I received my Associate in Science degree *summa cum laude*. Prior to this I didn't even know what that meant. I loved school. The sailors who were there were exceptionally bright and energetic. Classroom discussions were especially informative, as the sailors contributed with a level of experience that wouldn't have occurred otherwise. And the younger college students could always be counted upon for the fresh perspective. There was another group of students that consisted of first term military who had completed one hitch and was taking advantage of their G.I. Bill. They were around 21 to 24 years old. I was 29 years old. Most of the sailors were older than me.

After attending school for a full year, I learned there was a movement among some of the students to complain that the Navy ADCOP students were skewing the normal curve and making it difficult for them to obtain honors. The major complaint was the sailors were the "cream of the crop," and the average student couldn't compete. I found that quite humorous and recalled the adage: "Lead, follow, or get the hell out of the way!"

There's no question the Navy people did well and worked hard at it. Many Navy students were selected for officer programs. Some of the students were officers. In retrospect, I believe not having to contend with puberty and dating may have had a positive effect upon the sailors. Education certainly broadens one's horizons. It gives a larger knowledge base upon which to build, and it certainly increases options. When I transferred back to NSGA Maryland after Tidewater Community College, I determined to finish my bachelor's degree at the University of Maryland. This was accomplished in December 1975. When I was getting ready to leave the Navy after my twenty years, I interviewed for a job with Tracor in Rockville, Maryland. Much of the Tracor staff was made up of former Navy and retired officers. One retired Commander who interviewed me made the following comment: "I've seen many enlisted who begin college; I see very few who finish." The degree, at that point in time, resulted in a job offer three thousand dollars higher than other chiefs who had gone to work for Tracor.

Promotion to Chief Petty Officer

While at ADCOP I took the chief's test in 1971. This was my first time up for chief. I'd applied for Limited Duty Officer before I left Maryland. Sandra and I decided if I got selected for officer, I would stay in the Navy for 30 years. If I made chief first, I would complete 20 years and move on. That's what happened!

The promotion opportunities were exceptionally limited in those days. Worldwide there were only three chief petty officers in my field to be promoted from that 1971 test. Those not selected for promotion received a summary of how well they did on the test, which included what score was needed to be promoted. As I reviewed my results I could tell my total multiple had not been properly counted, and, if it had, I would have been, at least, the third individual promoted in my field. The multiple, as I remember, is made up of a combination of the test score, the average of the last number of evaluations, and credit for awards. My awards were not properly considered.

Remember my previous comments regarding the administration of the records of NSG enlisted that participated in the submarine support program? Well, many of the missions in which we participated were awarded unit citations. Each of these was worth one point in multiple. Plus personal awards such as the Meritorious Service Medal or the Navy Commendation Medal earned for a period prior to the test were worth three points each. I had learned through my contacts in Maryland that I had been put in for a Meritorious Service Medal for my three years of service and the six submarine missions I had made while attached to that command. Additionally, I knew I had been submitted for a Navy Commendation for my contribution to the success of the *Hammerhead* mission. Each award was worth three points. If just one was approved, I would have been promoted to CPO (Chief Petty Officer).

I brought my problem to my present command, which was Fleet Training Group, Norfolk. They advised they simply didn't have the information needed to support my challenge. I had also taken the initiative to maintain my clearance while in ADCOP to give me access to the Security Group facilities in Norfolk with the idea of keeping current while in college. I was the only sailor to do this. So I took my errata sheet and went in to this office with the purpose of calling my previous command in Maryland. My friend Jesse James had been promoted to Warrant Officer, and he was the individual I went to see when I was there. When I explained my situation to him, he assisted me with the contact to NSGA Maryland actually making the call himself on my behalf. He was told the command would *not* do anything to assist me, and that I would likely be promoted the next year. This total lack of support or consideration from this command hit me like a ton of bricks. Remember the cup of coffee in the Crew's Mess during my qualification saga? Well, I had a similar cup of coffee there at NSGD, Norfolk. The more I thought about it, the angrier I got. That old stubbornness kicked in, and I finally made a decision. I told Jesse I was going to drive to Washington, DC, and seek the assistance of my congressional representative, who, at the time, was William Cohen of Maine. I left Jesse and drove home to Portsmouth. By the time I got home, the phone was ringing. It was Jesse. He asked for a few days before I went to DC. I agreed.

The Navy universally frowns upon seeking congressional assistance by active duty personnel for military problems. The administrators will deny it, but that's the way it is. It means outsiders were going to look into Navy administration, and somebody was going to have to explain the situation to the satisfaction of a member of congress. This could only mean considerable embarrassment for somebody, probably me. I was also well aware that even if I succeeded in getting promoted through this process, future promotions were unlikely. Now I'm not certain if this is actually true, but you can understand I firmly believed it to be true. Those of you with a military background know of which I speak. However, most enlisted sailors have a goal of making chief petty officer while active. I didn't really believe I would be further promoted, so my decision was to go for it. I firmly believed I was being treated unjustly, and I was totally disappointed—read crushed—at the failure of those for whom I'd worked so diligently to support me. It wouldn't have been such a big thing, except somebody would have to admit the command didn't take the time to keep this sailor's records properly current.

Within a few days I received a call at home from a gentleman who identified himself as Commander Reindo from the COMSUBLANT staff in Norfolk. He told me he had been directed to review my situation regarding promotion to chief petty officer. I was totally floored. I answered his questions regarding the unit awards and the two personal awards for which I was submitted for activities prior to taking the CPO exam. He took all the information and advised he would get back to me. I immediately called Jesse to report this change of events. Jesse was not in the least bit surprised. I asked how this happened. Jesse was evasive and simply would not tell me. I certainly wasn't about to look a gift horse in the mouth or question this sudden source of support. I have never learned the total truth, but I have enough circumstantial evidence to have arrived at a probable conclusion, which I will hypothesize below.

Commander Reindo confirmed the unit awards for which I was eligible and the recommended award of the Navy Commendation Medal from *Hammerhead* was probed and awarded. Then a letter from COMSUBLANT, who was Admiral R.J.L. Long, to the Navy Examining Center stated that an administrative error at COMSUBLANT resulted in awards not being properly credited and requested consideration be given to promoting me to CPO. When I read that letter, it brought tears to my eyes. Sports fans, the Submarine Service went out on a limb for me. As a "spook," I was never a direct asset of COMSUBLANT. The only difference was the submarine dolphins. The Naval Security Group made me an orphan; the Submarine Service adopted me. I vowed right then and there to dedicate the remainder of my active service to support submarine operations. This I did! COMSUBLANT's request for my promotion was approved, and I was promoted to Chief in December of 1971. I was given the opportunity to challenge my date of rank, but I did not pursue it.

Over many years, including after retirement, I picked up enough information about what happened to suppose the following occurred: I believe Jesse James approached Captain Whitey Mack, who was at COMSUBLANT at the time as a full Captain. I suspect Captain Mack approached Captain Ken Carr, who was the COMSUBLANT Chief of Staff at the time, with my legitimate promotion problem. Commander Reindo worked directly for Captain Carr. I asked Captain Mack a few years ago about this, when Sandy and I were his guests at lunch in Groton. I could tell by the twinkle in his eye he knew much more than he was going to share with me. Following my promotion and subsequent initiation to chief, I put on my new chief's uniform and went to COMSUBLANT and personally thanked Captains Mack and Carr and Commander Reindo. Captain Carr assured me he would pass on my gratitude to Admiral Long. When my original record *Take Her Deep* was published, I sent courtesy copies to Captains Mack and Carr and to Admiral Long, who was at the Pentagon at that time. I received a nice thank you letter from each. I could not find Commander Reindo.

I also learned the Fleet Support bosses at NSGA Maryland were literally incensed at my success by going outside of their channels. The fact this issue did not go to Congress was never credited to anybody. My recommendation for the Meritorious Service Medal was pulled. That's all they could do to me. Yes, it was a slap in the face, but it didn't hurt my career. As I said previously, of seven personal awards, none came from the Naval Security Group. The unit awards I received in my career were one Presidential Unit Citation, eight Navy Unit Citations, and two Meritorious Unit Citations. While that doesn't tell anybody much, it's clear that significant things were happening in these units where I served. They were submarines.

I thought I could stay at Tidewater Community College for a second full year, but by that time the Navy was interested in getting the ADCOP students graduated and back to service ASAP. I made the mistake of getting my core requirements for the degree satisfied as soon as I could. My advisor, a retired military officer, obtained credit for me from my Navy Russian Language School, and I was graduated in May of 1972. Prior to graduation I drove to Alexandria, Virginia, to visit my detailer at BUPERS (Bureau of Naval Personnel) who was Chief Bobby Kays. Bobby and I attended that electronics course at submarine school together back in April of 1968. He was very accommodating. I asked to go back to the Fleet Support Division at NSGA Maryland. Most of the officer structure had changed while I was in college, and the second in command, LCDR Tom Pressley was still there, but he was a friend. I moved back there to fulfill my intent to remain in support of the Submarine Service. To get in everybody's good graces, I volunteered to do the Christmas trip that year. A couple of guys I knew volunteered to make the trip with me based upon my reputation. We were going to be gone for Thanksgiving, Christmas, and New Years. The ship was the U.S.S. *Bergall.*

Back to Work in the Atlantic

The *Bergall* was another great 637-class submarine. Captain Wyatt was a great leader and exceptionally competent. The XO was also a full Commander named Jack Maurer. He was the former commanding officer of the NR-1. He'd been involved in some pretty neat stuff with that vessel. I would later ship with Captain Jack aboard the U.S.S. *Parche*, where he was the commanding officer. It was aboard *Bergall* that I had the honor of meeting and serving with Ray "Pappy" Kuhn. He was Chief of the Boat. This great submariner passed away on March 21, 2005. He had 41 years of active naval service. What a legend!

Another strange experience occurred the evening our team went aboard *Bergall.* I was sitting in the Crew's Mess working with my own team taking care of administrative functions when a sailor sat down across the table from me. He had his service record in his hand, which he placed on the table. I glanced down at the record, and, rather than read the name, I read the service number which was one number different than mine. I looked up and there was Leslie Dionne from Fort Fairfield, Maine. He and I had joined the Navy together back in August of 1960. He was a First Class Hospital Corpsman. He was assigned to *Bergall*, but he was not making the mission. It was good seeing an old friend. That was the last time I saw him. He's now retired and living near Pensacola, Florida.

Bergall had a great trip. One particular evolution provided vital information required by the U.S. We were getting ready for our responsibilities and participation in this event, when an officer we had with us, not the OIC, rang the buzzer to Radio. He was a second officer sent with us as a training run to learn the business. He had sound-powered phones on, red goggles on, and he had the connector jack for the phones in his hand. This was not a good time to be bothering the people in the Radio Shack. When we opened the door, there stood this guy with the phone jack in his hand and asked, "Where do I plug this in?" I almost busted up laughing but controlled myself and did not suggest to him what immediately occurred to me. I told him to go to control and ask where he should plug in the phones to receive from Radio. When he was situated he should test the circuit. I advised I would be on the phones in Radio, and I would report to him. He would then report to the officer who had the deck and the conn. In this case, it was Captain Wyatt. We all performed flawlessly.

As *Bergall* was return from the mission, there were all the administrative functions left to do. As the leading chief for the spook team, I had to write the trip evaluations for each individual in our embarked group. I was sitting in the Chief's quarters at a small desk there, writing my rough drafts using a dictionary and a thesaurus. One of the chiefs came in and was making fun of me for using the thesaurus to find "officer words" to make the evaluations sound "highfalutin." I let the teasing go and handed the evals to our OIC for his approval. Then they would be signed by the XO, and these evaluations would be entered into each sailor's record. These evaluations were significant for promotion as described above.

Several days later the ship was holding field day to clean up the ship prior to entering port. I was in the Goat Locker (CPO Quarters) with the other chiefs helping to clean up. The chief who'd given me a hard time over my evals was present. Executive Officer Jack Maurer knocked and entered the quarters. He looked directly at me and said, "Chief Cox, I understand you are responsible for these evaluations." The XO was using his command voice, and my first thought was he would make me defend what I had written. I stood ready for the grilling and answered, "Yes, Sir." Then the XO said, "This is the finest and best, well-written evaluations I have ever received from a division chief. Well done!" And before I could say anything, he turned and left. I was totally surprised. In thinking about it later, I suspect Master Chief Kuhn, Chief of the Boat, had overheard the other chief giving me a razzing over my approach to doing the evals and took the opportunity to use it as a lesson to my heckler and the other chiefs.

My next submarine was the U.S.S. *Trepang*. This was the mission I made with LT Normand Houle. LT Houle was a very young looking individual who reminded one of a geek. He was an exceptionally intelligent individual. It did not occur to me he was a career NSG officer, or I might have conducted myself differently. The enlisted people referred to him as "Slick." We had a significant event brewing, similar to the one on *Bergall*, and I was awakened and called to Radio to supervise. When I entered Radio I was apprised of what was going on. When I understood the situation, I began directing the activities of the team, and I donned the sound-powered phones to communicate with LT Houle in Control. Somebody told me Slick wanted the team to do things somewhat differently. After listening to what they were telling me, I responded by stating, "F— Slick! We're going to do this right." I assured them I took full responsibility for all our activities. What I didn't know was the sound-powered phones I was using did not work correctly. The sound-powered phones had a push-to-talk feature. When the button on the mouthpiece was not pushed, nothing was supposed to be heard at the other end. However, this set was defective, and LT Houle could hear everything that we were saying in Radio. I fully commend him for not interfering with my directions to the watchstanders. Perhaps he agreed with what I was telling them to do. But, once again, our participation went off without a hitch, and we scored another coup in support of the national effort. Had I been a better chief, I would have explained to him why I was doing what I did as a part of his continuing education. It did not occur to me that the better he understood what we were doing, the better he could have represented our contribution to the success of the mission. Mr. Houle did an excellent job as OIC on this mission. According to others who had shipped with him, he didn't do well on their missions. In retrospect, I was guilty of forming an erroneous opinion of him based upon faulty input from others.

Mr. Houle made a trip a couple years later with my buddy, Lew Bearden. Mr. Houle castigated the team members on one occasion, so Chief Bearden asked to speak to him in private. Chief Bearden explained that if the Lieutenant had a problem with the team, he should advise his chief, and the chief would take care of the problem. Lew also explained to Mr. Houle that his remarks were detrimental to team morale, and Lew would have to work with the team to reconstruct their attention and dedication to the mission. When Captain Houle retired many years later, he spoke very highly of Chief Bearden's superb leadership. It was a discussion with Lew Bearden that made me realize I had not fulfilled my responsibility to assist in training of the OICs when I had the opportunity and obligation to do so. For those with whom I served and specifically to Captain Houle, I apologize for this failure. My second run in 1974 and an early run in 1975 were both aboard U.S.S. *Hammerhead*. These were four more missions in the Atlantic arena, all as a Chief Petty Officer.

Following my last mission aboard *Hammerhead*, I went to BUPERS to feel out the new detailer on what my next assignment would be. He wanted to send me to Turkey. I told him under no circumstances was I going to take my family to Turkey. Americans were being killed there. He jumped at that and said I could go unaccompanied to one of their remote sites in Turkey. Once again, I got angry and told him, "The only thing I could see to do is take the decision out of your hands." We parted as adversaries. I had no idea what I was going to do about this.

Special Projects

At one point in time around 1975 I was offered to work in a special project in which some of my contemporaries were involved. My name had been given to the OIC as a competent operator, and he approached me with his offer. I declined to participate, as I would not be deployed in a submarine. The officer blew up on the spot. He told me I was turning down a great opportunity without even knowing about it. His project was exceedingly important to national security, and I should really consider working for him. Well, I knew more than he expected about his project, and I knew he was having trouble keeping his team. I didn't think I could work with this guy. His attitude attack confirmed it for me.

Following my disappointing trip to BUPERS, I received a visit from two guys I had worked with before, Mack Empey, from *Lapon*'s first run, and Mark Rutherford, whom I had met on *Greenling*. I knew these guys were participating in a super secret special project that very few people in the Fleet Support Division knew about. They were looking for a dedicated linguist to support their project. My only question was, "Is this aboard submarines?" When they answered in the affirmative, I agreed to work with them. One of the special projects members was Frank Courtney, with whom I had served aboard *Sea Devil* and *Greenling*. The fourth member of the team was Bob Ellenwood. This took my next assignment out of the hands of the detailer at BUPERS. The family got to stay in Maryland. I had three and a half years to go to retire on twenty years. Good move!

As I got briefed on the various levels of the project clearances, and the multiple compartmented categories to which I was going to have access, it boggled the mind there was so much of it. I think the total was fifteen special accesses. I already had some of the clearances, but it just got bigger and bigger. The sorry part was a lack of guidance regarding who knew what and at what level. The basic program had three levels of access. For example, level two included everything about the project except where in the world it was located. Several times I have gone to high-level conferences regarding the project, which was supposed to be at level two, and they invariably exceeded the classification content. After a while you could only laugh. The project was too big. There were too many bosses. Because of the project successes, all the major players in the intelligence community wanted to claim ownership. Ashore, everybody was in civilian clothes. Everybody was introduced by first names. Then the high-ranking guys would get upset if we addressed them by their first names. You couldn't tell an admiral from a chief. Then there was a civilian contractor, who prepared all the equipment, hardware and software. When we visited at the contractor's, we didn't tell them we were in the Navy, we used our driver's licenses for identification and listed our jobs as DOD (Department of Defense). Somehow we kept it all straight.

Mark Rutherford and Mack Empey were the only two guys from the original group who remained on the special project team. Their part of the team consisted of four watchstanders, two on watch at a time. The two other original team members quit. The space where these men worked was called "The Chartroom."

The first two boats assigned to this project were *Halibut* and *Seawolf*. Others have written about this, so I can retain my position of neither confirming nor denying. Both submarines were very old and far from competitive tactically with modern nuclear submarines of the 1970s. If we had had to go up against any hostile force of any nation in these relics, we would have been seriously disadvantaged. My first boat in the project was *Seawolf*. She had a great commanding officer in Captain Charles MacVean, a great crew, and we learned to love and respect this ship. *Seawolf* served her country longer than any other submarine. Captain MacVean achieved the same respect and support from his crew as Whitey Mack, with a totally different approach to leadership. Captain MacVean, in addition to being a superb naval officer, is a Ph.D. in nuclear physics. He is a very personable individual, respected and admired by all of us.

Everything in *Seawolf* seemed to be patchwork. The old, out-of-date equipment was falling apart. Many systems had been jerry-rigged to get them to work. That she was still in service was a great credit to Captain and crew. These guys knew their business. The thing that troubled me personally was that she was acoustically noisy. This is not a good thing for a submarine attempting to operate covertly. Be advised, I wouldn't be saying these things about these old submarines if they were still operational.

Knowing how noisy *Seawolf* was, I once suggested to Captain MacVean that we shut down the reactor and proceed through a chokepoint on the battery. The quietest submarine acoustically is a diesel boat on the battery. Now I don't know how realistic this idea was, but the Captain didn't act like it was total lunacy. He simply advised he didn't dare shut the reactor down by saying it might not restart. That got my attention. I suppose if he shut it down, he would have to file special reports ad nauseam in explanation of his action. We went through the chokepoint, but no reaction to our presence was detected. I guess we sounded more like a merchant ship than a submarine. Lucky! I made two special project missions in *Seawolf.*

The next submarine involved in this special project was U.S.S. *Parche.* Captain Jack Maurer, previously met as XO of *Bergall,* was the commanding officer. Captain Jack had a distinguished naval career, and he contributed greatly to national security during the Cold War. It was an honor to work with him again. The XO on *Parche* was Archie Clemens who retired as a three-star admiral. I made one mission aboard *Parche.* Later publicity reported the splendid history of this ship and its contributions and service during the Cold War.

A couple years after I retired, I got a call one day from Mark Rutherford. It seems our beloved special project had been compromised, and our security people were looking for the culprit. A couple of our team members were really raked over the coals due to this issue. It was later learned that a traitor, Ronald Pelton, sold us out for a paltry amount of money. The scary part was this breach of security could have cost us an entire submarine and crew. This traitor jeopardized the lives of many of my shipmates.

Since the "end" of the Cold War, many keynote speakers at submarine veteran reunions, birthday balls, and conventions have stated what a contribution to national security was made by the U.S. Submarine Service. As Mr. Richard Havre stated in the *Blind Man's Bluff* History Channel Special, "The American people got their money's worth from the Submarine Service during the Cold War." This includes not only the activities of the fast-attack boats, but also the service of our boomers in their deterrence role. This made all the difference!

Submarine Songs

Around 1993, my daughter Cher Maria (Cox) Hebert got the idea of putting my record album *Take Her Deep* on a CD. At first it was supposed to be a surprise for my birthday, but to get it done she had to have the original master tapes. These I had at home. So we contacted producers in Scarborough, Maine, with the idea of producing 500 copies. The cost per unit was high, but I didn't know any better. This was not a very professional operation. In my experience with them, I often received complaints of CDs that malfunctioned. On one occasion, I had an entire order of 200 CDs that were defective. I'd already sold nine of them and offered to replace them all. But I'd given a few away and couldn't contact those folks. I paid the bucks and started advertising in the American Submariner, the periodical of the U.S. Submarine Veterans, Inc. I found that many submariners who had heard of the earlier vinyl record were glad to be able to get the collection on CD. When another submariner, Gus Pedersen who I call Pete, who worked for Wooden Ships Music contacted me, he wanted to obtain copies of the *Take Her Deep* CDs to sell through their website of sea shanties.

Pete was a former *Ben Franklin* boomer sailor. He had contacts for CD production. I sent him a disc and requested he evaluate it. The disc he reviewed that was made by the Scarbourough, Maine, company was absolutely horrible. When we next talked he offered to remaster the album again and have real professionals, Disc Makers, who do the CDs for the real stars, do the album for me. Since then I've had no bad CDs. Gus Pedersen is the Executive Producer for my last two CDs, *In Honor of...* and *Spirituals*.

By this time the Internet was in full swing and a few shipmates allowed me to advertise for free on their Internet sites. I was slow getting started in this medium, as I knew very little about the Internet. The first shipmate who established a business relationship was Don Merrigan of Graphic Enterprises of Marblehead at www.subnet.com, and the only CD he ever sold was *Take Her Deep*. The second to assist was Ron Martini, now at www.rontini.com. Ron placed a review on his bulletin board, and he continues to do that occasionally today. Ron has been a good friend. Later on, I learned of Don Gentry's bulletin board at www.submarinesailor.com. For a while, I would harvest the e-mail addresses of submariners from this website and send ads via e-mail for the CDs. Usually, I would get about half a dozen orders from about 200 e-mails. Yeah, this is spam. I got some real nasty responses from submariners who were offended that I did this. And I started receiving a plethora of viruses. So everybody who sent a virus, you can rejoice. Somebody finally got me. Yep, it was costly. Anyway, I stopped doing this about three years ago, so the virus that got me shouldn't have come from that source. The biggest and best retailer for the submarine music is The Submarine Store, in Gaithersburg, Maryland, at www.submarinestore.com. I had the pleasure of meeting Harry Lieberman and his lovely wife, Toni, and "Bodega" Bob Homme at the 2000 Convention of Submarine Veterans, Inc., in Atlantic City. These are some real nice people who have virtually every product of submarine paraphernalia known. Their products are high quality, and everything is submarine related. Master Chief John Crouse, of the Saint Mary's Submarine Museum in Kings Bay, Georgia, also began selling the CDs. I could not have continued without the kind assistance of these generous webmasters and the gent who was to become my partner for a new CD, Bobby Reed.

In 1999 a fellow from Milford, Massachusetts, named Bobby Reed bought one of the *Take Her Deep* CDs. Being a submarine sailor himself, having served in the *G.W. Carver*, a boomer, he liked the music. Bobby also turned out to be a singer and songwriter who formerly owned a recording company in the Boston area. He and a partner specialized in doing radio commercials and air spots. When they dissolved the business to pursue alternative employment, Bobby transferred some of the equipment and set it up in the basement of his home. He had kept current with technology, and he'd modernized everything with digital technology. He had digital effects modules, and he was recording on an eight track digital audiotape. Bobby downloaded the *Big Black Submarine* cut from the *Take Her Deep* album and added guitar, bass, and backup vocal to the original track. It took him a time or two to realize I had not recorded with a standard tuning. In fact, when I arrived at Omega Studios, I tuned my guitar with a studio piano that had the European tuning. This is half a step lower than the standard tuning. Then as I retuned by ear before each song was recorded, the actual tuning in relationship to the standard tuning was further compromised. Bobby figured it out right away and simply tuned with the CD. Bobby sent me a cassette tape that included my song with his enhancements plus a bunch of songs he wrote, including one entitled *Brothers of the Dolphin*. I liked the enhancements to my song. I'd always felt the album was deficient, because I could not afford sideman musicians and professional vocal backup. And I loved his song *Brothers of the Dolphin*. We began an e-mail correspondence.

Bobby invited Sandy and me to attend a reunion of the *G.W. Carver* in the fall of 2000 in Norwich, Connecticut. We agreed. There was another function in the Groton/New London area that I was attending which was a lobster night at the SUBVETS Headquarters at 40 School Street. Bobby arranged for us and his shipmate, Bob Devitt, to do a few songs at the *Carver* reunion. On Thursday, Sandy and I drove to Bobby's house in Milford, Massachusetts. We were invited to spend the evening with him and his wife Margie, and we would all head for Groton in the morning. Of course, in the evening following dinner, we were sitting having drinks in the living room, and we were speaking about music and recordings. Bobby asked me if I expected to do any further CDs. I told him what my sales history was and admitted another CD would probably not be very cost effective. While I had several songs to record, I simply couldn't afford to rent another studio at the current prices, and I didn't want to do another album without professional background music. I could not afford the backup musicians. Bobby asked if I would do another album if I didn't have to pay those costs. I answered in the affirmative. He asked me to accompany him to his basement studio. There he showed me a complete, state-of-the-art, digital recording studio. He offered to do the recording, play backup music, and he showed me his computer music program. This is a program that allows the musician to enter the chord progressions for a song into a computer then include a broad variety of instrumentation, all computer-generated, including drums at whatever tempo desired. Bobby is also an electrical engineer. He had my interest. He also offered his song *Brothers of the*

Dolphin to me to sing. For submariners, that is a great song. He offered his studio and services free of charge.

Bobby's generosity made a big impression on me. I gave his offer a great deal of consideration, and over the holidays I made the decision to ask Bobby to record an album with me. I could have done this on my own and taken advantage of his generosity, but that was not the right thing to do under the circumstances. When I contacted him, he thought I wanted to record the whole album myself but use his facilities. I had to explain that what I was offering was for us to record the album together, and we would split the costs and the sales proceeds. After the recording was over, and there was a lot of work that went into the album, I would send the tape to Pete at Wooden Ships, and take care of the CD sales. We were going to premier the album at the SUBVETS for that year's anniversary celebration but we didn't make the deadline. Bobby agreed to do the album with me, and we set a date for me to come to Milford to do my share of the recording of my songs. I also intended to include two songs I'd recorded back in 1980 for a 45-RPM record called *Bring the Nautilus Home* (Chapter 14) and *Paybacks Are Hell* (Chapter 18). These were professionally cut songs, done in a studio in Connecticut, with the musicians from the original Tommy Cox Band, Gerry Rucker and Jim Corbett. Bobby had only two songs of the Navy and Submarine Service, *Brothers of the Dolphin* and *If You Didn't Get Enough While in Navy Blue*. But he had two more songs respecting the U.S.S. *Constitution*, *Lady of the Water* and *Every Now and Then*. It was during this session that we wrote the first two verses and the bridge of *Blind Man's Bluff* in just about an hour. I added the last verse a year or so later. I suggested he include a couple of his standard songs and I would do the same. The album got done. Bobby knew a graphic artist from Massachusetts named Margie Jump-Cecco, who would do a drawing for the cover. We called the album *Brothers of the Dolphin*, using Bobby's song as the number one cut. Bobby went to Connecticut and beseeched the Groton SUBVETS Base Commander John Carcioppolo to record the "Dive, dive" and "Surface, surface, surface" at the beginning and end of the album. This was an idea used in my original *Take Her Deep* album. Gus Pedersen did a great job on the tray card and liner. It was truly a submarine undertaking by cooperating submariners. Never before has Bobby's line in the song *Brothers of the Dolphin*, where he said: "depend upon each other" been more true.

When our son Bill was taken to Brigham and Women's Hospital in Massachusetts in a coma in August of 2002 to evaluate the possibility of recovery, Bobby and Margie graciously opened up their home and allowed Donna, Bill's wife, to camp out there for the time Bill was in Massachusetts. This is something for which we will be eternally grateful. The Reeds are wonderful people, and we love them dearly.

To go forward with this music we had to get past one significant hurdle. While the potential was always there, the likelihood of making a significant amount of money, given the financial track record of the *Take Her Deep* album, was very tenuous at best. Our mission became the creation of the music collections for the purpose of preserving the history expressed in these songs, and to support the United States Submarine Veterans, Inc., and the Submarine Veterans of World War Two organizations. Once this transition was made, and the profit motive taken out of the equation, the ability to go forward was much easier. I think we may have lost sight of this intention a few times, but opinions can differ greatly when faced with possibilities of losing money in a project. This is what happened with our intentions to do a second album together.

Bobby and I continued to write submarine music with the intention of producing another album together. Once again, Bobby had written a dynamic song called *Proud to Be an American Veteran*. One idea we bounced around was putting together original creations by several submarine and military songwriters and artists with a collection that would span all services. The problem of dealing with several musicians regarding the splitting of profits, if any, was horrendous. It is surprising how many people associate having a song on a CD equates to instant wealth. It became clear that the humorous definition of a band would prevail here: "A band is several musicians working together each knowing he would be a star if the rest weren't holding him back." Additionally, we had met Don Ward, former Marine and submarine Torpedoman, who is an excellent guitar player. I wanted to use his guitar playing to supplement the computer-generated music from Bobby's program. I called the computer stuff "plastic music." Don offered to work without pay for the credit on the album, so cost was not a factor. I also wanted to include, at least, one track of an artist with whom I worked in Maine, who did a great song about the Vietnam War. How to properly credit him with a fair remuneration from the album became an issue. Also the logistics of including Don Ward on the album became problematic, as I would have paid him to come to Massachusetts to record in Bobby's studio, but the apparent final solution was to have Don add the guitar tracks at home.

At this point in time, Bobby's life was getting pretty complicated. His new job was extremely demanding and required extensive travel to the Far East. This greatly diminished his ability to focus on producing a new album. Managing the logistics of sending tapes back and forth to Don Ward required more bandwidth than he could muster. To add another layer of stress, Bobby had to deal with the fact that his son, Mike, was serving a one-year tour of duty in Iraq as a soldier of the 101st Airborne. His stress level was nearing the maximum, and producing another joint album at this time didn't seem likely. Bobby ultimately lost his job in an ownership change and restructuring. Bobby and Margie sold their house in Milford and moved to Albuquerque, New Mexico. These were all high stress events. Additionally, three things were happening in my life that created excessive turmoil during this period: (1) my son Bill passed away on August 22, 2002, and I was named as the Personal Representative for his estate, (2) my mother passed away on December 8, 2003, and I was the Personal Representative for her estate, and (3) I was approaching retirement age from my position with the State of Maine in child support law enforcement. There was too much on my plate. A second joint album was simply not to be. Murphy's Law prevailed.

I wholeheartedly encouraged Bobby to proceed to do his own album. When the time was right, Bobby did just that and kept the original name for his song, *Proud to Be an American Veteran*. It's a great collection. Bobby timed his album to be released at the 40th Anniversary of Submarine Veterans in Groton in early May of 2004. I'd been invited to attend the 40th SUBVETS Anniversary with Bobby, but I knew that simply by attending I would have detracted from Bobby's moment in the spotlight. Unfortunately, some folks misinterpreted this as a rift between Bobby and me. Trust me, Bobby and I remain the best of shipmates, and we continue to cooperate in matters of our submarine music albums.

In 2003 I had decided to retire from music completely, and I did final shows at the 39th SUBVETS Anniversary and one final gig at Norm's Lounge. Bobby joined me for those two gigs as well as Don Ward and two musicians from my original band, Hank Schaffer on Drums and Gerry Rucker on bass and vocals. Patty Benjamin, who also worked with me as a bass player and vocalist, and husband Nate drove down from Charlton, Massachusetts, to surprise us at Norm's Lounge. I publicly announced I was going out of the music business.

The geography between Maine and New Mexico now serves to mitigate against Bobby and me ever recording together again. When the BRAC (Base Realignment and Closure) commission included the New London Submarine Base in its closure recommendation in 2005, John Carcioppolo contacted Bobby and me to write a song immediately to challenge the BRAC decision. Bobby and I discussed it by e-mail, and I recommended Bobby go forward solo on the project. There was no way we could execute a joint venture. In the meantime a local rock group in Connecticut came forward with a tune called *Submarine Town* that seemed to fill the bill. I listened to the song, and I wouldn't have gone with it. Fortunately the BRAC Commission backed down and the New London Submarine Base was saved.

In 2001 Bobby and I ordered 2,000 copies of *Brothers of the Dolphin*. Now in the new year of 2006 we still have five or six hundred CD's left. Once again, we've given away a significant number. But it's par for the course.

While I still worked on new songs, in the next two years I was overcome by the events of the deaths of my son Bill and my mother. I retired from service to the State of Maine in May 2003. After my son's death, my tolerance for people who did not want to be parents virtually disappeared. This was not a good attitude for a person in child support law enforcement. It was time to get out of there, as my ability for remaining politically correct had significantly diminished. If I remained, the eventuality of getting the State of Maine and myself in litigation was increasing by the day. I retired and declined any retirement ceremony. The thought of having people who dislike me stand up and say otherwise was disgusting. And I didn't think it would be good to offer me another forum to express myself. The leadership I'd admired had retired, and I was singularly unimpressed with the replacements. In the meantime I became a Registered Maine State Guide.

Last Two Albums

By the end of 2004 and many exchanges of e-mails with guitar player Don Ward in Wilmington, North Carolina, I decided to go ahead and do two more albums. I had some new songs to offer, plus one of my mother's requests was for me to sing spirituals. She always wanted me to sing in church, which I rarely did from the congregation, as I either didn't know the song or the key was wrong for me.

Don Ward has the heart of an artist. He's not only an accomplished musician and performer, he's an abstract artist, an accomplished photographer, and he's written a book himself. He started his military service in the U.S. Marine Corps. He then changed over to the U.S. Navy and became a submarine Torpedoman. Don Ward is certainly an individualist. He seems to care little what others think. He does his own thing in his own way. If he were a youngster, he would certainly be called a "rebel." I admire him greatly for his way. He has the hopes of a dreamer combined with the pragmatic reality of a submariner.

I know very little about his personal life. I do know he had a first marriage that didn't last but produced a very beautiful daughter named Shevaun. Don sent me a picture of her once. He also had two sons, Ben and Nathan. Today he is married to a lovely lady named Melissa, and they live in Wilmington, North Carolina. All I can say is that it is apparent they love each other deeply.

I liked working with Don a lot. He had an 8-track digital recorder that we both learned how to use during this week in March of 2005. Much of what we were doing was trial and error. We worked on the *In Honor of…* album first, which was probably a mistake, as it took a lot of experimenting to get things right. My first mistake was in thinking we could record two albums to perfection in one week. Recalling my experience with *Take Her Deep*, where I recorded the whole album in two and a half hours, I believed a week would be more than enough. The second mistake was something beyond my control. Our motel and Don's house seemed to have a mold common to the Wilmington area that affected my voice. I thought my voice was in fine shape when I got there, but this strange mold resulted in a bronchitis that, of course, affected my singing. This troubled me greatly and gave me considerable problem during the recording.

My original idea was for Don and me to do both albums with his music on rhythm guitar, lead guitar, and bass, and I would sing. When these parts were done, we would bring in a keyboard player and drummer and, perhaps, add more background vocal. Don did do some of the vocal enhancements on a few of the songs, and I added some harmony and a vocal bass track on *Ballad of Whitey Mack*. We never got beyond the original plan for Don and me, and that is how the albums remain to this date. Contrary to what may be written on the albums, every note from guitar and bass was done by Don Ward on both albums. We simply ran out of time.

I was under two time constraints. First and foremost, I had to get master discs to Gus Pedersen of Wooden Ships Music in New York before March 12 in order to give Disc Makers time to get the projects done to have the albums ready for sale for the Submarine Veterans anniversary the last week of April. Pete brought the albums to Groton in his van to meet this deadline. Secondly, Don and I had agreed to go to the VA Hospital in Fayetteville to play music for the veteran patients on the afternoon of March 11. I also had a commitment to meet and sing for the Northern Virginia Base of Submarine Veterans at an American Legion Saturday morning and also at another SUBVETS gathering in Glen Burnie, Maryland, that evening. So my cup runneth over. Talk about getting ten pounds in a five-pound bag!

Major Kristine Armstrong, U.S. Army, the daughter of Robert "Dex" and Solveig Armstrong of Alexandria, Virginia, made the arrangements at the Fayette-ville VA Hospital. Don and Melissa in their car, and Sandy and I in ours, arrived at the VA Hospital early in the afternoon. Don did a recon and found where we were to go to play our music. We got all our gear and rode the elevator up several floors to a room where about thirty veterans, most of them in wheelchairs, were waiting. We learned later that one gentleman who seemed to be asleep in his wheelchair had not been communicative for quite awhile. They didn't use the term catatonic, but that's what I thought of when they explained his condition. Don and I decided to start our performance by doing Don's instrumental version of the *National Anthem* just as recorded on the *In Honor of...* album. As Don began playing, this gentleman came alive and started singing the words. The nurses were astonished. There were veterans there from all services, and we tried to do songs that would be significant for them. We did some of the submarine songs. We did *Frenchie* for the Marines. We did *The Green Beret* for a fellow wearing a 5th Special Forces blue ball cap. After we played for an hour, the nurses and orderlies started moving the patients out for some other function they had planned. We stopped playing and I went to each of the veterans remaining, shook their hand, and thanked them for their service to our great country. The older fellow who appeared catatonic when we arrived shook my hand, kissed it, and thanked me with tears in his eyes. I knew that a good thing had happened there that after-noon. Many thanks to Kristine Armstrong and Don Ward for doing that. The original idea to go to the Fayetteville VA Hospital was Don's.

Dex, Kristine's father, is a big-hearted diesel boat submariner who served aboard U.S.S. *Requin* out of Norfolk circa 1958-61. Dex was a hard working young man who never got promoted beyond Seaman (E-3) who was full of mischief. He is also a prolific writer who has contributed greatly to the AFTER BATTERY RAT at www.olgoat.com administered by Ray Stone. This is a collection of submarine stories that captures the essence of submarining during that era in the best of sailor vernacular. Dex is also a GS-15 and is the Deputy Director for GSA (Government Services Administration) at the Pentagon. Dex is married to a wonderful and lovely lady from Norway who he calls "The Metric Blonde." Solveig passed away in December 2005 from cancer. This was truly traumatic for her family and all who knew her.

Kristine Armstrong is another unique person. She enlisted in the Army, served in country during the first Iraq War to free Kuwait, became a combat paratrooper (a pioneer for women in the Army), and received a commission. She is also very attractive. Sandy and I were her guests the evening of March 11. We got up at 0430 on the morning of March 12, and she guided us to the Interstate to make it to Northern Virginia before noon. We made it.

I performed at the American Legion for the Northern Virginia SUBVETS. Sandy and I were treated like royalty. Dex had several challenge coins to present to me at the meeting, including one from the Chaplain's Corps, where a Master Chief, who worked in that office at the Pentagon, provided the coin to Dex to give to me in appreciation for the song *Sailor's Prayer*, which had been used in a variety of naval ceremonies. I was presented with the Pentagon Recovery coin as a participant in the reconstruction following the 9-11 disaster. While I was not at the Pentagon in person, Dex took his boom box in to work and constantly played *Paybacks Are Hell* from the *Brothers of the Dolphin* album. Dex said the song did much to inspire the recovery workers. Then he presented me with a coin from the Joint Chiefs of Staff, also in appreciation for my patriotic music for the military, especially the Submarine Service. He also presented me with a print of an artist's conception of the U.S.S. *Wahoo* sitting on the bottom, sunk during World War II. This was Dudley "Mush" Morton's boat. Somehow I believe Dex paid for all this himself. But it sure was a moment of honor for me.

Additionally, Solveig made a large table cover with my name on it for me to use when I set up a table to sell CD's at conventions and gatherings. They had bought these little holders that were perfect for displaying the CD's, so they could be viewed by the public. They had a frame that held clippings from the *Blind Man's Bluff* book with the pictures of me. They also provided me with a ceramic statue of the famous sailor kissing the young lady in New York City following the end of World War II. This was just too much. What generous and gracious people! We were truly blessed for meeting and knowing the Armstrong family.

We attended the SUBVETS gathering in Glen Burnie, Maryland, the evening of March 12. I set up my equipment and sang for about forty-five minutes while the real band set up for the evening. I mainly premiered some of the new songs as I did earlier at the Legion for the Northern Virginia SUBVETS. It was at this gathering where I saw an old *Lapon* buddy, Don Salisbury, who was a Sonar Technician in *Lapon* when we served together in 1968 and 1969. Don was the Sonar Tech who was on the stack when the torpedo in the water incident occurred that resulted in the song (See Chapter 3). We also met with our dearest friends Lew and Cathy Bearden, who we had not seen for twenty-two years. It was a great reunion. As we drove back to Alexandria following Dex and Solveig at 0130 in the morning, I commented about the bumper-to-bumper traffic. Sandy and I were following Dex and Solveig, and we were going about ten miles per hour over the speed limit. Dex contacted me later, as he received a speeding ticket from a remote camera that got his license number. I guess they just ignored us, since we had Maine plates (we didn't know any better). It was a wonderful visit. We spent Sunday just visiting and talking with Dex and Solveig. Solveig would say we simply listened to Dex, which is pretty close to reality. I'm sure he'd been vaccinated with a phonograph needle. That man can talk! But what he has to say is very interesting. They were exceptionally gracious hosts, and they treated us famously.

While in the area, Sandy and I visited with Evelyn Williams in Laurel Maryland, who is godmother to our son James. Then we spent the next two days with Dave LeJeune and family in La Plata, Maryland, before heading back to Maine. Dave is a dear friend and shipmate from *Seawolf* (See Chapter 10). We missed many friends in the area that we wanted to see. But we were maxed out for time.

CHAPTER 1
SCORPION

Look out on the wide Atlantic
At the bottom lie our souls
Ten thousand feet below the surface
That is where we met Our Lord

Nobody knows just what had happened
On that day, May twenty-nine
We went deep for the last time
S-S-N five eighty-nine

The Lord was waiting to receive us
Davy Jones stood by his side
And as the Captain read the roll call
Standing tall and filled with pride

We are the men of the ship Scorpion
All present and accounted for
Ninety-nine pairs of dolphins
Ready for inspection, Lord

S*corpion* was my first song in the submarine genre. This song is my personal, emotional reaction to the loss of a modern nuclear submarine. This was a tragedy that touched the very being of every sailor who ever did "Take Her Deep" in a submarine. But, in retrospect, *Scorpion* is much more than a song. Scorpion was the beginning of a lifetime dedication for me to establish a collection of music to honor the U.S. Submarine Service. This mission has led me on a fantastic voyage of nearly 40 years. The original inspiration for this crusade is owed to the 99 young men who lost their lives in U.S.S. *Scorpion.*

Scorpion was one of six submarines in the *Skipjack* class. The U.S.S. *Scamp*, my second submarine assignment, was a boat of this class. It did not have the super-sensitive sonar of the subsequent classes of submarines, but it was certainly superior to other submarines of the same era. It was also the fastest class of submarine in its day. The *Scorpion* was 252 feet long and displaced 3,515 tons submerged. *Scorpion* was built by the Electric Boat Division of General Dynamics Corporation in Groton, Connecticut, launched on December 29, 1959, and commissioned on July 29, 1960.

I was about to make my first submarine run in the Atlantic at the end of May in 1968. This trip was my fourth having done three patrols in the Pacific all in the year 1967. Our team was to be embarked in U.S.S. *Lapon* (SSN-661). We had been conducting a workup for the mission obtaining final briefings, putting our kit together, and learning to work together. A day or so before departing NSGA Maryland, a message was received at our command postponing the departure until further notice. The *Lapon* was working on the SAR (Search and Rescue) operations for *Scorpion.*

On May 27 COMSUBLANT (Commander Submarines Atlantic Fleet, Vice Admiral Schade, Norfolk, Virginia) made an announcement that *Scorpion* was "overdue." By May 29th, *Scorpion* was "presumed missing."

Submarines don't have accidents; they have catastrophes. While nobody I know gave any consideration to quitting submarines, all certainly experienced the loss of shipmates, whether we knew them or not. This was a deeply felt tragedy.

Along with my teammates, we talked about the loss and wondered if any of our teams were aboard when she went down. One of our officers advised that the spooks got off *Scorpion* in Rota, Spain. *Scorpion*'s previous mission had some of our people assigned. I believe it was that evening on May 29 when I was back at my quarters with my family that I wrote the above lyrics primarily as a prayer. At the time, there was little thought of putting it to music. Sandy, my wife, could see I was a little moody, but I didn't want to discuss anything about this with her due to security constraints at the time. It didn't make sense to bring this to her attention shortly before I deployed for a couple months or so. At the time, it was still not well known to the wives that our teams were being embarked in submarines. I was new to the Atlantic theater and didn't want to break any rules I didn't know about. Within the next year the command began advising the wives of our assignment to submarines as well as surface craft and aircraft.

The guess of a depth of 10,000 feet in the song was simply pretty lucky. I believe the actual depth is another thousand feet for a total depth of 11,000 feet. No, I had no inside knowledge about this whatsoever. The song was written within days of the loss of the boat, while it took five more months to find the *Scorpion* wreckage. The actual date of the sinking is thought to be May 22, 1968. The official date of declaration of the loss of *Scorpion* was June 5, 1968.

Another criticism has been my line of "99 pairs of dolphins." Clearly some of the crew had not attained submarine qualification for dolphins, but it is my song and, as the composer with literary license, I have unilaterally granted all non-quals aboard *Scorpion* their dolphins.

Bobby Reed shared this story with me: Bobby was a Missile Technician. On an off patrol cycle he was attending a Navy school on "Launcher Power Supplies." There was a sailor sitting beside Bobby. He revealed in conversation that he had been aboard *Scorpion*. Just prior to deployment, this young man suffered an appendicitis attack. He was hospitalized just hours before the departure and did not make the mission. His next assignment was to a fleet ballistic missile submarine, which is why he was attending this class with Bobby. In their conversation, Bobby asked him if he ever asked himself, "Why me?" The sailor stated this thought was with him everyday. Frequently, before falling asleep, he commonly experienced a flashback where he visualized the *Scorpion* crew standing topside as if for muster with one space vacant, his. He told Bobby he simply renders a hand salute in farewell to his shipmates before drifting off in peace for another day.

Here is the list of names of the crew of *Scorpion* lost on that fateful day. Perhaps there is a spark of their lives passed on each time the song Scorpion is played. Their personal sacrifice has certainly inspired me, and they have been with me as I continue to write songs honoring the United States Submarine Service. Together we have reached out to our shipmates across generations in ways that cannot be expressed in the written word. These songs shall always be their songs.

99 Shipmates on Eternal Patrol in U.S.S. Scorpion *(SSN-589)*

Francis Atwood Slattery, CDR - (CO)
Walter William Bishop, TMC - (COB)
Keith A.M. Allen, FTG2
Thomas Edward Amtower, IC2
George Gile Annable, MM2
Joseph Anthony Barr, Jr., FN
Michael Jon Bailey, RM2
Michael Reid Blake, IC3
Robert Harold Blocker, MM1
Kenneth Ray Brocker, MM2
James Kenneth Brueggeman, MM1
Robert Eugene Bryan, MMC
John Patrick Burke, LT

Daniel Paul Burns, Jr., RMSN
Ronald Lee Byers, IC2
Duglas Leroy Campbell, MM2
Samuel Cardullo, MM2
Francis King Carey, MM2
Gary James Carpenter, SN
Robert Lee Chandler, MM1
Mark Helton Christiansen, MM2
Romeo Constantino, SD1
Robert James Cowan, MM1
Joseph Cross, SD1
Garlin Ray Denney, RMC
Michael Edward Dunn, FN
Richard Philip Engelhart, ETR2
George Patrick Farrin, LT
William Ralph Fennick, FTGSN
Robert Walter Flesch, LT
Vernon Mark Foli, IC3
James Walter Forrester, Jr., LT(jg)
Ronald Anthony Frank, SN
Michael David Gibson, CSSN
Steven Dean Gleason, IC2
William Clarke Harwi, LT
Michael Edward Henry, STS2
Larry Leroy Hess, SK1
Richard Curtis Hogeland, ET1
John Richard Houge, MM1
Ralph Robert Huber, EM2
Harry David Huckelberry, TM2
John Frank Johnson, EM3
Robert Johnson, RMCS
Steven Leroy Johnson, IC3
Julius Johnston, III, QM2
Patrick Charles Kahanek, FN
Donald Terry Karmasek, TM2
Richard Allen Kerntke, MMCS
Rodney Joseph Kipp, ETR3
Dennis Charles Knapp, MM3
Charles Lee Lamberth, LT
Max Franklin Lanier, MM1
John Weichert Livingston, ET1
David Bennett Lloyd, LCDR

Kenneth Robert Martin, ETN2
Frank Patsy Mazzuchi, QMCS
Michael Lee McGuire, ET1
Steven Charles Miksad, TM3
Joseph Francis Miller, Jr., TM3
Cecil Frederick Mobley, MM2
Raymond Dale Morrison, QM1
Michael Anthony Odening, LT(jg)
Daniel Christopher Petersen, EMC
Dennis Paul Pherrer, QM3
Gerald Stanley Pospisil, EM1
Donald Richard Powell, IC3
Earl Lester Ray, MM2
Jorge Louis Santana, CS1
Lynn Thompson Saville, HMC
Richard George Schaffer, ETN2
William Newman Schoonover, SN
Phillip Allan Seifert, SN
George Elmer Smith, Jr., ETC
Laughton Douglas Smith, LTjg
Robert Bernard Smith, MM2
Harold Robert Snapp, Jr., ST1
Daniel Peter Stephens, LCDR
Joel Candler Stephens, ETN2
David Burton Stone, MM2
John Phillip Sturgill, EM2
Richard Norman Summers, YN3
John Driscoll Sweeney, Jr., TMSN
John Charles Sweet, LT
James Frank Tindol, III, ETN2
Johnny Gerald Veerhusen, CSSN
Robert Paul Violetti, TM3
Ronald James Voss, STS3
John Michael Wallace, FTG1
Joel Kurt Watkins, MM1
Robert Westley Watson, MMFN
James Edwin Webb, MM2
Leo William Weinbeck, YNCS
James Mitchell Wells, MMC
Ronald Richard Williams, SN
Robert Alan Willis, MM3
Virgil Alexander Wright, III, IC1

Donald HowardYarbrough, TM1
Clarence Otto Young, Jr., ETR2
...Sailors, Rest Your Oars!
Compiled by SUBNET from U.S. Navy press releases and *U.S. Naval Submarine Force Information Book*– J. Christley.
Thank you, Jim.

CHAPTER 2
BIG BLACK SUBMARINE

Take her deep and take her down
Where no other human being can be found
Below the surface where it's dark and green
Down to the sea in a big black submarine

Left the wife and the kids behind
Most other people say I've lost my mind
Can't see the sun, and I can't see the sky
But it's my life, and I don't know why

The silver dolphins that I proudly wear
Remind me that I'm among the few who care
Out on patrol and loaded for bear
And when it comes my time, well, I've done my share

This is the second song in my submarine genre. After putting music to *Scorpion*, I started thinking about a song that could be universal for all submariners. In fact, this is the point where I started to think of myself as a submariner with new ambitions of qualifying in submarines. The U.S.S. *Lapon* was my fourth submarine, and something just clicked. The crew members were great guys, competence radiated, and their camaraderie and esprit de corps filled the boat. The crew loved Captain Chester M. "Whitey" Mack and would do anything for him. I wondered if I was merely being more in touch with the spirit of the crew or if

Lapon was something special. Within a few years I learned the latter was true. Even as a rider I was part of this crew.

I lived in the Torpedo Room and got along famously with the room watches, "Sarge" Mauras, Terry Knepper, and "Joe" Joseph. I think "Sarge" was a former Marine. "Sarge" was a topside line handler, and he invited me to go topside with him when we pulled into Holy Loch on that first run. I remember he almost fell overboard, and I grabbed him to keep him from falling in the water. See, I did something right!

I found the tune to *Scorpion* in this Torpedo Room, and I wrote this song *Big Black Submarine*. This is one of the simplest songs ever written, two chords. The words were very direct and to the point. The lyrics suggest that submariners are unique people, dedicated to service of country, and allude to certain hardships. When I wrote the words: "The silver dolphins that I proudly wear," the handwriting was on the wall. I would wear dolphins at some point. In fact, crew members aboard *Lapon* were the first to suggest that I go through the qualification process. This song is also a tribute to the enlisted men nationwide who serve in submarines.

Big Black Submarine has since become the signature song of the U.S. Submarine Service. At least that's what I would like to believe. The *Take Her Deep* album began with the old style diving klaxon from the U.S.S. *Seawolf* (SSN-575), followed by "Dive, dive," and it goes right into the *Big Black Submarine* song. Almost every show I have done begins with this song.

What nature of man becomes a submariner? Certainly he cannot be claustrophobic. And he must be both an optimist and a realist. He must be technologically competent and curious. Phenomena must have explanations that make sense. The submariner has a good sense of humor and can take a joke as well as give it. He is gregarious and is proud of his own abilities and respects the abilities of others. He develops a bond and a sense of trust with his shipmates and a dedicated loyalty to his own ship. He is altruistic and patriotic. Whether he admits it or not, most submariners have already come to terms with their own death in consideration of the perils of submarine duty. Hazardous Duty Pay is not granted to submariners because somebody likes us. It's dangerous! There is an aura of elitism in being a submarine sailor. Not everyone can be a submariner. It's certainly not for everybody, and those who can't hack it are soon transferred or they de-volunteer. A submariner will complain vociferously about the rigors of submarine life, then turn around and defend it vigorously if outsiders criticize.

Submarine sailors and veterans are a stubborn, cantankerous lot who are opinionated and recalcitrant. Yet they are kind and generous to a fault. You've got to love and respect the old curmudgeons. I'm honored to be among them. I enjoy being in the company of submarine veterans, and I am delighted with the history, experience, and opinions of my shipmates. Rarely can you get universal agreement on any subject. One thing they will agree on is safety of the boat. The members of a boat crew will argue tirelessly about every subject known to man, yet will work together cooperatively as a well-trained team during boat casualties, drills, and action.

I recall the business meeting of the USSVI in Atlantic City in 2000. One of our members from Charleston, South Carolina, attempted to obtain organizational support for the Confederate submarine *Hunley* from the Civil War, which had recently been recovered. Technically, the *H. L. Hunley* was the first "American" submarine to score a kill in warfare with the sinking of the *Housatonic* on February 17, 1864. All eight crewmen in *Hunley* drowned. Analysis of the sunken vessel showed that musket balls had penetrated the hull.

The advocate for the *Hunley* support presented his case for the SUBVETS organization to support what would eventually become a *Hunley* Memorial. Unfortunately, this gent was literally shouted down by those who immediately took the opposing view that the *Hunley* was not a U.S. submarine, and, therefore, not entitled to the recognition and support of the USSVI. The *Hunley* was a Confederate submarine. I was personally disappointed in this response, and the young submariner who supported the *Hunley* simply sat down and maintained his dignity. Personally, I would have voted to support the *Hunley*.

At one point in the *Hunley* dedications a few submarine veterans from the Northern Virginia Base drove down to Charlston, including Dex Armstrong and a World War II veteran named Art Smith. Art was in his 80s. He was publicly recognized as being the oldest submariner present. Art had been awarded the Silver Star in World War II, and the SUBVETS urged him to wear the medal at the *Hunley* ceremony. This earned him a round of applause. It was my honor to meet Art Smith on March 12, 2005, when I joined the Northern Virginia Base at the American Legion in Arlington.

I've got to let you know how Art won his Silver Star. His submarine was on pilot rescue duty in shallow water when they were going in for a downed pilot. A Japanese aircraft spotted the sub on the surface and made a strafing run. To save the boat the Captain ordered a reverse course to take the submarine down. At this point Art dove into the water and swam to the pilot. The pilot slipped in and out of consciousness, and Art kept the pilot from drowning. The Japanese plane made repeated runs at Art and the pilot until he either ran out of ammo or became low on gas. Art says the closest the guy got to them was about a hundred yards. After about an hour and a half, the submarine returned to pick them up. The Captain called Art to the wardroom later, with the rescued pilot present, and berated Art for his reckless action that created a danger for the safety of the submarine. The Captain turned to the pilot and emphasized that he owed his life to Art, as the Captain would not have returned to pick up the pilot if Art was not with him. Then the Captain submitted Art Smith for the Navy Cross for his heroism under fire. I suspect the Captain knew his recommendation for such an award for an enlisted man would be bumped down to the Silver Star. I expect if he'd put Art in for the Silver Star, it would have been downgraded to a Bronze Star. Art Smith is a submarine veteran icon. These are great men!

CHAPTER 3
GITMO BLUES

Life for a sailor boy was dull on Gitmo Bay
Everything was old routine, then there was that day
Orders came from JFK, terrorized the crew
So what's new for Gitmo Bay? Everything's SNAFU
Gitmo blues, Oh, yeah! Got those Gitmo blues, ah huh!

Russians got their missile sites and Castro thinks he's bad
Everything's turned upside down, best time we ever had
Marines out there in the hills, first line of defense
Throwing rocks at the Cuban guards made for great suspense
Gitmo blues, oh, yeah! Gitmo blues, o-hoo!

Admiral's in a panic, don't know what to do
Captain said, "The atom bomb!" But that would get us too
Gitmo blues, Gitmo blues

Now as the burning sun sets on Gitmo Bay
The same way it always does every single day
Us sailor boys, we just sit back, ain't nothing here to sweat
Just the day we leave the Bay, ain't got our orders yet
Gitmo blues, crazy Gitmo Blues (fade)

This song is actually the first song I wrote about the Navy or the military, so it's a bit out of sequence chronologically and historically. This was written in Gitmo in 1962 during the Cuban Missile Crisis. Naval Security Group Detachment, Guantanamo Bay, Cuba, (NAVSECGRUDETGTMO), was my first duty station after finishing two years of schooling. Jerry Henley and I were the anchormen in our class, and we got sent to Cuba for a twelve-month tour (six months short of a regular tour) in the event they ended up needing Russian linguists. Jerry had made third class, but I had flunked the test, and I was still a Seaman. Jerry got put in a watch section, and I got the gofer duty (go for this; go for that, etc.) I did all the running around for everybody and burned all the burn bags on a daily basis. But, at least, I worked days. I had to come in every Saturday for a few hours and sometimes on Sunday, but that was OK. There was no liberty to be had. The gates were closed. The entertainment was the EM Club (Barrel Club), movies every evening at an outdoor theater, which was great when it rained, golf, tennis, basketball, baseball, and football, and swimming and scuba diving at some superb beaches. One of my favorite pastimes was playing my black, Harmony, flat top, jumbo guitar and singing either at the beach or the Barrel Club. That old Harmony cost me $65.00 and had a fast neck with a light touch and a real good sound.

I don't remember what drinks cost at the Barrel Club, but during Happy Hour you could get a screwdriver for a dime, and you could back them up as far as you could stand. Playing guitar and singing supplemented my meager income of $22.00 per payday (later $36.00) as my shipmates bought me drinks to keep me tuned. Somehow, I managed to buy a $25.00 bond a month while receiving this pay. These disappeared fast when I went on leave.

The Navy sent the dependents home as the Crisis broke out, but they left the married guys in their family quarters. Jerry Henley and I teamed up with a First Class named Nick Owens who had a three-bedroom unit. We bought food at the commissary and all the beer we could afford and lived the bachelor life for a while. It was during this period that I wrote "Gitmo Blues." I was twenty years old.

The song was written in a contemporary rock and roll style, beat, and chord progressions. Somebody like Elvis could easily have done it. It was a catchy tune and certainly appropriate to the point at that time in history.

It was after the dust had settled when Perry Como came to Gitmo to do his TV variety show and to entertain the troops. In the chow hall one day, I was no more than thirty feet from him. In retrospect, I consider this my biggest, missed, lifetime opportunity. I just didn't think of it. All I had to do was walk up to him, introduce myself, and tell him I'd written a song called "Gitmo Blues," and I'd like to sing it for him. The old Harmony guitar was in my locker across the street. I could have been back with it in five minutes. In retrospect, I'm certain I would have obtained the opportunity to perform that song on his show. I'm confident it would have "brought down the house." And I suspect my future would have been considerably different. The stupidity of youth!

There are points mentioned in the song that recall the historical events. The line "Orders came from JFK, terrorized the crew" was based upon listening to President Kennedy's speech while the arms and ammunition were being passed out at our site at Radio Range. Radio Range was a half mile from the fence and two hundred yards from the beach. It could easily have been overrun had the Cubans attacked. The most important information contained at Radio Range was crypto stuff. There was a cyclone fence around the compound. Under normal conditions a Seabee would guard the perimeter during the hours of darkness. Prior to the Crisis, if we were coming back from the beach with extra beers, we'd share them with the Seabee.

However, when the Crisis broke out, the Navy sent in the Marine Second Composite Radio to supplement our guys. They mustered at Radio Range and hung out there with their guns and ammo while their gear was catching up to them. Jerry and I had been in school in Pensacola, Florida, with some of these guys, and we remembered each other. They'd pulled Jerry and I in off the beach early in the day, so we were back near the Radio Range Compound with a case and a half of beer on ice, dressed in beach clothes, standing by to stand by. We shared the beer with the Marines, and we had a beach party right there.

One of the first actions the detachment took was to get the major part of operations out of Radio Range and set up in the Admiral's Command Bunker. This was a casehardened facility designed to withstand a direct artillery hit. It was a good place to be if the bombs started flying. Anyway, our people were required to provide armed guards for the compound that night. That meant Jerry and I, who had been drinking all day and were still in our beach outfits, got stuck with guard duty. I'd had a nap, so I took the mid watch, midnight to four. My weapon was an M-1 Garand with an ammo belt. When the trucks left the compound, they would leave the front gate open, so they didn't have to keep unlocking and locking it. After all, an armed guard manned it. At about 0200 after one truck had left, I was standing by the gate directly under a light. Considering my precarious position, I decided to get out of the light and into the shadows, so I wouldn't present such an easy target. It was during this time when LT James Pierce drove up to the compound in his vehicle with the tape over the top half of the headlights. This was supposed to reduce the night-light from enemy aerial targeting. LT Pierce walked up to the gate, and I could hear him cussing from my shadowed position. I knew he thought he'd found the gate open with nobody around, and that was bad juju. So I spoke up and said, "Good morning, Mr. Pierce." He damn near had a heart attack on the spot. He then composed himself, recognized me, and said, "Nice uniform, Cox!" I kept my big mouth shut. LT Pierce was a very well liked mustang (former enlisted) officer. He was killed aboard the U.S.S. *Liberty* when the Israelis attacked that ship on June 8, 1967.

Of course, the big issue in the Cuban Missile Crisis was the Russian surface-to-surface missiles installed 90 miles from the U.S. mainland. That made it into the song. The biggest comical happening was what was going on at the fence around the base. The Marines were out there agitating the Cubans around the perimeter by throwing rocks at them. A Marine Brigadier would send his driver every morning to the pistol range where he would pick .45 slugs out of the berm (the dirt that served as a backstop). These were 230-grain bullets that really could hurt somebody if one hit them. The General's jeep had a windshield that would fold down, with a .30 caliber machine gun bracket mounted on the hood. The General had installed rubber bands there that made a real good sling shot. He'd pick a spot where he could launch that pouch of .45 slugs at the Cuban guards. We loved that guy! "Marines out there in the hills, first line of defense. Throwing rocks at the Cuban guards made for great suspense, Gitmo blues." Luckily the Cuban guards could take refuge in small wooden shacks along the fence line where they would stay when it was raining. At least, they could be protected from the rocks and slugs being hurled at them. Also luckily these confrontations didn't degenerate to bullets.

The Navy wound up extending Jerry and I for a full 18-month tour. Then, as that point became near, they asked us both to "voluntarily" extend our tours until we reached the end of our enlistments. Jerry agreed, as he had only four months. I did not agree, as I had nine months left. Now for some reason CT's didn't seem to want to do any sea time. Now, why would somebody join the Navy and not want to go to sea? I got transferred to the U.S.S. *Oxford* (AGTR-1). So I got to do a cruise to the Caribbean, Canal Zone, and Peru and Chile before I got out. It was great, and I nearly reenlisted during that cruise.

OK, I'll tell the short story why I didn't reenlist. I liked the sea duty; I loved the liberty (that's going ashore in foreign ports and playing sailor). And I could have gone to French language school (I always wanted to be fluent in French). There were some pretty good chiefs and leaders on the *Oxford.* I put in my chit to reenlist. We had pulled into Valparaiso, Chile. My division officer had found a message that was misfiled. He was angry and blamed me for misfiling the message. The fact was, I'd never handled the message. I knew it for a fact! When liberty went down at 1300, I could not go ashore until 1600. I used my time "wisely" to find and destroy my reenlistment request. Had that issue been handled justly, my future would have been very different.

One of my concepts of peace and tranquility were the evenings sitting on an antenna base on the forecastle of the *Oxford* playing Robbie's (H.B. Robbins) guitar and singing during sundown and enjoying the warm Caribbean breeze, viewing a calm, rolling sea, and watching flying fish scoot above the surface and diving back down again. The world was right and so was I.

After being stationed in Cuba, I was somewhat sensitive to the defense options available to us on *Oxford*. The older, more experienced, *Oxford* sailors stated all we had to do was radio for help, and we would have air cover instantly. That seemed to satisfy my curiosity until years later when I recalled how efficient those radios worked for the U.S.S. *Liberty* and the U.S.S. *Pueblo*. For armament we had two .50 caliber machine guns and a variety of small arms. There was a Thompson .45 caliber in a locked bracket mounted on the bulkhead in our spaces up forward. Nobody seemed to know where the key, magazines, or ammo were located.

The *Oxford* communicated with U.S. radio receiving stations using a unique system dubbed CMR (Communications Moon Relay). We simply bounced our radio signal off the moon back to earth. The antenna for the CMR system was a huge parabolic dish, roughly twelve feet in diameter, mounted on an after deck housing. The dish could be raised at an azimuth of zero to ninety degrees and rotated 360 circular degrees. One of the famous stories aboard *Oxford* was when the Cubans (or Russians) sent PT Boats and Soviet KOMARS out to challenge the *Oxford* as she steamed outside Havana Harbor on one particular mission before my time aboard ship. It just so happened that the ship was raising the CMR gear as these fast moving boats approached *Oxford* from Havana Harbor. As they approached *Oxford* they could observe this huge parabolic dish in motion. Within minutes, all the boats were heading back for the harbor just as fast as they came out. The best guess was they were backing down from this "secret weapon" that appeared to be being readied to be used on them. Our sailors started calling it the "secret death ray." Let's face it; the *Oxford* was just lucky it was never attacked, as her fate could have been similar to *Liberty* and *Pueblo*.

By the early '70s my father had concluded that because I seemed to be stationed in areas where social upheaval or actual war seemed to exist. He mused, "I think we could do much for world stability if we just kept you home."

CHAPTER 4
TORPEDO IN THE WATER

Torpedo in the water and it's closing fast
It's on a steady bearing heading straight down the stack
Kick her in the tail, boys, break her back
Torpedo in the water and it's closing fast

The 2MC rang loud and clear
Those frightful words I didn't want to hear
I was about as scared as any man can get
And the seat of my pants were all wet

I cursed the day that I'd first seen
This big black (bleep) submarine
If we ever get this pig back to the pier
You can bet your boots I'm gonna leave her there

We heard the steady screaming of the screws
I was not in the least bit amused
Is it four hundred pounds of T-N-T
That will blow us to eternity

Or could it be a practice fish by chance
Whatever put me in this circumstance
Gee, I hate to see a grown man cry
But Goodness knows I'm just too young to die

54

On *Lapon*'s first mission we got into a situation, which certainly got my attention. Every time I tell this story, I begin by stating the following: "I won't tell you where we were in the world, but..." We were closing on a submarine of another nation when *Lapon* Sonarman Don Salisbury reported, "Conn—Sonar, loud bang from the target... Conn—Sonar, the contact just started up a big motor... It's a torpedo, Conn, torpedo in the water." As Salisbury made each report his voice got more and more excited. The next voice we heard was that of Chief Sonarman McNally. I don't remember his first name. His voice was as calm and controlled and professional as any I've heard: "Conn—Sonar, torpedo in the water bearing ???... Conn—Sonar, torpedo in the water bearing ??? (the same bearing as before)... Conn—Sonar, torpedo bearing ??? (the same bearing as the two previous reports), closing fast." By this time it was clear this torpedo was heading straight for *Lapon*.

At this point Captain Mack stated: "Oh, (expletive deleted)! I am the Captain, I have the deck and the conn, right full rudder, come right to course ??? (which was the reciprocal of the torpedo bearing) make your depth 380 feet, ahead flank, Maneuvering—Conn, cavitate." (That means we were going to move away from that torpedo at best possible speed.) *Lapon* came alive. The Main Cooling Pumps shifted to high speed with a loud clunk, and we were making "get out of Dodge" turns post haste. By telling Maneuvering to cavitate, the Captain was superseding the standing orders to increase speed without exceeding the threshold of cavitation. Cavitation is created when a submarine moves rapidly through the water creating bubbles with the screw that are quite noisy when the bubbles collapse. This is a sound submarine sonar technicians listen for to detect and classify a contact as another submarine. Certainly the launch platform would not hear *Lapon*, as the torpedo was between them and us.

Now chances were this torpedo was a practice "fish," but could Captain Mack take the chance? Nope! He had to take evasive maneuvers, just as if this torpedo was fired at us in wartime. And, do we think the torpedo was intentionally fired at us? That answer also seems to be in the negative. We were just in the wrong place at the wrong time. The torpedo had a mind of its own in the form of its own acoustic search and acquisition system. So when the torpedo was launched, the first thing it heard was *Lapon*, and that's where the torpedo headed.

At this point those not familiar with torpedoes are wondering if *Lapon* can outrun torpedoes. The answer is: Probably Not. However, for the sake of explanation, let us say this particular torpedo has an effective range of 10,000 yards (that's about five nautical miles). Now let's say *Lapon* was 7,000 yards away from the launching submarine (that's three and a half miles). To successfully evade the torpedo, the *Lapon* must boogie 3,000 yards (that's a mile and a half) before the torpedo can go the full 10,000 yards. Make sense? As I understand it, that's pretty much what happened. Yes, there are different types of torpedoes that activate and operate quite differently than what I've just explained, but this was back in 1968, when things were a little simpler. And there are torpedoes that do move very slowly in the water while they are in long-range search and acquisition.

Now while this was transpiring, I was sitting in the Radio Shack listening to the action on what we called the "White Rat." This was an open microphone in the Control Room (Conn) that let the watchstanders in Radio and Sonar know what was going on in Control without the Officer-of-the-Deck having to pick up an interior communications microphone for each acknowledgment. All they had to do was speak, and the OOD could be heard in Radio and Sonar. Sitting with me in Radio was (Joseph David) Jesse James, CTT1. Laying on the Radio Room deck (floor) was a young R-Branch operator named Bobby who was listening to music from a tape recorder with headphones. I can't remember his last name, but this was to be his first and last mission, as he was leaving the Navy and getting married shortly after the patrol was over.

Somehow, call it a sixth sense, I knew what the loud bang (opening the outer door of the torpedo tube) and big motor sounds (starting the torpedo motor) from the contact were, even before Chief McNally took the sonar stack. I *knew* it was a torpedo. For about thirty seconds, from the time of the original report and while Captain Mack was giving his evasive maneuvers orders, I thought, "This was it; I'm going to die." Jesse and I looked at each other, and the significance of all that was transpiring was well understood by both of us. I was totally numb (with fear). Bobby, who felt the main cooling pumps shift and felt the surge of vibration, looked up at Jesse and me, took off his headsets, and asked, "What's going on?"

I replied, "Torpedo in the water heading right at us." Bobby got this sheepish grin on his face, laid back down on the deck, put his headphones back on, stuck his thumb in his mouth, and curled up in a fetal position. It was clear he was clowning around rather than having a psychotic reaction to the situation. Jesse and I looked at each other, and, in spite of the possibility of dying within a minute or less, we started laughing at Bobby's antics.

Within the next minute or so, Chief McNally reported to Conn that the torpedo had shut down. It was out of power. Jesse and I both breathed a sigh of relief. I got out a cigarette (most everybody smoked in those days) and gave one to Jesse. He reached for his lighter and tried to offer to light my cigarette. His hand was shaking so bad, he couldn't hold the lighter so I could get a light. I then put my hands around his, and my hands were shaking just as bad. We did get the cigarettes lit, then Chief Russ Krause came into Radio (he felt the main cooling pumps and the ship vibration and got up out of bed). The Chief took one look at Jessie and me and said, "Geeze, you guys are white as ghosts. What's going on?" I told him we just had a torpedo scare.

That was one of the most intense experiences of my life. It also served to make me aware of just how dangerous these missions could be.

CHAPTER 5
BALLAD OF WHITEY MACK

This story is about Captain Mack
And his nuclear powered fast-attack
S-S-N six sixty-one, a second boat to none
And after we've dogged down the hatch
The Lapon's the lady in black

And Whitey's got the deck and the conn
Nobody else can handle this big Amazon
And we won't be back till we finish our track
Whitey's got the deck and the conn

Now he had quite a job to do
And every man on board he knew
When the going got rough in this game of blind man's bluff
Somehow we'd pull her through
And his faith in us was true

With trust in the Navy restored
And faith in a system reassured
Beneath the Union Jack they presented Whitey Mack
The Distinguished Service Medal Award
It sure is a fitting reward

I once stated publicly, the only man I respected more than Whitey Mack was my Dad. I also spoke in an interview to say, "Whitey Mack is the kind of man John Wayne wants to be when he grows up." Of course, this was long before John Wayne's death, and the statement was intended to show Whitey Mack to be a great and charismatic individual rather than detract one bit from the Duke's persona. I always thought if they ever did a movie portrayal of Whitey Mack, John Wayne should be the actor to do it. Whitey Mack was indeed an imposing figure.

Whitey Mack stood 6' 6" and weighed a constant 240 pounds. This was his weight in 1968, and this was his weight in 2003 when Sandy and I met him in Groton for the 39th anniversary of the U.S. Submarine Veterans, Inc. And he was then and still is a very intense individual who simply radiates confidence. His crew loved him.

If you could point to one thing in *Lapon* that made the most difference it would be the capability of the crew. *Lapon* had some exceptionally competent individuals in the crew. Whitey Mack reviewed the record of every sailor assigned to *Lapon*. If a man could not live up to expectations, if he was a defeatist or quitter, Captain Mack arranged to have him transferred. *Lapon* definitely was a crew of high achievers. Three of her officers became admirals, Ralph Tindal, Charles Brickell, and Richard Buchanan. I don't know of others. One of *Lapon*'s sharpest officers, LT Bruce Mouw, an Academy graduate, became an FBI Special Agent and was a key individual in the conviction of John Gotti. Jim Marin became an attorney. Some enlisted men who were exceptionally competent who became officers that I can recall are: Commander Herschel Hobbs, Lieutenant Commanders Dan McGovern and my guitar pickin' buddy Howard Jones. Donald Duck (yes, that's his real name), Don Bolling, Roger Dyer, and John Hicks became Master Chiefs. I'm sure there are others. Captain Mack had a significant role in each of these individual's career achievements.

There must be a mutual confidence between Captain and crew. The Captain must know the crew can and will execute orders unhesitatingly and competently when given. The crew must be depended upon to keep everything in tip-top condition, and all watch stations must be ready for the full spectrum of action required of at all times. The Captain must also be confident that key watch standers will take unilateral corrective action in the event of emergency. At the same time the crew needs to be confident in the Captain's ability to maneuver the submarine with skill and aplomb and not needlessly endanger the ship.

One of the advantages of serving in eleven different submarines in as many years is the unique opportunity to merge with eleven different crews. During mission deployments that lasted between 56 days on a diesel boat and 120 days in *Seawolf,* most around three months in duration, I served with a broad sampling of Captains and crews. The best of these in my humble opinion was U.S.S. *Lapon* (SSN-661) under the command of Chester M. "Whitey" Mack. It is no coincidence that I chose to qualify in submarines in *Lapon*. I made my fourth, fifth, and sixth submarine SPECOP missions in *Lapon*. I became totally acclimated, socialized, and integrated with ship and crew. I was accepted as a shipmate. I had complete faith and trust in Captain Mack's skill, aggressiveness, courage, and leadership. And I felt the same way about my shipmates. *Lapon* did things, and I was proud to be part of it. After qualifying in *Lapon*, I did everything I could to learn about technology that could impact on anti-submarine capability. One incident that significantly impressed me was Captain Mack's ability to assimilate everything that was going on around him. I'd taken the liberty of wandering into Control and simply began conversing with the Captain. He asked me if I'd learned anything new between missions, so I took the opportunity to tell him about a mine that sat on the bottom and armed itself whenever discrete frequency sources were in the immediate vicinity of the mine. As I spoke he was receiving reports from the Officer of the Deck. When the officer spoke, I would stop talking to wait until their conversation ended before continuing. The Captain told me to continue talking. So I kept right on with my report while the Captain and the OOD continued their discourse. Then just about the time I thought I was going to have to repeat the most important parts of my report, Captain Mack turned back to me, repeated the frequencies I had reported, and equated them to sources on *Lapon*. He'd heard and understood everything I said (not exactly what could be called a casual conversation), received reports from the OOD, gave direction to the OOD, knew everything about depth, course, speed, and trim of the boat, and all contacts held by Sonar. I read in books later that Admiral Rickover was famous for this ability.

Each commanding officer in whose boat I served was, above all, an individual. None was a carbon copy of another. I can safely say all were very intelligent and capable officers. Some considered themselves aristocrats. Some were automatons that would never deviate from standard operating procedure or an operational order. Others were more adventurous and would push the envelope. Many were very conservative, much like the peacetime submarine commanding officers prior to WW II. The personality and attitude of the submarine crew is a direct reflection of the personality and leadership of its Captain. I believe Captain Mack was much like Captains Slade Cutter and Ned Beach. These officers were tactical geniuses, courageous, and knew the full capability of their ship and crew. I heard many a *Lapon* sailor say, "I would go anywhere with Captain Mack." So would I, and we did.

Some may have seen Whitey Mack as arrogant. But in my opinion, there are two sides to this coin. There is an undeserved arrogance that is cocky and replete with overconfidence. Then there is the arrogance of real confidence earned through experience and ability that radiated from Captain Mack. He didn't brag; he didn't assume; he didn't guess. He knew what he was doing, he was confident in his own ability, and he executed with skill, confidence, and finesse. Yet he was personable and would take the time to assist a junior rate with a technical matter or praise a sailor for doing well.

On our first *Lapon* mission spook Jesse James was in the process of changing a wideband tape when Captain Mack came to the door of our room to see how much longer this evolution would take. The wideband recorder door, when opened, blocked access in and out of the compartment. Jesse didn't even look to see who was at the door, he just handed him the new tape and directed the individual to take the plastic wrapper off the new tape while he cleaned the recorder heads. Captain Mack dutifully removed the plastic and handed the fresh tape to Jesse when he was ready. When Jesse finished and the new tape was running Jesse turned to thank whoever had assisted him and did a double take to see it was the Captain. Then, and only then, the Captain asked how much longer would be "required." Jesse humbly requested 15 minutes, and the Captain checked the time and agreed. When the tape was finished, we informed Conn and *Lapon* went deep.

On another occasion I was operating the AN/BRD60-6 Radio Direction Finder. The Bird-6, as it was called, was notorious for having a "sense button" failure. With a good signal, in the DF (direction finding) mode, the signal was displayed in a figure eight pattern on a 360-degree presentation. When the sense button was pressed, the display would break away from the bearing of the direction of the signal. In this case the emitter was one of interest. Captain Mack came to the compartment and asked which direction the signal came from. I lightheartedly reported with the two bearings 180 degrees from each other. When the Captain asked again, I understood the seriousness in the command voice of Captain Mack. I picked one of the two bearings. Then he simply said, "Why?" I responded, "Because we can see all the way to the beach on the reciprocal bearing and nobody is there, and Sonar has a noise level at the bearing I selected." Captain Mack just nodded and left for Control where he ordered the boat deep and to change course for our contact. He'd taught me a real lesson to think beyond the problem and to use common sense to support my ship. He didn't have to criticize me for giving a flippant response. He showed me I knew the right answer with one repeated question, which he shouldn't have had to repeat, and made me express the logic of the answer by asking, "Why." Of course, he knew the answer long before I realized I knew the answer. Then when he ordered the ship to close the contact on the given bearing I had provided, I realized how I had contributed to what was about to happen. I was a *Lapon* crewmember.

Some of our submarine commanding officers attempted to establish a relationship aboard their boat where the crew feared the Captain. While this may have worked in the German U-boat community in the world wars, it did not go well in the U.S. Navy. All they accomplished was alienating an entire crew by making life miserable. This was not Captain Mack's way. He was, and still is, a charismatic leader who was exceptionally professional, firm, and fair. He was admired, trusted, and above all, respected. Crewmen were likewise respected by the Captain and treated with courteous dignity. I've seen officers and chiefs attempt to stifle a lower rate by interrupting him, where Captain Mack would listen to the senior man then ask the lower rated man to finish his statement. Captain Mack was receptive to new ideas and gave most suggestions due consideration. At times he would not respond for several days, but then he would return to the man who made the suggestion with appropriate feedback. Sailors knew he could be trusted with their ideas, and it was complimentary for the Captain to remark on a suggestion. While many of us would have said we loved the man, a more apropos term came to my attention later, and we would agree we had all "bonded." Shared experiences and literally being in the same boat does create an everlasting bond among shipmates. Bobby Reed called it *Brothers of the Dolphin.*

CHAPTER 6
THE SACRIFICE

It's time for me to say goodbye again (boy)
And it's time for me to start to cry again (girl)
Another two-month submarine patrol (boy)
And another two-month wait till you come home (girl)

It's leaving you behind that makes me sad (boy)
And the children really miss and love their dad (girl)
If I wasn't needed, darling, I would stay (boy)
I know, I wouldn't have it any other way (girl)

The sacrifice that we must make just tears my heart in two (both)
But it's the life I chose for us; now we must see it through (boy)
The sacrifice that we must make somehow seems so extreme (both)
But at least the other woman is a big black submarine (girl)

The days of missing you are hard and long (boy)
But we never once believed it wrong (girl)
Soon we'll surface on the briny foam (boy)
I'm looking forward to that welcome home (boy)

Yes, looking forward to that welcome home (both)

This is the first song I wrote with boy-girl parts. This song turned out to be quite a hit with the wives and girlfriends of submariners. I did write the song for my wife and children. The song expresses the loneliness of the family separation that must be experienced by most submariners with families and girlfriends who waited ashore while their men were deployed. The song is timeless, as well as the pain of being apart.

Bruce and Kathy Bowie were stationed in Norfolk at the Main Navy Base. Bruce's Dad, CTICM Robert Bowie, was my leading chief from my previous duty station at Fort Meade. The Bowie family was originally from the State of Maine, so we were maniacs or Mainers together. I'd lost my proficiency pay when I went to college, and Bruce was a Third Class Personnelman. We'd frequently get together to play pinochle, often searching for pocket change, so they could pay the toll to get back through the tunnel from Portsmouth to Norfolk. We were so poor; we couldn't even pay attention. Well, it turned out that Kathy had a superb singing voice. Bruce was also a guitar and bass player, and we taught Kathy to sing the girl part to *The Sacrifice*. Then Bruce and I collaborated to write a second boy-girl song called *Long Separation*. This was how Kathy became part of the original album *Take Her Deep*. Kathy and Bruce eventually divorced. After the CDs were made, I sent her a copy, but I never heard from her. I have received many compliments and requests for future recordings by her. Sandy and I felt very bad that they divorced. We love them both.

With the high divorce rate for military families and the even higher divorce rate for submariners, family stability and longevity of submarine families always seemed in jeopardy. The ladies who conducted all family business, paid the bills, cared for the children, solved all the problems, and handled the emergencies while their submariner was deployed rarely seemed to get the credit they deserved for their uncommon family contribution. Frequently, us guys focused more on the missions than the families. We frequently felt our part was more important, because it was our life that was on the line each patrol.

But, folks, we missed our families while we were away too. We had time to think about how important they are to us, how much we love the wife and children, and became knowledgeable of the things in their lives we missed while we were away. I remember returning from an extended patrol in *Sea Devil* when Sandra was ready to have our third child. Many submariners have been deployed while children were born. The fact is, I was supposed to have been returned by the time the baby was born, but the extension of the mission cancelled that plan. But these women knew how to take care of themselves while we were away, and they learned to help each other as needed. In Sandra's case, possibly through sheer willpower, she held off two weeks having the baby until I did return. I took two weeks leave immediately upon return, and Sweet Baby James was born four days after my return on December 5, 1970. This child Jim turned out to become a Navy Nuclear Power Electronics Technician submariner. Sandy agreed it was nice to have hubby at home to take care of the two older children, while she took a few days at the Kimbrough Army Hospital in Maryland to give birth to James. I agreed—that was my job and my role.

I never really was the domestic type (housebroken). But the two older kids and I got along fine. We put up a large (too big) Christmas tree, which totally dried out and had to be replaced before Christmas. I cooked the things I knew how to cook, but the children were really happy to eat at McDonald's frequently. We had a good time. But it was those times when I learned to appreciate all that Sandy did in her role as mother and homemaker.

As the submarines I rode pulled into their home ports following a mission, I always enjoyed witnessing the welcome home reunions on the pier where the ship tied up. Very frequently the spooks used this diversion to offload the many packages of classified material needed to accomplish such a mission, our personal luggage, and us. We would quietly and unobtrusively slink off when nobody was looking, so to speak. In the special projects we traveled in civilian clothes. Nobody seemed to pay any attention to us.

In a couple interviews I made the following statement, "At that time I put my country ahead of my family." The statement never made it to print or screen. I suppose the thought and the statement sounded borderline fanatical, and probably would have created an image different from the stereotype. Of course, everybody did not share this notion and sentiment. But there certainly were those of us who were dedicated to the missions at this level. The homecoming for spooks occurred in private, sometimes days and thousands of miles later.

CHAPTER 7
BOOMER PATROL

Men extraordinary living in solitary
Inside a big black submarine
Big birds of death we carry; it seems so necessary
Prepared if we must intervene

Nerves of steely ice; we make the sacrifice
Of the deterrent force at sea
Sure ain't no paradise, but it's a simple price
To give our home some form of guarantee

Peace is the goal of the Boomer Patrol
Poseidon, the protector of the sea
So we pay the toll to maintain control
And do our share to keep our country free

Men extraordinary living in solitary
Inside a big black submarine
We are boomer sailors all serving voluntary
In this underwater war machine

Serving to keep our country free

The *Take Her Deep* music collection would not be complete without at least one song honoring and recognizing the service of the fleet ballistic missile sub-

marines called boomers. I believe this was the last song written in the original collection. I have never served on a boomer, and, at that point in my life, I had never
set foot aboard a boomer. All I knew was what the boomer sailors who served on
the fast attack boats that I was assigned to would say about FBM duty.

The big difference between boomers and fast attacks boats is the boomers
had two crews, called Blue and Gold, while the attack subs had a single crew.
The general idea was to keep the submarine at sea on patrol ready to respond to
national emergencies as much as possible. As one patrol terminated, the boomer
would pull into port. The crew who made the patrol would leave the ship, the
second crew would come aboard, load stores for the next patrol, do required
corrective and preventive maintenance, and leave for patrol with a fairly quick
turn-around time. It also provided a ready-made alibi for anything that did not
work correctly. The other crew did it!

The off crew would return to their main home port, receive a period of basket leave to be with their families, friends, etc. Basket leave did not count as regular leave against a sailor's regular thirty days of annual leave. Usually the crewman
would have to call in on a daily basis for mustering purposes. Then the sailors
would attend schools to improve their skills within their rating or learn of modifications to submarine equipment that would affect their performance.

While at sea, the boomer submarine, in those days, would monitor communications as continuously as possible using a floating wire as a radio antenna
for what is called an EAM or Emergency Action Message. Every message of this
nature, received since the inception of the concept of deterrence through fleet
ballistic submarines, has been a drill. Deterrence worked. No ballistic missile was
ever fired in anger throughout the Cold War to this date.

The routine of the boomer was to steam around, usually at 3 knots, within a
given area of assignment. Not even the United States command authority knew
exactly where the boomer was at any given point in time. Upon detection of
another vessel, the boomer submarine would sneak away in the opposite direction to avoid any possibility of contact or detection. Boomer sailors referred to
this routine as "poking holes in the ocean." It was also very boring for the crew
and took a certain kind of individual to accommodate this kind of duty. But it was
very necessary. The constant threat of nuclear war required a certain guaranteed
response should any country initiate a nuclear confrontation with the United
States. The primary feared potential enemy at the time was the Soviet Union.
Both sides feared the ambition of the other for world domination. Thank God
both sides possessed the wisdom to avoid what would have been a nuclear holo-
caust. With time on their hands to meditate on the probable aftermath of firing
their weapons, many boomer sailors wrestled with the moral issues surrounding
their great responsibility. There is no doubt in my mind that, if required, the missiles would have flown. Submariners are a dedicated lot who will do everything
required to accomplish their mission.

Without the personal experience of serving in boomers, I sat down with my guitar and my *Wood's Unabridged Rhyming Dictionary* and wrote down the lyrics above. I always described this song as the most "mechanical" song I ever wrote. It is a strange quirk of fate this song was the first to be used on national television in a Discovery Channel special first published on May 5, 2000, entitled *Submarines: Life on a Boomer.* The Full House Films folks got in touch with me to execute a document with them to permit them to use this copyrighted song in their special. Of course, these folks don't pay for this right. If I didn't agree, they simply wouldn't use the song. I did agree hoping the public would hear the tune and, perhaps, think enough of it to purchase the CD. I also learned the viewing of the credits at the end of the program, while giving me credit with special "Thanks" for the song, is something the public rarely gets to see. Oh, well! It's a good thing my revised goal is to support the memory of the U.S. Submarine Service.

Two places referring to previously written songs in the collection are the lyrics *Big Black Submarine* and *The Sacrifice.* The reference to Poseidon is made, as that was the latest and greatest submarine launched ballistic missile in the U.S. inventory at the time the song was written. There were a total of 41 FBM submarines deployed during the main periods of the Cold War. Bobby Reed wrote and recorded a song called *Forty-one for Freedom* to honor these boats. Bobby himself served aboard the *George Washington Carver* submarine. It is the boomer sailors who paid the price in isolation, boredom, loss of family time and the like. As we frequently point out today, freedom is not free. Every day we live in freedom in the United States, we should thank God there are men willing to accept and accomplish the responsibilities of deterrence by serving in boomers and fast attack submarines. All these old boomers are now retired, and the boomers in service today are the Trident submarines. The payload power in these submarines is totally awesome, and we pray this power will never need to be released in the national interest.

CHAPTER 8
DIESEL BOATS FOREVER

We go to sea on diesel boats; they call us bubblehead
Our blood is laced with diesel smoke; we're sailors to the end
Our diesels whine through the salty brine until we take her deep
Then we turn her loose on battery juice and we all go to sleep

Diesel boats forever! Hear the diving klaxon sound
Diesel boats forever! Take her deep; take her down

No conning tower - nuclear power - Hymie's fairy queen
For bolts and nuts and gravel guts of the diesel submarine
The mighty brass would sink our class; we are a dying breed
Lift voices high and shipmates cry the diesel sailor's creed

The Submarine Veterans of World War II is a dying organization. These intrepid submariners who have earned War Patrol pins are presently in their late 70s or 80s. Many have joined the United States Submarine Veterans, Inc., and we honor them greatly. These gents set the standards high for the submariners that followed.

Diesel Boats Forever or "DBF" is the "battle cry" of the old time submariner. There is even a set of dolphins to support the diesel boat sailors. And every submariner who has shipped in a diesel boat submarine savors the experience as a badge of honor and irrefutable evidence of a "salty" old timer. Well, you get the idea! The diesel boatmen will hang on to this distinction as long as they remain.

68

It's like the VFW members referring to the American Legion members as "non-combatants."

Diesel boats have a unique odor that permeates the clothes and even the skin of submariners. Diesel boat sailors were commonly referred to as "pig boat" sailors. There were reasons for this. Diesel boat sailors could rarely take a shower while at sea. The biggest reason was because operation of the potable water stills was very noisy acoustically for covert operations. The potable water created at night while charging batteries was used for cooking and the limited shaving and sponge bath requirements of the crew.

The routine of a diesel boat is to operate on the surface or at periscope depth while snorkeling to charge the batteries at night away from compromising contacts. The World War II boats would surface at night and do their running on diesel power while charging the batteries at the same time. Whenever a diesel boat submerged, the diesels would be shut down, and the submarine operated on the battery. The faster a diesel-electric submarine operated while submerged, the faster the battery (juice in the can) would be used (depleted). Of course while the submarine was submerged, the boat would operate on what is called "reduced electrical," which means all non-essential electric equipment would be shut down to conserve battery power for as long as possible. Additionally, during this submerged mode of operation, the oxygen inside the boat that was fit to breathe was also being depleted. In the days of the diesel boat, since the sub must either surface or come to snorkel depth so frequently, there seemed to be no requirement for a system of generating breathing oxygen. However, we know of many World War II and some Cold War situations when the diesel boat was held down for as long as possible while the surface units prosecuted the submarine to its limits. During these incidents a substance called lithium bromide would be placed out on trays inside the submarine to absorb the carbon dioxide to make the air as breathable as possible until outside ventilation could be made available. Every diesel boat sailor has seen the air on board so bad that a cigarette could not stay lit. Then there was the fear that lit cigarettes would form phosgene gas which is harmful to submarine sailors and other living things. Submarine batteries, if mixed with seawater for any reason, would form chlorine gas. And submarine batteries, like any other storage battery, were prone to explode. You didn't have to be crazy to serve in diesel-electric submarines but it helped.

For the folks who are not familiar with submarines I point out that diesel engines cannot be operated when the submarine is submerged. Diesel engines need air to operate. Most of the diesel submarines had four diesel engines and the air intake for the diesels came through the main induction valve that is about a foot and a half of hull penetration. It was this main induction failing to close that accounted for several submarine accidents, including the sinking of the U.S.S. *Squalus*. The deepest a submarine can operate on diesel engines is periscope depth, and only when the submarine is equipped with a snorkel.

The operation of the diesel engines, whether on the surface or at periscope depth, is a relatively noisy evolution. Typically, if a submarine were operating off the coast of the country of a potential adversary, the submarine would have to pull out to sea at night to run the diesels and recharged the battery. The World War II boats would run on the surface at night to make best speed and for the purpose of charging the batteries. The diesel boats of the World War II type were much faster on the surface, while they went very slow submerged. Remember, the faster they went underwater, the quicker the battery life would be depleted.

One advantage of the diesel electric submarine, submerged and slow, is that it is exceptionally quite. It was very difficult to detect when deep on the battery. However, active sonar, the acoustic pinging you hear in the movies, doesn't care what form of propulsion is used, it will detect a submerged object equally well. The only way a submarine could hide was to either out maneuver the searching surface vessels or hide below a thermal layer that was dense enough to reflect a sonar signal. Submariners could only hope and pray these layers exist should they need to hide from surface searchers.

One way of describing the typical diesel boat is to categorize them as surface ships with the ability to submerge for short periods of time. The first true submarines, submarines that could remain submerged indefinitely and still return to the surface when required, were the nuclear powered boats beginning with the *Nautilus* and the venerable *Seawolf.* The one individual who's contributions to this technology that made this capability possible in the forum of our history is Admiral Hyman G. Rickover. That made Admiral Rickover the bane of the diesel boats. Old habits die hard. There was much to overcome in the nuclear submarine force. Those who idolized Admiral Rickover really bristled at the term, "Hymie's fairy queen."

Where in diesel boats the engines needed air to operate, in the nukes the crew needed air to survive. The production of a suitable amount of oxygen for breathing became quite a problem to solve. As I recall, the first method was by burning what were called "oxygen candles." I never really did understand it but the candles gave off O_2 through the oxidation process. The system I am more familiar with was oxygen generators. This system was affectionately called "The Bomb." The general idea was to separate the oxygen and the hydrogen from water (H_2O). Of course obtaining oxygen was a good thing, but the hydrogen can be exceptionally volatile. The oxygen was retained, and the hydrogen was dumped overboard. Additionally, the impurities, such as carbon dioxide in the atmosphere, were removed through utilization of burners and scrubbers, which I remember at this point as magic. And let's not forget the problems associated with the isolation of radiation, which can be harmful to people and other living things.

So while the learning curve in nuclear submarining was being experienced, the diesel boat sailors sat back with multiple predictions that "this will never work." Change comes slow in institutions, and the submarine Navy was no exception. The whole idea and philosophy of submarine tactics were in flux, so there was much to learn, experience to be gained, and people of vision were making giant steps of progress.

But the respect of the diesel boat sailors remained and continued to be venerated in the Submarine Service. The danger, and the element of courage, that went with service aboard a diesel submarine were not lost on the nuclear sailors. Besides, diesel boat sailors were usually "old timers" who brought with them the courtesy and honor that went with their senior rank. The advent of nuclear boats also created a dilemma of what to do with diesel boat officers. A class of officer was created called "surfaced submariners." Commander Lloyd Bucher of U.S.S. *Pueblo* fame was one of these individuals. Lieutenant Steve Wood, an academy graduate who became a spook officer, was such an individual. He graduated from the academy during the transition from diesel to nuclear, but he was assigned to a diesel submarine. The handwriting was on the wall by the time he made O-3 that diesel submarines were on their way into obscurity. Mr. Wood had earned his dolphins aboard a diesel boat; however, that did not translate into a career in the nuclear boats. Mr. Wood chose to apply to Russian language school and become a Naval Security Group officer. I suspect, as he experienced the caliber of the officer structure in the Security Group, he made his decision to resign his commission, go to Yale to earn an MBA, and move into defense industry. I had the privilege of making one mission with him aboard *Hammerhead* and, subsequently, working with him at A&T Technical Services, Inc., in New London, Connecticut, were he was the General Manager.

The vernacular jargon for diesel boats is "smoke boats," and the nuclear boats are called "glow boats." I believe these terms came to be used subsequent to 1980, after I retired from active naval service. But that diesel smoke always brought back memories to every submariner who ever experienced service in these vessels. The cold air, the rapid changes in pressure in the boat experienced when snorkeling at periscope depth, the waking up with the obligation to equalize the pressure in our ears, or having your ear attached to a flash cover created by a vacuum in the boat are all experiences of diesel boat duty. Flash covers are used to contain the bedding on submarine racks.

I was an E-4 with seven years of active duty when I first served aboard the diesel boat submarine *Barbel*. It was quite a culture shock, but I was in a whole new world that fascinated me greatly. Observing the submariners carrying out their duties with skill and professionalism was totally intriguing for me. I never forgot this trip in *Barbel*, and, for me, it represented the hub of the "Diesel Boats Forever" attitude.

For many years I would be contacted when the boat chiefs were being promoted, as part of their initiation was to learn and sing *Diesel Boats Forever*. While it did occur to me that these guys could have bought the CD and learned the song that way, I never failed to e-mail the lyrics that are listed at the beginning of this chapter. This is also the song that brought a "thumbs-up" from Captain Slade Cutter, as Dex Armstrong continuously played this album at a *Requin* reunion on the eastern shore of the Chesapeake several years ago

(Top) Author at age 4. The sailor suits were popular for boys, and perhaps an omen of things to come.

(Bottom L) The high school teenage idol, age 16, 1958.

(Bottom R) Cox Scouting family portrait on 1961 Christmas card. (Front) Jeff, James, Lorraine, Ina. (Back) Tommy, Alan. (All photos private collection)

(Top) Russian Language School class. U.S. Naval Intelligence School, Washington, DC, 1961.

(Bottom L) Author with Mother in July 1962, after Russian language training, jut prior to Cuban Missile Crisis.

(Bottom R) Top Hands country band, Japan, 1966. Tommy lower left.

(All photos private collection)

CTI George T. Cox

904 01 18, USN

Having successfully completed the rigorous professional requirements for qualification in submarines, having gained a thorough knowledge of submarine construction and operation, having demonstrated his reliability under stress, and having my full confidence and trust, I hereby certify that he is

Qualified in Submarines

Given this 4th day of June 19 69

On Board U.S.S. (Classified)

C. M. MACK, CDR, USN
COMMANDING OFFICER

Qualified in Submarines aboard U.S.S. (Classified), signed by Captain Whitey Mack, June 19, 1969. I'd found a new home.

By virtue of the authority vested in me as President of the United States and as Commander-in-Chief of the Armed Forces of the United States, I have today awarded

THE PRESIDENTIAL UNIT CITATION (NAVY)

FOR EXTRAORDINARY HEROISM TO

USS LAPON (SSN-661)

For extraordinary heroism and outstanding performance of duty during a period in 1969. Throughout this period, the USS LAPON successfully executed its unique mission. The results of the mission were of extreme significance to the United States. The outstanding courage, resourcefulness, persistence and aggressiveness of the officers and men of LAPON reflected great credit upon the Submarine Force and were in keeping with the highest traditions of the United States Naval Service.

Richard Nixon

(Top) *Lapon*'s Presidential Unit Citation, signed by President Richard M. Nixon, when Captain Whitey Mack proved the U.S. Submarine Service could counter the Soviet ballistic Missile threat.
(Bottom L) Scuba diving with Marine sergeant, Pensacola, 1961. Author on left.
(Bottom R) On patrol in U.S.S. *Greenling* (SSN-614) in 1970.

Sailor of the Month, September 1971, NSGA, Maryland. (Private collection)

(Top) Author at NSGA, Maryland, 1968, after first run on U.S.S. *Lapon*.
(Bottom) Aboard U.S.S. *Seawolf* (SSN-575), 1976. (L-R) Dave Lejeun, Tommy
Cox, Mark Rutherford. (Photo by Dennis Nardone, private collection)

Aboard U.S.S. *Seawolf* (SSN-575), 1976. (Photo by Dennis Nardone, private collection)

(Top) Family photo after promotion to Chief Petty Officer, 1971, Portsmouth, VA. (L-R) Cher, Bill, Sandra with Sweet Baby James, Tommy.
(Bottom) Receiving Meritorious Service Medal from Admiral Bobby Ray Inman for service in U.S.S. *Seawolf* (SSN-575) at undisclosed government agency, 1977. (Photos private collection)

A bearded Tommy in Admiral Zumwalt's Navy after submarine qualification in 1969. (Private collection)

U.S.S. *Parche* (SSN-683), the most decorated submarine of the Cold War. (U.S. Navy photo. Private collection)

(Top) Receiving Joint Service Commendation Medal from "the Doctor", 1977, at undisclosed government agency. (Private collection)
(Bottom L) Senior Chief Cox, 1979, shortly before retirement. (Bottom R) Publicity photo, 1978. (Bottom photos by Judy Taylor, private collection)

Publicity photo with Top Secret Gibson guitar, 1980. (Photo by Ruby Norton, private collection)

(Top) James and Lorraine Cox, Tommy's parents, who received community citations for service as Mr. and Mrs. Santa Claus, 1980. (Private collection)
(Bottom) With the future President of the United States, George H.W. Bush, after performing *Bring the Nautilus Home* during 1980 primary, Groton, CT. (L-R) Jim Corbett, Cox, Gerry Rucker, Bush. (Photo by Ruby Norton, private collection)

(Top) The Tommy Cox Band, Norm's Lounge, 1982. (L-R) Jim Corbett, Tommy Cox, Gerry Rucker. (Photo by Rocky. Private collection)
(Bottom) Brooklyn, CT Fair, 1982. (L-R) Howard Jones of *Lapon*, Hank Shafer, Jeannie C. Riley, Cox, Patty Benjamin, Gerry Rucker. (Private collection)

CERTIFICATE OF RECOGNITION

GEORGE T. COX

In recognition of your service during the period of the Cold War (2 September 1945 - 26 December 1991) in promoting peace and stability for this Nation, the people of this Nation are forever grateful.

William S. Co
SECRETARY OF DEFENSE

(Top) Brooklyn, Connecticut, Fair, 1982. North Star Band. (Private collection) (Bottom) Cold War Service Certificate. Just as intense as any hot war in the Submarine Service.

Tommy and Sandra, 1990, Caribou, Maine. (Private collection)

(Top) LTC Oliver North and Philip "Frenchie" Sirois at USMC reunion in 1998. (Bottom) At U.S. Submarine Veterans 2003 Anniversary in Groton, CT. (L-R) Cobey and Sherry Sontag, Don Ward, Tommy Cox. (Photo by Chumley, private collection)

Tommy Cox, 1971. (Private collection)

CHAPTER 9
LONG SEPARATION

I am a sailor going to sea (boy)
At home sits a wife and a family of three (boy)
It grieves me knowing the love I leave behind (boy)
Long Separation weighs heavy on my mind (boy)

I am the wife of a man dressed in blue (girl)
Although he's out there my love will be true (girl)
It hurts me knowing we must be apart (girl)
Long Separation weighs heavy on my heart (girl)

Long separation tears our hearts in two (both)
Long separation, what are we to do (both)
Long separation, it's something we both knew (both)
That we'd have to live with while I'm in Navy blue (boy)

We need each other now forevermore (both)
I'm here at sea and my love's back ashore (boy)
And I'm here alone waiting for his return (girl)
And the love that we share continues to burn (both)

Long Separation is the second boy-girl song written for the *Take Her Deep* album in Portsmouth, Virginia, during my college period in the ADCOP Program. Kathy Bowie was singing *The Sacrifice*, and I firmly believed, if one song of this structure was going to be included on the album, a second song was necessary. Kathy's husband, Bruce, and my old buddy from Caribou, Harry Anderson, wrote this song together in about an hour and a half. Harry was driving the country for Bama Pies out of Oklahoma, and he had to spend a few days in Virginia while waiting to be told where to deliver next, so he visited with us. It was great seeing him, and he still had his musical ability. Harry was a great country singer. He knew a lot of tearjerkers. I loved hearing him sing, and he had a great influence on the fact that I even played guitar and sang songs.

I also loved singing with Kathy. Besides having an excellent voice, she was an exceptionally beautiful young lady. She and Bruce made a perfect couple. We spent so much time together, because we couldn't afford to do anything else. We played a lot of pinochle, did a lot of cookouts, and spent time at the beach. These were all things that cost little or nothing.

This song is not specific to the Submarine Service, but it was specific to the U.S. Navy. Family separation is a way of life for sailors of all eras and countries. That doesn't make the separation any easier to endure. Fidelity is the one thing on the mind of virtually every Navy family who must endure the hardship of separation. There is a broad bandwidth of attitudes regarding the sanctity of marriage in our world. We come from all walks of life with a variety of attitudes and commitment to responsibility in our lives. Some of us are totally dedicated to our wedding vows, consistent with the expectations of our early family life, our role models, and our own experience. Some of us are not. It helps when we know the expectations of our partners, and we are able to agree on a standard. It is when these standards between marriage partners are not in total harmony that each goes forward with separate agendas. It doesn't always work.

While the divorce rate nationally hovered around 50%, the divorce rate in the military approached 65% in those days. When I first read these statistics, they were applied to the Navy and the Submarine Service, but I later learned it was common to the entire military across the board. It stands to reason during times of extended deployment, strains on marriages will occur.

While I was stationed in Japan and still worked in a country-western band, I recall driving a spook team to Yokosuka in the morning to deploy on a submarine, then seeing one of the team member's wife at the Seaside Club, where our band provided the music that evening. Certainly she knew who I was, but she didn't care and was having a high old time with some stranger before the submarine had made its first trim dive outside Tokyo Bay. Similar scenarios were common. Of course, some of the guys, when opportunity existed, also took advantage of the separation to do their own thing. I guess the standard was: "If you're not with the one you love, love the one you're with." And there were notions that while we're away, somebody is going to "mow the grass."

Jokes abounded about how things went while the submariners were at sea. If a sailor returns home to find all the shoes in his closet spit shined, he could suspect there was a marine hanging around. Another clue was tank tracks in the yard, especially on an Army post. The CPO Club in Norfolk was so famous for the abundance of wives who would hang around to meet men while their husbands were deployed that the club was affectionately called "The Body Exchange."

I don't expect the attitudes differed that much between the military and the general U.S. population. Society changes constantly and we're all social animals. There are a lot of liberalizing forces in our great country. Some of us readily accept change and adapt; some of us hang on to the old tooth and nail. Some of us let our conscience be our guide; some of us adjust our conscience to suit our behavior. Some treated the last few days ashore like it was their final days on earth, and sometimes, considering the danger, the notion wasn't that farfetched. I choose not to judge. My primary concern is the mettle of the man when the brow goes over. In sixteen missions I was fortunate to be deployed with dedicated experts.

There's a song I used to sing for the submarine sailors when I would perform in the Crews Mess usually on the way home. The song was Dave Dudley's *Six Days on the Road*. I would introduce the song about this poor trucker who had been away from his honey all week, but he was making it home after six days. That usually got quite a laugh from the crew who were on the tail end of an eight to twelve week mission.

CHAPTER 10
SEAWOLF

Big S-S-N 5-7-5 on Seawolf's conning tower
The second boat to log it out, "Underway on nuclear power."
The back aft nukes have quite a job just torquing on the screw
Between steam leaks and reactor scrams they haven't much to do

She may be old but she's still bold at the helm Captain Charles MacVean
No finer ship or finer crew ever sailed the bounding main

Where Linda Lovelace is a queen and the Happy Hooker too
Hawkeye said to Short Time, "There's still a lot to do."
Research of the ocean depths bring men from Project Dive
More grapes than brains a rowdy bunch, and don't forget Act Five

If she ain't out she must be in, Mare Island is her home
You'll find the crew at the Horse and Cow prob'ly getting stoned
Seawolf is a part of us, forever homeward bound
She'll take us there and back again and never let us down

Seawolf is the second oldest nuclear powered submarine of the U.S. Navy. Of course, the first nuke was the *Nautilus*. When *Seawolf* was commissioned, the Navy experimented with an alternative type of reactor in *Seawolf*. I believe *Seawolf* served our country with distinction longer than any other submarine. The *Seawolf* was launched on July 21, 1955, and served our country proudly until decommissioning on March 30, 1987. In 1958 the *Seawolf* set a record of 60 days totally submerged. In 1976 *Seawolf* set another submerged record of 87 days while on a special projects mission. This record would have been longer except we spent several hours on the surface dealing with a casualty in the mid-Pacific after being in transit for twelve days or so.

Having served in the most modern 637-class submarines, deploying in *Seawolf* did cause me some consternation. It couldn't run with any great speed while submerged, compared to the 637-class of submarine, and it was especially noisy. But after the '76 mission, we'd become *Seawolf* sailors, and we loved our ship. It was this sentiment reflected in the song. Others may disagree with me, but, in my opinion, the brightest group of sailors in the U.S. Navy are the nuclear ratings that serve in U.S. submarines. This was certainly true of the nukes aboard *Seawolf*. They kept this old tea kettle (nuclear reactor) brewing, making power, and pushing the old boat through the water and history. God bless 'em one and all!

A fairly humorous situation occurred due to the publication of this song. *Seawolf* had four ROVs (Remote Operating Vehicles) used for oceanographic research that had some strange names based upon popular Americana of the period. Two ROVs were deep divers and two were shallow vehicles. I don't remember which was which, but their names were: *Deep Throat* (after the X-rated movie), *Happy Hooker* (after another X-rated movie and an advice column in *Penthouse* Magazine), *Hawkeye*, and *Shorttime*. When it came to writing the lyrics I need four syllables, so I used the name of the movie star Linda Lovelace in the song instead of *Deep Throat*. Some of the stuff I've seen in print has reflected my use of literary license to reflect an actual misuse of the truth. I got a kick out of it.

Something I regretted after the song was published was the lyrics: "You'll find the crew at the Horse and Cow prob'ly getting stoned." The use of the term "stoned" in today's colloquialism refers to drug use. I never did intend to suggest there was drug use by *Seawolf* sailors in any way. In fact, a good portion of the *Seawolf* crew were involved in "reliability programs," and any drug use would have ended the careers of such sailors. To my knowledge, there was no drug use by submariners involved in these projects. It is also true that if somebody were to use drugs, I would not be one with whom this information would be shared. I was a Senior Chief and a spook. Most crew members had no idea what agencies I represented. For all they knew, I could have been DEA.

The Project Dive division contained a group of Navy divers essential to *Seawolf*'s mission. ACT V was the name of the spook group aboard *Seawolf*. We used to joke that ACT V was a really long play. One of the *Seawolf* divers, David LeJeune, became a life long friend. We've hunted together in Maryland, Virginia, and Maine. Our families know each other. And we've stayed in touch. Dave is one of the few enlisted men to have earned a Legion of Merit. Dave retired as a Master Chief and a Master Diver. He's one of the few people that I trust explicitly. Dave was also the Master Diver for the recovery operation of the Air Florida Disaster in Washington, D.C., on January 13, 1982. He is also a qualified submariner. He earned his dolphins in *Seawolf*.

Dave was also the ship's barber. Shortly after we first met, at the Horse and Cow in Vallejo, California, and after the *Wolf* got underway for the mission, Dave was cutting hair in what was called the Project's area. Dave and I didn't know each other very well at that time. Dave likes to tell the following story: "As I was cutting hair, this short, dumpy looking chief (Tommy Cox) comes into the area and sits down on a skid there in the room. This chief picks up a guitar that didn't belong to him and starts tuning, and tuning, and tuning (it was a 12-string). So I (Dave) thought to myself, yeah, this guy's going to sit there and strum the guitar with two or three chords of the only song he knows, then he'll strut off proud and full of himself. Well, when he finished tuning, he blew his nose, strummed a few chords, then he opened his mouth and out came music."

I sang for about an hour and a half doing request after request including some of the early submarine songs that were included on the first album. I also got together with some of the other crew members, and we would perform in the Crew's Mess for a larger number of the crew. Once the ship diversions, such as movies, were established as routine, any departure from that routine was welcomed. For example, when we were on our way home, we held what is known as "spook night." This is where the spook team gave the mess cooks a break and served the evening meal. We would put our fingers in the food making sure all could see. (Yeah, our hands were clean.) We never messed with anybody's food, but we sure made comments like we had, such as getting the gravy from Number Two Sanitary Tank. I would also sing a song or two for these evolutions. I often wrote special verses on these occasions. No, I don't think they were really suitable for children and clergy. On the 1976 mission, Mark Rutherford and I served in the Wardroom for the officers. By that point in time I'd written "*Seawolf*," and I sang it for the officers. So this song actually started out as a big joke for "spook night" and got cleaned up for the record album.

Dave LeJeune helped Mark and I in the Wardroom although he was a diver. I'd blackened my face for the event. Dave blackened half of his face to show he was half a spook. Actually, we adopted him. Dave is one of those gifted individuals who is good at anything he does. Dave went to Kuwait with a "civilian" company following the first Gulf War. He has yet to be paid for his employment. Today he and his wife Cheryl own a furniture store near Gambrills, Maryland. He's lost most of his hearing due to his Navy diving activities.

When Dave and family lived in California, he invited Frank Turban and me to his house for a meal of abalone. It's the only time I've ever had it, and I found it very tasty. While visiting, I sang some songs for Dave and Cheryl's daughter whose name is Julie. I knew two songs that had that name in it, so I sang them for her. We saw her again when we visited with them in March of 2005, when Sandy and I were on our way back to Maine after returning north from North Carolina, where we cut the last two CDs.

Captain MacVean, always the gentleman, autographed a picture of *Seawolf* to me by saying, "Your song will do much to make the memory linger." *Seawolf* had such camaraderie that I couldn't help but develop a strong fondness and loyalty to that boat. In fact, I had that famous picture of *Seawolf* in one of the panels on the album cover of *In Honor of...* That great crew took care of *Seawolf*, and *Seawolf* took care of us.

The spooks who served in *Seawolf* were a pretty unique group. The guy who started out as the Leading Chief was Malcolm "Mac" Empey. Mac was a Senior Chief Communications Technician Maintenance Branch. In my personal opinion, Mac was nothing short of an electronics genius. For one thing, he was color-blind. Therefore, he could not follow the electrical color code. He compensated for this by knowing the full function of each discrete circuit. He never ceased to amaze me when he looked at an electrical schematic. You could follow the direction of his head, as he would scan the print from side to side then top to bottom. We frequently joked that when he did that he was in raster scan as in radar. What never ceased to amaze us, and the college level electrical engineers we came in contact with, is that Mac would immediately grasp any specific problem with the equipment in relation to the function it was to perform or its interface with ancillary equipment. As far as I know, Mac had no formal college. He was just that good. One of his favorite tricks was to increase the efficiency of standard submarine antennae by inserting pre-amps (amplifiers) into the signal path. On *Lapon*'s first mission both oxygen generators died. After several days of trouble-shooting by the ship's experts, who had been to school on the system, Mac offered to assist. The problem module had been identified, so Mac just asked what it was supposed to do. Then he redesigned the module to accomplish the function. In fact, this was the biggest complaint about Mac: He would redesign units and modules. But he rarely left any documentation as to what he did. Technicians who worked the same system after Mac would go nuts trying to figure out what he had done. Mac's approach to problems was to fix it and make it work by any method available. This is a submarine standard. I made three missions in special projects, and Mac Empey solved problems every year that allowed the mission to continue. In every instance, the contractor providing hardware that was computer driven had software problems every year when the hardware was hooked up through the boat. Every year Mac corrected the software programs to make the systems work.

Mac's colorblindness was also apparent in his apparel. He commonly wore a pair of green pants, an orange shirt, and a gray sport jacket. The tie he selected from day to day could be any color. He wore a beard and was balding on top. In fact, he resembled what I imagined the typical absent-minded professor would look like. Mac's philosophy was to work hard and play hard. It was not uncommon for him to be out most of the night drinking, come in and get a few hours sleep, and be totally mentally alert by the time the workday started in the morning. Mac was getting ready to retire when we made that first project run aboard *Seawolf* in 1976. In fact, during that mission, Mac was promoted to Warrant Officer 1, so he moved to the wardroom to be with the officers. Since I was also a Senior Chief, that made me the senior enlisted man in the team from that point forward. I will hasten to add, none of us paid much attention to rank, as each individual was respected for the expertise each brought to the team. I remember once when we were at Mare Island in our khaki uniforms. Mac and I were riding together, and Mac had talked the OIC (Officer in Charge) into lending him his lieutenant's bars. Mac put them on his collar himself, but I noticed he had them ninety degrees off from the proper alignment. We stopped the car and changed the collar devices and headed for the gate. Of course, Mac got the proper salute from the marine guard, and we headed for the Horse and Cow. A lot of the *Seawolf* enlisted sailors were surprised to see Mac wearing the officer insignia. These guys didn't have a clue who we were, and we were rarely seen in uniform off the boat. Oh, yes, folks, impersonating an officer is against military regulations. Mac, rest his soul, is deceased.

Mark Rutherford was another very unique individual. I introduced him briefly in the Prologue as the former submarine radioman from *Greenling* and *Flying Fish* who managed to buck the system and convert to a spook. He was a Chief Communications Technician Technical Branch, but he could install and repair equipment as well as any Mat man (the name for the Maintenance Branch technicians like Mac). In fact, Mac and Mark worked together quite a bit when problems existed. It's a shame he made this conversion so late in his career, as he ended up retiring as an E-7, Chief Petty Officer.

Mark loved being a "spook." He was smooth and debonair and took on the persona of his screen idol, James Bond. He was exceptionally articulate and a master of double talk. He could make you understand what he was talking about by speaking all around a subject regardless of classification or location. He was exceptionally technically competent and a hard worker. He could drink all night and never appear in the least bit intoxicated. He could easily rub shoulders with the Commodore or the seaman gang. A late night phone call when Mark was uptight about something was a marathon. We'd been provided with a credit card number for making phone calls, and Mark used this feature more than any other member of the team. Mark had a brilliant second career with Mitre Corporation. He is now retired full time.

The third ACT V member was one of the spooks who received his dolphins on the *Sea Devil*, Frank Courtney. During this period Frank was a First Class Communications Technician "R" Branch. The books say the "R" stands for "Collection." Frank was an excellent operator, but an unlikely member of ACT V. This is not what you would normally consider an "R" branch assignment. But he was certainly up to the challenge and performed very well. Frank was a good writer and was a great help with the recommendations for awards. Frank was a polished gentleman who frequently stood on ceremony. I often thought he should have been an officer. He would have had this opportunity, as he was assigned to Auburn University under the Navy NESEP program (Naval Enlisted Scientific Engineering Program). Just to qualify for that program was quite an accomplishment and reserved for select, very bright, enlisted personnel who would be promoted to officer upon graduation. Frank did not finish this program, and I never knew why. At one point Frank had changed rating from Communications Technician (CT) to Ocean Systems Technician (OS). He did not stay there very long and returned to being a CT and joined the special project. Frank Courtney retired as a Master Chief Petty Officer (E-9) and works for a defense industry company.

It seemed every other special projects mission had roughly a 50% attrition rate following each mission. Two CT's who made the first run on *Halibut* dropped out after the first mission. That's when Frank Courtney and Bob Ellenwood came aboard to make the second mission on *Halibut*. Bob was a younger fellow, who was a First Class Communications Technician Maintenance man, who was actually stationed at Skaggs Island, California, near Napa Valley. However, he spent his working days at Mare Island taking care of the equipment on a full time basis. Bob was the fellow who was informed his wife was going to apply for a divorce as we were boarding for the *Parche*'s first special projects mission in 1978. Bob was a hard worker who was a little less mature than the rest of the team. He was also the youngest. In Bob's case, if it weren't for bad luck he'd have no luck at all. Poor Bob seemed to be our doom and gloom sailor. But he could get snot-flinging, puke-throwing drunk, and stay that way for days. However, when aboard ship, he worked like a trooper and got the job done. Bob Ellenwood made more of these special projects missions than any other individual over the years. After the second *Halibut* trip the team decided they needed a permanent team member who spoke Russian and who could be trained and dedicated to support the special project. This is when I came aboard.

After the first *Seawolf* mission, we lost two more team members. Mac Empey was retiring and Frank Courtney moved on to other challenges. This is when we selected two more individuals to join the team, Charlie Miller and Frank Turban.

I suspect the detailers at BUPERS (Bureau of Naval Personnel) were getting upset with the project team having *carte blanche* to select anybody we wanted for the team, while they had no control whatsoever. Remember, that's how I came aboard, after a fight with my detailer? It was a control issue. We had already talked to a fellow named Bill Stringfellow, who was a Maintenance Technician assigned to the Sub Base in New London. Bill was a qualified submariner. However, when we put in our request for him, the Bureau went ballistic and demanded we check out the people they suggested. So, to play the game, Mark Rutherford and I drove to Sugar Grove, West Virginia, to interview Charlie Miller. Quite frankly, our intent was to find reasons we should not bring Charlie aboard. But we were honest about the process and came away with a favorable impression of Charlie as a good choice. Charlie was willing to be away from his family for one extended mission per year, several TAD trips for training and consultation, and accept the fact that this kind of mission aboard a nuclear submarine was very dangerous and could result in canceling our birthdays. Charlie was easy going, not a party animal, but a responsible worker, fast learner, and self-motivated.

Frank Turban, on the other hand, was a steamer, an outstanding technician, and my friend. Frank was instrumental in helping me get two singing jobs in the Laurel, Maryland, area, one at a Holiday Inn and another at a Howard Johnson's. For this assistance I paid Frank the standard 10% booking agent fee. Frank was a Chief Communications Technician Technical branch. He was also an accomplished magician who had a routine that he did. He would do his magic program using a lapel microphone that I would plug into my music sound system. We did a few shows that way. When we were out west for the project, we would tell people we were working for the USO. We remain good friends even to this day.

I would include similar summaries of the spook officers we worked with aboard *Seawolf* and *Parche*, but the lieutenant who was our boss on *Seawolf* wants absolutely no publicity, and I have not been able to get in touch with the *Parche* spook boss for this purpose. Both are fine gentlemen who continue to serve our country in defense industry.

I'm not going to use names here but, as expressed in an alternate chapter, there were several divorces in the ACT V cadre. I don't know the details of these marriage breakups, but I do know the general state of mind of our team members prior to leaving on one of these patrols. Remember the first two boats assigned to the projects were *Halibut* and *Seawolf*. I'm told these boats were released for this purpose because they were derelicts, in the opinion of Admiral Rickover, who would not release a first line submarine for something that was not controlled by him. The ACT V team knew exactly where in the world these missions were to take place, the hazards of getting there, and the constant danger of getting detected. We knew that, if detected, the prosecution could be intense and perhaps fatal. Without talking about it, team members treated the last few days ashore prior to departing for the mission as a possible final party before meeting the Grim Reaper. We not only knew the dangers of the mission, we also knew how important this project was to the security of the United States at that particular point in time. In fact, we'd been advised our material was going straight to the White House; it was that important. We literally lived like we were dying in those days. The specter of not returning was very real. In our military minds the results were worth the risk, and we were willing to take the chance. Like I said before, you don't have to be crazy to work here but it helps. In this sense, these could be viewed as suicide missions.

CHAPTER 11
FREEDOM PATROL

The word came this morning our orders are in
My submarine's got a new mission again
We're leaving tomorrow for places unknown
It hurts me so, darling, to leave you alone

I'll be gone, sweetheart, for two months or so
We've got a long cruise, and I must go
While I'm gone, darling, I'll leave you my soul
For I won't need it while out on patrol

So kiss me tender and hold me so near
Whisper sweet nothings that I like to hear
Burn me a memory and my heart console
God, love, and country; the freedom patrol

Freedom is costly, but, dear, I don't mind
It's just that each time I must leave you behind
Pray each night, darling, for a quick, safe return
My reason for living is for your concern

It is commonly said today, "Freedom isn't free." This should be well understood by every American taxpayer. Taxes are so much a part of the United States way of life now that it's a "given," and it is such a sure thing that it is described as being the "only sure thing" in life as in death.

Most of us cannot know what it costs in dollars to keep a nuclear submarine at sea. First there is the cost of the submarine itself. These days the *Tridents* and newer attack boats cost more than a billion. The figures were equally astronomical back in the '60s and '70s, when the new boats were the *Sturgeon* 637 class and our 41 for Freedom boomers. But this song is not about dollars.

This song is about the cost to the young sailors. A submarine crew pays dearly in the loss of the very freedoms they have sworn to defend and to protect. It has frequently been said a convict in prison has more personal space and can walk further than a submariner at sea. The same goes for prisoners of war. One drunken sailor, who had to spend a night in the Dunoon jail in Holy Loch, Scotland, joked this was the first night in a long time he didn't have to hot rack. Hot racking is when three guys, each in a different watch section, share two bunks. One crewman is always on watch in three-section duty; therefore, two of the bunks (racks) are always free. Or, in the case of two-section duty, called port and starboard, two sailors share the same rack, so when one man is on watch the other is off. The only time a crewman has any privacy is when he is in his bunk. Sometimes even that privacy isn't available, as when makeshift racks are constructed in the Torpedo Room, where sailors sleep on air mattresses. Nobody can be asleep in the Torpedo Room when weapons are being maintained. This may mean a sailor may have to go for some time without sleep if he is not resourceful to "borrow" a bunk from another shipmate.

Eating must be done quickly, especially for the on-going watch, so the next guy can sit and have his meal prior to assuming the watch. Meals are served every six hours. They are the standard breakfast, dinner, and supper. For the on-going and off-going watch at midnight, the meal is called "mid-rats" (midnight rations). There are usually cold cuts and soup available for this meal. After the supper and mid-rats meals, and after clean up, a 16MM movie was usually shown. Now I guess they use DVDs and VHS tapes. Typically, after the breakfast and noon meals, the Crews Mess is used for School of the Boat, where lectures and presentations are made to assist in crew training.

Movies on submarines were a unique experience in themselves. Every movie, regardless of genre, was a comedy when you factored in all the comments and observations made by crew members during the course of the show. Of course, ship's alarms superseded any movie at any moment.

Most of the movies were pretty bad. I don't know what criteria were used for content selection for movies that would be appropriate to be viewed by submarine sailors. Of course, the guys liked the submarine movies like *Run Silent, Run Deep*, *Destination Tokyo*, and *Operation Petticoat*. Every time Hollywood made an error in the movie, the *faux pas* would earn a unanimous "Bullshit" from the viewers. Films got rated by the number of "Bullshits" detected. The crew usually enjoyed the *Silent Service* made-for-TV submarine series. Many of us enjoyed the history and the legacy of the U.S. Submarine Service. The guys would always comment on the opening scene where the U.S.S. *Pickerel* did an emergency blow with a 45-degree up angle, and almost lost the boat for the sake of the camera. An emergency blow is where the water is purged from the submarine ballast tanks by high-pressure air to bring the submarine to the surface much like a balloon. The displaced water is replaced by air, which, in effect, makes the submarine lighter and pop to the surface. As I recall, an emergency blow must be done each quarter (every three months) to exercise the system from a nominal depth of 400 feet. Annually, an emergency blow (also called EMBT, Emergency Main Ballast Tank, Blow) must be done from test depth. Usually a surface ship is near for safety. Once the submarine doing an emergency blow starts an ascent, there is no stopping it. Physics rule!

The typical scenario would be for the BCP (Ballast Control Panel) operator called the COW (Chief of the Watch) to activate the EMBT Blow switches, commonly called the "chicken switches." This would cause high-pressure air to blow the water out of the ballast tanks. The sub would usually remain at depth for as long as a few minutes before ascent would commence. At this point a small degree of rise would be ordered by the Officer of the Deck through the Diving Officer on the fairwater and diving planes (front and back). Once the submarine starts to ascend, the bet is on to see if it can be controlled to the ordered degree of rise, around 10 to 20 degrees. Thirty-five degrees is a lot, so the *Pickerel*'s 45 degrees was out of control. When the submarine broaches the surface, almost half of the boat comes out of the water, as shown on the TV series *JAG* and the History Channel's *Blind Man's Bluff*. At the point of surfacing, the digital depth gauge on the 637 class boats has not caught up to the boat and is a blur, too fast to read. The submarine then sinks back down again before settling on the surface.

Now just prior to a planned emergency blow, it would not be uncommon for crew members to get a new guy to make a coffee run, shall we say six cups stacked one over the other, three in each hand. With luck, the newbie would be on the ladder between decks with coffee in hand when the boat starts its ascent. Balance under these conditions is precarious, and the usual result is coffee everywhere.

More seriously, it was the emergency blow system executed upon the initiative of a very knowledgeable Chief of the Watch that saved the U.S.S. *San Francisco* in the Pacific last year. May God rest the soul of MM3(SS) Joseph Ashley who was killed in that accident. I remember reading the great concern over the delay in ascent in the emergency blow system described above. I imagine those few minutes were an eternity to the crew in Control watching their depth gauge.

Submariners are generally quite tolerant of others. Almost all the time one shipmate is within arm's reach of another. Varying personalities and standards can create conflict. Each individual brings a different set of circumstances and experiences to the crew. Individual talents recognized can be appreciated or despised. Where the crew joins in unison is in the safely and operation of the submarine. Here the crew members think as one. Each is respected for individual ability and knowledge, and lack of it brings resentment. New guys are encouraged to qualify as rapidly as possible and woe be unto the non-qual (not qualified) who becomes delinquent (dink) in the ship's qualification schedule. Most qualification programs are designed to be accomplished in one calendar year plus or minus a month or two. I've seen a few complete a qualification card in a month. Notice I said, "complete a qual card." Personally, it took me three months of qualifying to complete my qual card, but I actually spent six months, in earnest, learning about submarine systems aboard *Lapon*. It helped that I had no formal, professional duties while in transit, and I could work on qualifications sixteen to eighteen hours a day. The ship's schedule, which included an ORSE (Operational Reactor Systems Exam) in Scotland, gave me the opportunity to complete watch standing requirements of planesman, helmsman, lookout, and topside watches. After this diligent program, I was suitably embarrassed when a few spooks were given their dolphins aboard a different submarine for completing their qual cards in one month. While there is no doubt these were highly intelligent individuals, I don't believe they were genius prodigies. But that's my opinion, which caused me to question the qualification integrity of that submarine.

Perhaps the biggest cost to submariners and most seagoing sailors is the loss of quality, family time. When I added the actual sea time of my sixteen missions, it totaled four years. This is time that can never be recovered. Sometimes neither wife nor children can understand why husband and daddy has to be gone. My own wife brought it home one time by complaining about all she had to do taking care of everything "while I was out having fun." According to her perspective, submarine missions were "fun." I never forgot that. I do recognize it takes a good woman to do all that was necessary while the husband and father is gone to sea. Seafaring families have had to deal with this issue through the ages. It's not easy. If it were easy, anybody could do it.

At one point in time it was estimated that, while the national divorce rate was near 50%, the Submarine Service divorce rate approached 65%. There were several divorces with every mission. I've seen sailors return home after being gone for nearly three months to find their personal belongings out on the front porch or the wife gone with another. Who was having "fun?"

A close friend and teammate was told just hours before leaving on a special projects mission that his wife and two daughters would be gone when he returned. He had the most miserable time at sea of anyone I'd ever seen stewing about a situation to resolve or influence while deployed. He couldn't even protect himself financially while he was gone. His wife had the checkbook and the credit cards, all the marriage property, and the vehicles, and she was free to do whatever she wanted while he was away. What she certainly didn't concern herself with was his state of mind while deployed. As his leading Chief, I was pleased that he did his duties with typical outstanding professionalism and contributed greatly to the success of the mission. This was one of the cruelest things I've ever witnessed.

She gave no thought whatsoever to the importance of the mission. But she gave a great deal of thought to a very efficient way of tormenting her husband. Was he out there having "fun?"

Of the original six members of the ACT V special projects team that served in *Seawolf* for the 1976 mission, half divorced. The other half could have. Some of us took our vows very seriously. Some of us took our parenting very seriously. We were all at the stage of the seven year itch, eleven year split. Marriage and parenthood notwithstanding, collectively the most important thing in our lives at that point in time was the continued success of our special project. Without doubt it was of great significance to national security, and nobody could do it better than we could. While many of our contemporaries withdrew from the special submarine program in response to family crises, not one of us in projects would do that. We were totally committed to the project and would have sacrificed our family life if that had to be a choice. I once said in an interview, "At that time in my life I put my country before my family." That's how important it was to each of us. We were totally dedicated. It was the ends justifying the means issue. Many intellectuals, philosophers, teachers, and pundits disagree with such a value system in the face of political correctness. This is the freedom given by those of us who will not tolerate failure under any circumstance and will do anything, yes anything, to serve national security. Thank you, Oliver North. Thank you ACT V.

CHAPTER 12
SAILOR'S PRAYER

Lord, Thy sea is so vast
And, Lord, our boat is so small
Guide us home to the ones we love
Lord, hear our call

Lord, You've a mighty sea
And we are in your care
Lord, hear this call from below
Lord, hear a sailor's prayer

Lord, the cruise is so long
And the loved ones that we leave behind
Wait patiently for our return
Lord, ease my mind

Lord, it's so lonesome out here
And Thy sea looks so empty and bare
Guide us home to the ones we love
Lord, hear a sailor's prayer

And, Lord, when our ship comes to rest
And we have done our share
Raise us up to the One we love

Lord, hear a sailor's prayer
Lord, hear a sailor's prayer

In the U.S.S. *Hammerhead* Radio Shack there was a plaque mounted on the plate cover to Power Panel 14 that read: "Lord, Thy sea is so vast and my boat is so small." I believe it was placed there by A.J. Long, submarine Radioman. Every day I worked in that space on three missions, I would see that plaque and read the words many, many times. A.J. turned out to be a good friend. He was very helpful to the embarked team. And he was a guitar player who liked country music.

A.J. owned a Gibson Hummingbird. It was a beautiful guitar with a great sound. It was with this guitar that I compared my own. The necks were identical. They played equally as well, and they sounded just alike. I always wanted to know what model my guitar was. At the time of purchase, the dealer advised me this was a "Gibson Southern Jumbo." Inside the body of the guitar an "SJ" was stamped. But the guitar never fit any of the standard models for Gibson. Some call it a J-45, but I know that is not correct. I did run the serial number of my guitar on the Gibson website and learned it was made in 1963, the year I bought it. Essentially, it's a J-45 jumbo body with a J-200/Hummingbird neck. It's a great guitar!

When writing the songs for the *Take Her Deep* album, I believed the collection should contain at least one hymn. The *Hammerhead* plaque always came to mind when considering this particular effort. All I can say is this song was not written, it just happened.

The lyrics are quite straightforward. It is simply a prayer. The average observer will not see that this song pertains to submariners. It is only the Submarine Service that refers to its ships as "boats." No, we are not still running PT boats.

The final verse to this song was written when Master Chief Bobby Kays passed away in 1979. This is the song that was so difficult for me to sing. Bobby's wife had asked that I sing the *Navy Hymn*. At that point in time, I did not know the words, let alone the chords, to the *Navy Hymn*. I finally fulfilled this request when I did my album of Spirituals in March of 2005. Don Ward assimilated the chords for that recording. The song is still beyond my musical ability.

Submariners know the might of the oceans intimately. The North Atlantic has been historically infamous for rough seas of the type that claimed the U.S.S. *Cochino* back in the fall of 1949. This was the first patrol where a "spook," Harris "Red" Austin, was assigned to a submarine. This was a most inauspicious beginning.

Most of the diesel boats were obligated to ride out storms on the surface. Rough seas were hell on the topside watches. When in a trough the boat was frequently underwater as the peak of a 40-foot wave broke over the submarine. Those topside could only hold their breath and ride it out. The only escape was to submerge and hope the boat could get beneath the fury. The nukes could generally dive beneath rough weather, but I've seen the boat rock and roll in heavy seas at 400 feet. That's rough!

Many of our operations required our submarine to be at periscope depth. Maintaining depth control in rough seas was an art form, rarely mastered. Some of the boats made "wings" to be "earned" as a badge of shame by the Diving Officers when the submarine broached. Broaching is when the sail or any other part of the boat is above the surface. I remember watching the periviz (TV attached to the periscope) and seeing the boat's single screw turning in the breeze (up in the air). The Officer of the Deck was usually shouting, "Get me down!" We joked that we were maintaining our covert cover by impersonating a helicopter.

Depth control at periscope depth had a lot to do with the actual location of the fairwater planes. The fairwater planes for diesel submarines were on the bow and referred to as bow planes in the old days. The nukes with the albacore hull typically had the fairwater planes on the sail. Some of the 688 class boats did have their fairwater planes up on the bow for this very purpose.

The best nuclear class of boat in periscope depth operations was the 585 *Skipjack* class. These six submarines, of which *Scorpion* and *Scamp* belonged, had an exceptionally tall sail with the fairwater planes near the middle of the sail. The next class, the 594 *Thresher/Permit* class, had their fairwater planes high on a short sail. This class of boat was relatively difficult to operate at periscope depth. I served in two boats of this class, *Guardfish* and *Greenling*. The 637 class, the workhorse of the Cold War, was a compromise between the 585 and the 594 classes, but the fairwater planes were still on the sail. The 637 boats in which I served were: *Lapon, Sea Devil, Hammerhead, Bergall, Trepang,* and *Parche.*

These characteristics of our submarines notwithstanding, the might of the oceans was still something to be respected and never taken for granted. Every seagoing vessel is constantly probed by the ocean for any weakness. Usually such weaknesses are found at the most inopportune moments. Constant vigilance is required from the perils of the sea.

When I had the opportunity to edit the card tray of the *Take Her Deep* CD, I opted to dedicate this song to my friend A.J. Long who died all too young. This is my way of remembering him, his plaque, and *Hammerhead* forever.

Lastly, the love of God is much like our beloved oceans. You can see the beginning of it, but you can't see the end.

CHAPTER 13
BRING THE NAUTILUS HOME

Bring the Nautilus home
Bring the Nautilus home
Bring the Nautilus home

Bring the Nautilus home to Groton
Grant her history's honor, peace, and fame
Rest her in the river by the Croaker
Berth her by her birthplace on the Thames

Submarining is a way of life for folks in Groton town
E.B. builds 'em tough, and sleek, and mean
From Mystic sails to atoms, it's hometown family pride
To build the first nuke-powered submarine

The Nautilus served with honor from shakedown to ninety North
From New London to Mare Island ever proud
She's dearly loved and needed here, oh, bring the Nautilus home
Lift your voices high and sing out loud

At the end of 1979, when I retired from active naval service and moved to the Groton/New London area of Connecticut, I became aware of the efforts of a local developer named Frank Sheetz to bring the U.S.S. *Nautilus*, the first nuclear submarine, to Groton as a tourist attraction. Mr. Sheetz already had the U.S.S.

Croaker moored at his facility on the Thames River just up river from Electric Boat. Tourists could visit the *Croaker* to see what a World War II submarine looked like. It was called the *Croaker* Submarine Memorial. Large signs on I-95 advertised its existence. The *Nautilus* could continue to serve in the same manner. Frank Sheetz was a retired submariner.

At the time my song *Big Black Submarine* was being played on a regular basis by DJ Bob Edwards on WCTY radio out of Norwich, Connecticut. I was slowly developing name recognition in the area. This was the time when Gerry Rucker, Jim Corbett, and I first formed our band. We began playing for three weeks at the Mousetrap, then Norman Brochu hired us for his New Year's party at Norm's Lounge on Bridge Street, and booked the band for four months on weekends, Friday and Saturday evenings.

I don't recall exactly how I got hooked up with Frank Sheetz, but something motivated me to write the song. I believe Frank called me and gave me some ideas plus a synopsis of his effort. At that time the *Nautilus* was at Mare Island being prepared for destruction. So early in January 1980 we went to Willimantic, Connecticut, to a recording studio to cut *Bring the Nautilus Home* backed with *Paybacks Are Hell* as a 45 RPM record. The first attempt was a total disaster, as an electrical storm shut down the electricity, and we were unable to complete the recording. We went back two weeks later to complete the project. To save time and money, we recorded the whole thing simultaneously adding vocal harmony and tambourine and punching out instances of lesser quality very quickly. *Paybacks Are Hell* was completed in a single take. Gerry, Jim, and I had practiced the songs extensively, and the preparation paid off in the studio. We obtained a reel-to-reel copy of the cuts for WCTY radio, got a cassette recording of the *Nautilus* song, and Gerry and I met with Frank Sheetz to let him hear the song. He loved it. By then the air play on WCTY had given the song some publicity. Frank Sheetz and I went on radio at WNOR, which was the AM side of the WCTY radio station at the same facility in Norwich.

Then something happened that was amazing as far as I was concerned. George Bush the elder was campaigning for the Republican presidential nomination against Ronald Reagan. He was to make an appearance at the *Croaker* Memorial on a wet, snowy Sunday in Groton. Frank Sheetz invited us to make an appearance to play the song for George Bush. We set up our equipment, practiced the song several times to make sure the sound was right, listened to the campaign speech, then played the song after Mr. Sheetz introduced us. Present in the room was an 18-foot model of the *Nautilus*. All the lights and cameras shifted to us while the song was being played. I told the boys not to play the instrumental break in the beginning of the song to save time, and when the song was over, George Bush came over to shake hands with each of us. I'd hired Ruby Norton to take photographs of us with George Bush in the same picture, and she did an excellent job. We heard from several of our Navy buddies around the world who heard short sound bites of the song in such places a Hawaii, San Diego, and Norfolk. So this was our first, and only, national appearance.

George Bush had been a Navy pilot in World War II, whose plane had been shot down. George Bush was among the many pilots to have been rescued by submarines, in Bush's case, the U.S.S. *Finback,* on September 2, 1944. So George Bush retained a soft spot in his heart for the U.S. Submarine Service, as, without *Finback,* we would have had a long swim, which he probably wouldn't have survived. In my humble opinion, this was one of the Submarine Service's greatest contributions to the future of the United States.

Gerry, Jim, and I ordered 1,000 copies of the 45 record. We hoped to, and did, recover our investment costs in the record by selling them for $2.00 apiece. Later, when Bobby Reed and I were putting together the *Brothers of the Dolphin* CD, I wanted to include these two songs on the album, as they were part of the history of the genre of submarine music and as a memorial to my good friend, Jim Corbett, who died of cancer. Bobby used the record itself to put the two cuts on digital tape using filters to omit the needle noise. Then he added some vocal enhancements to produce what is on the album today. Our dear friend, Norm Brochu, the owner of Norm's Lounge, personally knew the gent who placed records on the juke boxes in the Groton–New London area. We gave him 50 copies of the record, and they were included on the jukeboxes. Later we heard the proprietors of these establishments had heard these songs so much they were sick of them. For a time these records were the most played selections on these juke boxes.

Bring the Nautilus Home is one of the most professional songs I ever wrote. The opening, repeating "Bring the *Nautilus* Home," set the stage for the message of the song. Then the song went straight to the chorus, stating very clearly "We" wanted the *Nautilus* to be returned to Groton, Connecticut, to be berthed in the Thames River as part of the *Croaker* Memorial near Electric Boat, where the great *Nautilus* had been created.

The two verses contained a thumbnail sketch of the *Nautilus* history. Frank Sheetz himself gave me the line "From Mystic sails to atoms." Somebody had characterized the seagoing history of the area as "from sails to atoms," and the line was perfect for the song. There is no question that Electric Boat was the largest employer in Groton, Connecticut, and E. B. and the Sub Base contributed greatly to the economics of Groton and New London, Connecticut. As the largest submarine builder in the world, the initials "E. B." have been used historically to refer to its submarines. In fact, I have personally heard the following statement made on several New London submarines after surviving a particularly high intensity experience: "Thank God and E. B." Yep, they build great submarines.

How many folks in the public are aware of the location of "Ninety North?" Many people have asked me this. Of course, Ninety North is the North Pole. The *Nautilus* was the first ship to go there. Can you imagine what it is like to go under solid ice? These sailors had to have tremendous courage and absolute faith in their ship and nuclear power. A diesel submarine could not go under the ice for any extended period of time, because they could not surface or reach periscope depth when necessary to run the diesels to recharge their batteries. Any casualty that required the *Nautilus* to surface would have been fatal during under ice operations. This was undersea exploration at its finest. I certainly salute these *Nautilus* sailors.

"From New London to Mare Island ever proud" cites the beginning and end of the service of the U.S.S. *Nautilus* to our great country. She began her history home ported at the New London Submarine Base, and, at the time this song was written, she was in Mare Island, California, to be scrapped. I am not aware of all the machinations that occurred to get the *Nautilus* saved from the scrap pile, but she was. The U.S.S. *Nautilus* now exists as a National Park Museum Memorial to submarines just outside the New London Submarine Base. A friend sent me a newspaper clipping that made the statement that "somebody" was on the river shore with a boom box playing "Bring the *Nautilus* Home" very loudly as she was being towed up the river to her final resting place at the Museum.

I do not believe for a minute that the reason the *Nautilus* now rests in the Thames River is because of the creation of this song. I do firmly believe it helped to generate a public support for the effort. The real credit goes to Frank Sheetz who was a tenacious advocate for the effort. The *Nautilus* Memorial is also a memorial to this great submariner who worked and lobbied so hard to make it happen. May Frank Sheetz rest in peace in the knowledge that he made a great difference to the submarine community.

CHAPTER 14
KURSK

The Kursk is on the bottom of the Barents Sea
One hundred eighteen sailors for all eternity
Submarine disaster, Russian tragedy
The Kursk is on the bottom of the Barents Sea

On August 10 in Y-2-K the exercise did go
A missile fired at the target through the sleet and snow
K-1-4-1, the mighty one, destroyed the target foe
With much success they did their best; they put on quite a show

On August 12, torpedo launch, St. Elmo did arrive
Then it was told all hands were lost; no one did survive
K-2-1-9, Komsomolets, and K-8 all alive
Joined Thresher and the Scorpion and Kursk on her last dive

Crewmen of the mighty Kursk and sailors everywhere
All submariners of the world join as one in prayer
We're brothers of the dolphin; you know we really care
It could be you it could be me beneath the waves out there

*Kursk na dno Barentsevo Morya**
Sto vosemnadtsat' moryaki za sovsem' vsegda

---

*   Transliteration used in lieu of Russian Cyrillic alphabet.

Atomnaya podlodka, dvenadtsat' Avgusta
Kursk na dno Barentsevo Morya

On August 12, 2000, the Russians lost one of their newest submarines in the Barents Sea. NATO had ascribed the designator *Oscar* for this class of boat. It is a nuclear-powered, cruise missile submarine SSGN (Submarine Ship Cruise Missile Nuclear). By submarine standards, it is huge. It was intended to be the Russian answer to the U.S. *Los Angeles* class submarine. This was the *K-141*. In addition to torpedoes it carried cruise missiles, which NATO designated Ship-wheel. The *Kursk* was 505 feet long and displaced more than 14,000 tons. Only the Russian *Typhoon* boomer and the American *Trident* boomer submarines are larger.

I knew when this song was published it would be controversial. Although I wrote a song for *Scorpion*, I have not done so for *Thresher*, and here is a song "honoring" a Russian submarine. While I have maximum respect for the memory of *Thresher*, her loss occurred in 1963 while I was in Cuba and before I had the opportunity to serve in submarines. When *Thresher* went down, I had not yet developed the bond and emotion of the submariner. The Kingston Trio had a song about the *Thresher*.

When the *Kursk* went down my personal sorrow for this tragic loss of submariners was immediate and unconditional. I prayed for the souls of the dead, the rescue of possible survivors, and for the grief and loss of the sailors' families and loved ones. Besides being human beings, they were submariners and, without doubt, as Bobby Reed has written in his song, the concept of *Brothers of the Dolphin* truly exists and spans international boundaries. There is strong precedent for this brotherhood.

The best documentation is from the submarine experience in World War II in the Pacific. As U.S. submarines sank enemy shipping, with each torpedo hit there was an amount of jubilation among our crews for their successful attacks, even when it meant they would have to endure a depth charging, which certainly could result in their own demise. However, when an enemy submarine was sent to the bottom, that celebration of success was absent. While our submariners did not hesitate in their duty to sink enemy submarines wherever and whenever possible, the spirit of glory did not exist. The dead were fellow submariners, and appropriate respect was tendered. In my heart the loss of *Kursk* was similar, "it could be you it could be me beneath the waves out there." The world had lost another crew of submariners, and the world goes on.

As the saga unfolded and it was learned that 23 of the sailors survived the initial explosion in the after compartments, submariners cringed at the thought of their deaths by suffocation and hypothermia. Those of us who serve in submarines know the dangers of these hazards when machinery and technology fail and the mighty seas take more victims. This is the gruesome reality of the Submarine

Services of all nations. The sea is a constant challenge and frequently more deadly than any potential adversary.

What really happened to *Kursk* will baffle submariners forever, like the *Thresher* and *Scorpion*. We can only speculate and attempt to rationalize the existing evidence. North Cape, Norway, recorded two explosions in *Kursk*. These events could be ascribed to a torpedo explosion followed by a sympathetic missile explosion. This is based on the relative magnitude of each explosion which fit the suspected amount of chemical propellant in a *Shkval'* torpedo and a *Shipwheel* missile. This is the theory to which I subscribe. In fact, the original song ended with the spoken Russian phrase "*Shkval' unichtozhil Kursk*," the *Shkval'* torpedo destroyed *Kursk*. *Shkval'* means squall or storm at sea. Leaving this statement out of the song is my personal effort at political correctness. I suspect the Russians would have been upset over this presumption by an outside foreigner.

Perhaps this is the one big irony of the Cold War. It is likely the *Scorpion* was lost due to an overheated battery which ignited the warhead of a MK-37 torpedo, and the *Kursk* was possibly lost due to a malfunction of a *Shkval'* torpedo. The only casualties of our Cold War weapons were ourselves. This thought certainly bears meditation.

The Cold War had a variety of facets. It was a war of technology, sophistication, and industry. Nowhere was this so evident as in the undersea war, the "game" of Blind Man's Bluff. The big difference was in the percentage of our nations' gross national product that went to military costs. While the U.S. and what is called the free world invested at 10% or less of GNP, the Soviet Union dedicated as much as 50%. In short, this led to economic collapse in the long run for the Soviets, while in the U.S. it created a defense industry that really served to keep the economy active and growing. President Eisenhower called it the "military industrial complex." As in the two world wars, the United States out produced everyone.

The big question during the Cold War was the intentions of the Soviet Union and Communist China. Marxist-Leninist doctrine was well known, with its recipe for world domination. The secret war of spies was consistent with communist goals. However, if the fertilizer really hit the fan, what would the Soviets and Chinese really do? Would they attack or form the wagons into a circle and hope to ride out the siege? The stakes were too high. We could not afford to be "second best" in any conflict. Evidence seemed to indicate they were preparing to survive a nuclear battle. This was scary! Part of our major strategy was the guarantee of nuclear retaliation from our ballistic missile submarines. Those in power in the Soviet Union and China with enough wisdom to understand nuclear might should have been deterred by this capability. The Soviets thought so much of the concept that they incorporated the strategy themselves. Thank God the cooler heads prevailed throughout the Cold War. No nuclear weapon of mass destruction needed to be fired in anger during this period. The strategy of deterrence prevailed.

Doomsday books and films abounded. Few of us understood the full spectrum of consequences of nuclear war. But the submarine nuclear rates did. Nuclear qualified officers, electronics technicians, electricians, and machinist mates are among the brightest, most intelligent group of men I have ever met. My son James served in nuclear submarines aboard the *Trident* boats *Tennessee* and *Maryland* as a nuclear ET. He also taught nuclear power at the prototype facility in Ballston Spa, New York, for a number of years. We joked that he was the family "rocket scientist." There is no doubt he is a bright young man. While on active duty, like his father, he earned his bachelor's degree. And as of June 2005 he successfully completed a course of study through EXELON in Illinois and obtained his license to operate a nuclear reactor in accordance with criteria established by the Nuclear Regulatory Commission. He served twelve years in the U.S. Navy. Being retired myself, I strongly believed he was making a big mistake by not finishing his 20 years to retire. His success at EXELON has convinced me he made the right decision. Why did the Navy lose him? Without going into detail it boiled down to two reasons: (1) President Clinton's downsizing, and (2) leadership. Think about it; I did!

I spent 20 years of active naval service in opposition to the Soviet Union. I internalized the concept of "my country right or wrong." As far as I was concerned the ends justified the means. I would do anything to support our national security. My adversary was the Soviet government and the concept of communism. I had no animosity for the Russian people. In fact, the few real Russians I knew, the professors who taught the Russian language at the U.S. Naval Intelligence School in Anticostia, Virginia, were really great people. I read *Pravda* when it was under the management of Khruschev's son-in-law and understood it to be a propaganda organ of the party. I read other magazines, books, and periodicals from the Soviet Union. I had learned to think in the Russian language. And I learned all I could about life in the Soviet Union. I thought how nice it would be to visit there someday.

There were those in our country who internalized a real hatred for the Soviets. And there are those in Russia who feel the same way about Americans. This creates what I believe to be a very dangerous situation. Safeguards of weaponry are still in force in the United States, but the situation is considerably destabilized in Russia. The economic woes have created a privateer, capitalistic mentality. Organized crime is rampant. And weaponry safeguards are lax. Much has been written about weapons that are unaccounted for that could be finding their way to the terrorists of the world who have *beaucoup* bucks to spend. In my view the most dangerous situation in our world today is the possibility of a nuclear weapon in the hands of terrorists. A second threat is the Russian SAM-7, surface-to-air missiles, similar to the U.S. Stinger, an infrared homer in the hands of terrorists. This could result in the civilian aircraft of the world, those without countermeasures, disappearing at an alarming rate. While this may have happened to a limited extent, the fact that a great number of aircraft have not yet been shot down with these missiles suggests either discriminating terrorists or a very effective world counter terrorist effort. What do you think? The reality is the anti-terrorists must be successful and lucky every time; the terrorists need to be lucky only once.

Certainly the scope of international relations is much more complex, but these are some of my conclusions from the perspective of being a Cold War participant for 20 years.

At this point you're probably asking yourself, "What has this got to do with the *Kursk?*" Well, these are elements that were considered as the song was written. We are still building submarines and so are the Russians. Technology progresses on a daily basis. In fact, quite frankly, Russia, and possibly China, are the only two powers that could build a submarine capable of taking on a modern U.S. boat. Yes, there are countries that are building modern diesel-electric submarines on a smaller scale that have modern torpedoes for weapons. In the hands of the wrong people, these could present a threat. But I strongly suspect our submarine computers contain the specifications of these boats before they are even launched. Everything must be considered. Those of us who were high-tech wizards during the '60s and '70s are today's dinosaurs. An era has ended and a new one began.

My intention is that the *Kursk* song not detract in any way from U.S. submarines. This song is a recognition of the service and tragedy of another nation. As I review the two verses, in the *Navy Hymn* from my spiritual album, that apply to submariners, I note the prayerful lyrics do not apply to any one specific nation.

CHAPTER 15
BLIND MAN'S BLUFF

Way back in the Cold War when the going got tough
We played a little game and called it blind man's bluff
The U.S. and the Russians kept the action unseen
We played this game of chicken with our submarines
We'd sneak up on each other – steal the secret stuff
Muddied up the waters; called it blind man's bluff

We're young and patriotic and devil may care
The good guys and the bad guys made a deadly pair
We shadowed each other with antennas for ears
We were just high-tech buccaneers
We could get the booty from the Soviet bear
And bring it all together with a wing and a prayer

Blind man's bluff is not a childish game
Blind man's bluff can bring you fame or shame
A little bluff here or a little bluff there
Blind man's bluff could be a sailor's prayer

Back in '97 when the Cold War was through
Pretty Sherry Sontag and Christopher Drew
Set out to tell the story of the fast-boat nukes
Intelligence collection and high-tech spooks

They wrote about the SPECOPS and the secret stuff
Put it in a book and called it Blind Man's Bluff

After publication of the book *Blind Man's Bluff* by Sherry Sontag and Christopher Drew and the upcoming History Channel Special by the same name, I'd given some thought to a song that should have the same title. It should be sort of a fast song with a beat. (I classified songs as "slow," "fast," and "half-fast."—Please pronounce carefully.) I had in mind the possibility of having this song be the theme song for the History Channel Special and/or the theme song for a movie by the same name, which seemed to be the intent of Steven Spielberg. Sherry Sontag had informed me of Spielberg's interest in the book. He paid a fee for the movie rights to *Blind Man's Bluff*, just as he had with Admiral Gene Fluckey's *Thunder Below.* I'd heard Fluckey contacted Spielberg at one point asking if he was going to do the movie before Fluckey's death. My guess is that Spielberg is a brilliant man who cornered the market on the submarine publicity of the day to go forward with a movie himself should his perception of the public attitude regarding submarines remain focused and positive. In the meantime, by purchasing the movie rights to these books, he prevented anybody else from doing similar movies. Neat approach! If such movies are made, it would be a good thing for Bobby Reed and me to contribute to the musical score of these productions. In fact, this is probably the only opportunity we will ever have to make any decent money with this music while we are still alive.

At the end of March of 2001, Sandy and I drove to Milford, Massachusetts, for me to work with Bobby to record my contributions to the *Brothers of the Dolphin* album. Bobby and I had been working for two days straight recording. We were tired, and diverting our attention from what we were supposed to be doing was easy. We were discussing the appropriateness of doing a song with the *Blind Man's Bluff* title to add to the collection with the potential for becoming the theme song for any *Blind Man's Bluff* productions, as discussed above.

I picked up my Gibson and started strumming at a lively pace in the key of E. The words just started to flow: "Way back in the Cold War when the going got tough, we played a little game and called it blind man's bluff." That was the perfect intro to the flavor of this song. Then I thought of the old saying we used to have about going out to watch the submarine races. Have you ever tried to find words that rhyme with "submarine?" Well, "unseen" worked which gave us the next line. At this point Bobby went to work on the computer to write down what we had, before it escaped us. In the meantime, Margie and Sandy had gone out to get some Chinese food. When they came back, they heard us jamming with this new tune and said it really sounded good. By then we had two verses and a bridge written. We took a break for dinner and a few more drinks and decided the song was done. We went back in the studio, Bobby programmed the Band-in-the-Box, and we put it on tape.

Later Bobby developed the musical introduction to the song with lead guitar, added an additional rhythm guitar track, added a bass track, and three new vocal tracks. Something that really caught my ear was his use of the bass strings on the lead guitar to fill the gap between the first and second verse. I commented the two notes he used here and let them sustain sounded a lot like an AN/SQS-26 sonar. Cool! I also suggested we use an abrupt ending on the song. I was having trouble expressing myself to Bobby what I meant by this. Then I remembered that Bobby had a strong folk song background. So I suggested he listen to the ending of *Tijuana Jail* by The Kingston Trio. Success!

After all was done, the cut only came to one minute and 46 seconds. This was the shortest song we'd ever done. I continued to think about that and later wrote the last verse back in Caribou. The opportunity to put it out on an album did not present itself until Don Ward and I did the album in Wilmington, North Carolina, in March of 2005.

CHAPTER 16
STILL ON PATROL

Still on patrol, stout heart and soul; submarine sailors 'neath the sea
They give their all to answer the call. Courage runs deep through history

Fifty-two boats and some three thousand men lost at sea in World War Two
Amberjack, Barbel, Sculpin, and Gudgeon, the S-boats, Scamp, and Wahoo
The service of some; the honor they won, white stars on a field of blue
Cromwell, Ramage, Fluckey, and Gilmore, O'Kane, Dealy, Mush Morton too

And many survived; kept freedom alive, Submarine vets of World War Two
Tautog and Thresher, Tinosa and Sea Dog, and Guardfish to just name a few.
And one other threat is still with us yet as Ivan the bear grows strong and bold
But sure silent death still lurks in the depth; submarines still on patrol

Sleek big and black, nuke fast-attack, Parche, Lapon, for red, white, and blue
And 688s lurk deep and wait, Groton, Phoenix, Bremerton too
Big bad and mean, ballistic submarine, Carver, Marshall, Hale, Boone, and Clay
Patriots who protect me and you, and Trident force sing "Anchors Aweigh."

There was a Navy Chief submariner who worked at the New London Submarine Base Museum in 1980–81 time frame. I called there for some background information for this song. He started talking, all off the top of his head, about the Medal of Honor winners in World War II and some of the boats that were sunk and some that survived. I only met this man twice, once when I donated two vinyl records of *Take Her Deep* albums to the Sub Base Museum and once at the Sub Base Chief's Club when I did a gig as a single and sang the song. He communicated his recognition of the song by the smile on his face. I regret I do not remember his name to include here, but he was a fountain of information and a real gentleman.

The song's inspiration came from the famous plaque inscribed with the names of the 52 U.S. submarines lost during World War II. At the top of the plaque are the words "Still on Patrol." I first saw this plaque in the Navy Museum at the Navy Yard (Gun Factory) in Washington D.C. They used to have a small room to the left of the main entrance dedicated to submarines. The plaque was displayed there. An old submarine periscope was also installed there. The kids loved to play with it to gaze around the Navy Yard. At first view of the plaque, I resolved to write a song with the same name.

With this song I wanted to span the history from World War II to the *Trident* boats. This is actually the first song that I wrote that required any research effort. The words "Courage runs deep" are also found on a plaque and on T-shirts, coffee cups, and other submarine paraphernalia. *Still on Patrol* actually has a double meaning. When a submarine is lost, such as the 52 boats of World War II or the *Thresher* and *Scorpion*, "Still on Patrol" means they are still out there serving our country in death on "Eternal Patrol." "Still on Patrol" also alludes to the fact there are *always* American submarines on patrol serving our country's interests at all times. Navy families are always making "The Sacrifice" every day. Our undersea warriors are accomplishing their missions in war and peace at all times. It never ends.

In the first verse I wanted to pay honor to a few of the boats of the 52 that were lost during the war. I also wanted to include the names of two of the modern boats named for these historical legends in which I served: *Barbel* and *Scamp*. I also wanted to mention the names of some of the Medal of Honor winners in submarines, but I made an error. Dudley "Mush" Morton was not awarded the MOH, "white stars on a field of blue." Morton was such a hero in my mind that I just assumed he was awarded our nation's highest award. It didn't happen. So that mistake is mine, and in this song Dudley Morton is honored as a Medal of Honor winner, in my opinion, as he should have been. I feel the same way about Slade Cutter. More literary license!

In 1978, after the *Take Her Deep* record came out on vinyl, Sandra and I attended the convention of the Submarine Veterans of World War II in Norfolk, Virginia, at the invitation of Rudy Jacks, a noted World War II submariner. We certainly met a lot of great submarine warriors and heard a lot of stories. It was here we met Harold Ballinger, who played the freckle-faced kid in the *Spanky and Our Gang* movies of the '30s. Harold left the movies to join the Submarine Service during the war. Mr. Ballinger sure took a shine to Sandra, who was a slim and trim beauty at age 32. I took my sound system, set up in the hospitality room, and sang while Sandra sold records for $7.00 each. I sure learned to sing *Waltzing Matilda* at that convention. We had a great time meeting so many heroes. Mentioning a few of the surviving boats I included *Guardfish*, another modern boat in which I served.

When the song was written in 1980, the Soviet Union was still the major adversary of the United States. China was a major power, but their submarine service was not impressive as it is now. The Soviet submarine technology was getting better all the time and was the major threat for the U.S. Submarine Service. There was no indication the Cold War would ever cease. But our "submarines still on patrol" were up to the task of being the "silent sentinels" that Bobby Reed wrote about in his song *Brothers of the dolphin*.

Representing the 637 class fast attack submarines are my beloved *Lapon* and the submarine receiving the most Cold War accolades, the *Parche*. This class of submarine was the mainstay of the Cold War involvement during the mid-'60s through the '70s. The 688s were being launched as the '80s began. I was very partial to the *Bremerton*, as we met many of their commissioning crew at Norm's Lounge in the early '80s. Several members of this crew remain dear friends to this day. The Tommy Cox Band and Norm's Lounge can claim responsibility for several marriages for couples that met there to listen and dance to our music. The *Groton* was a submarine commanded by George Emery of Sanford, Maine, who I met on the *Hammerhead*. Since he was a Mainer, I assumed a hometown bond with him whether he liked it or not. He retired as a Vice Admiral.

The final lines of the song are to honor the boomers, fleet ballistic missile submarines that are constantly on patrol in their deterrence role in support of our country. There are five boats from the original Forty-One for Freedom, plus the *Trident* boats were being built at the time, *Ohio* and *Michigan*. The *Carver* is named, as that is Bobby Reed's boat. The power and might of the payload of a *Trident* submarine is nothing short of awesome. They were quick to point out, when deployed, they were the third most powerful "nation" in the world. We toured the *Michigan* at the invitation of their Chief of the Boat, Master Chief Bud Atkins. My Dad took quite a shine to the *Michigan*. It could be viewed from the Gold Star Bridge at Electric Boat, and Dad would always ask about the progress on the boat when we spoke on the phone. I shared this with Bud Atkins, and he arranged for us to receive invitations to the commissioning, and he provided a jacket and hat for Dad. We also got to tour the boat. My father was ecstatic. I am personally very grateful to Master Chief Atkins for his kindness to my Dad.

This must be the spot for an additional tangent regarding the *Bremerton* crew. A young Seaman Apprentice named Larry Tharp would visit Norm's Lounge with the *Bremerton* sailors. He met a young lady there named Marianne Dobrinsky and they fell in love. Marianne was 18 years old at the time. Connecticut had changed the drinking age to 18, and she would come to dance and listen to the band with her Mom and other members of her family. She was the spitting image of my high school sweetheart, so I liked her immediately. After a period of time, we received an invitation to their wedding, and they hired the band to play the music at their reception.

We attended the wedding Mass at the church, and then we all got together at Norm's for the reception. I had given them our rock-bottom price of $180.00 for our music services. Following the dollar dance, I could see they were putting together the money to pay the band from the dollar dance money. That's when it occurred to me, they didn't have any money for their wedding night. Sandy and Jim Corbett's wife, Veronica, made a few inquiries, and they learned they didn't even have any place to go for a honeymoon. So Sandy called the Ramada Inn in Mystic, Connecticut, reserved the Honeymoon Suite for them, we gave them back their money and sent them off to Mystic. The three of us in the band, Jim Corbett, Gerry Rucker, and I, all remembered when we were E-2s in the Navy and did what we could to make this a happy night for them. Larry and Marianne have kept in contact with me since 1980. We exchange Christmas cards. They are still together, and we compliment them on their life together. Yes, Larry is a submariner!

CHAPTER 17
PAYBACKS ARE HELL

In Iran you held us hostage for all the world to see
In Pakistan and Libya, you burned our embassy
And yesterday in Old San Juan you shot my brother down
Paybacks are hell; sucker, if you want to fool around

You're walking on the fighting side of me
When you're messing with our liberty
Mr. Terrorist, you'd better listen well
Get ready, Hoss, 'cause paybacks are hell

The Russians in Afghanistan are now invasion bound
In Bogotá, Columbia, another embassy went down
Yes, these states are united in the American dream
Paybacks are hell, fool, don't make that eagle scream

I hear your saber rattle with the unarmed in your land
Because we have respect for life you force the upper hand
You've burned one flag too many, it's no more other cheek
Paybacks are hell, coward, let's see your yellow streak

On December 3, 1979, terrorists attacked a Navy bus in Puerto Rico. The pictures showed bullet holes all through the bus including large holes from

12 gauge shotgun slugs. CTO1 John Ball and RM3 Emil White were killed. Ten others were wounded including five women. This was a shocking tragedy for the Naval Security Group. My close friend, Master Chief Jim Corbett, knew Petty Officer Ball personally. Jim and I discussed the event over drinks at the New London Sub Base Chiefs Club. By the time I got home, I was upset over the situation in particular and terrorism in general. I sat down and wrote this song in about thirty minutes.

Of course, the Iranian hostage crisis that occurred on November 4, 1979, was fresh in everybody's mind. An Iranian mob stormed the American embassy in Teheran and took the staff hostage. This lasted 444 days. The Soviets were doing their international *faux pas* in Afghanistan. American flags were being burned all around the world. Other American embassies were becoming endangered species. But it was always what could be described as a "sucker punch." It was the innocent being attacked, like the bus to NSG, Sebana Seca, Puerto Rico. Everyone on this bus was unarmed. All were non-combatants at the time. It was a hit and run by these terrorists. The attack can only be characterized as cowardly. This is the nature of terrorism. Those of us who had been or would be warriors experienced great frustration with these situations. Where would this condition end? How long was the United States going to sit and take it before some serious retribution was obtained? President Carter was a great humanitarian. He could always see the "good" in others. I believe his premise was along the lines of "I'm a good guy; you must be a good guy." Well, we weren't seeing much goodness from the Ayatollah. We were letting a mob govern United States actions. We were "turning the other cheek." We were the laughing stock of the world. The rescue attempt, while employing some highly capable people, turned into a real goat rope. The United States military effectiveness was perceived as a joke. The terrorists loved it! But I digress!

In the chorus of this song I wrote: "You're walking on the fighting side of me..." Merle Haggard had a song called *Fighting Side of Me* that was one of the original "kick-butt" songs in country music. I had just retired from the Navy and moved to Gales Ferry, Connecticut, to work for A&T Technical Services, Inc., a subsidiary of Analysis & Technology, Inc., in North Stonington. I'd hoped to parallel two careers at the same time while in Connecticut, one as a defense industry consultant and a second in music. I'd yet to break into the song writing market with the exception of my album, and part of my intention was to pen a sequel to *Fighting Side of Me* which had the potential of being of interest to Merle Haggard.

Later in 1980 I decided to record *Bring the Nautilus Home*, (See Chapter 14) I put *Paybacks Are Hell* on the flip side of a 45 RPM record and did, in fact, send the record to Merle's publishers out in Bakersfield, California. Of course, I never heard from them. One thing that became very obvious was the enthusiasm for the song when we played it at Norm's Lounge. The crowd loved the song. I was delighted with its polarizing effect on the crowd for American patriotism. Norm's

Lounge had quite a diverse clientele. There were sailors, of course, Electric Boat yard birds, civilians, and a large contingent of bikers. In fact, I was always amazed at how the ingredients for a real brawl always existed there at Norm's, but it never happened. I firmly believe when this song played, we could have put together a contingent of Norm's Lounge regulars and accounted well for ourselves against the Iranian mob holding our hostages. Isn't it great when hostility can be channeled?

One gent who took a real interest in this song in particular was a former sailor from the submarine tender U.S.S. *Fulton* in New London named Steve Corneliussen. Steve is quite an industrious individual who is an accomplished songwriter, unpublished, who is pretty good with a computer and is aggressive when it comes to business. In fact, Steve had an idea of doing a book similar to the one you are reading now. Following the September 11, 2001, attacks on the World Trade Center, the Pentagon, and the plane crash in Pennsylvania, Steve made copies of *Paybacks Are Hell* and sent media player copies to multiple radio stations. Here was an anti-terrorist song already on the market, and the United States had just become victims of terrorism. Quite a number of radio stations did play the song. He would tell me which stations wanted copies of the CD (*Brothers of the Dolphin*) that contained *Paybacks Are Hell*, and I would send them a copy. Conversely, many other radio stations refused to play the song. These were the radio stations that were courteous enough to reply to Steve who were more interested in political correctness. The complaint was essentially that the song incited violence. Well, that was the finest compliment they could give me. Wow! I have a song powerful enough to incite violence!

In the year 2001 Sandy and I visited our lifelong friends Judy and Rodney Sirois, who are the hosts at Northern Hideaway during bird season, October. Northern Hideaway is a set of woodland camps and guiding service near St. Pamphile, Quebec, Canada, just inside the Northwest Maine border. Rod is a retired Maine Game Warden and a retired CWO-4 Navy SEAL. Rod's guests at that time included Roy Maddocks and Dave Bixler, two Senior Chief Navy SEALS on active duty with SEAL Team 2 out of Little Creek, Virginia. Rod loves the song *Paybacks Are Hell*. I brought my guitar and sang for the guests. Roy made the comment that the song, "made the hair stand up on the back of his neck." Now there's a unique compliment! I gave him a CD, which got played for the guys at Little Creek during training evolutions "just to get the frogs in the mood." Up yours, Jane Fonda! Navy SEALs exercise to my music.

Roy and Dave are not your average enlisted men. Both are now Command Master Chiefs; both have bachelor's degrees. I remember suggesting they may wish to augment to become officers; they certainly had the qualifications. It would also increase their retirement. Nope! They'd reached their goal. Both wanted to be E-9s. This way they still made command decisions, but they got to remain active operators. I guess I understand that. More about these guys in Chapter 25!

The trouble with *Paybacks Are Hell* is that it's 25 years out of date. Several people suggested redoing the lyrics to make the song more modern. This is exactly what happened in the latest CD, *In Honor of...*, with the song *Paybacks*. (See Chapter 22) What the heck! I own the song; I can change the lyrics if I want to. That's exactly what I did.

CHAPTER 18
MIGHTY MINE DODGERS

In May of 1945 nine boats left Apra Bay
For Hirohito's hot tub, known as the S-O-J
Operation Barney, Earl Hydeman's Hellcats
To dodge the mines in all three lines to get on station fast

On the way to station Tinosa got the draft
Rescued ten downed airmen from their rubber raft
Transferred them to Scabbardfish to pacify their soul
Didn't want to hide deep inside Tinosa on patrol

Hepcats, Polecats, Bobcats all—Sea Dog, Spadefish, Crevalle tall
Skate, Tunny, Bonefish, heroes true—Flying Fish and Bowfin, Tinosa too

On June the 5th—Tsushima Straits—Snuffy had the con
Jeep Shelden at the helm on watch in the early dawn
The Hells Bells rang a warning there were mines ahead
Each man aboard could not afford to be among the dead

Right full rudder; left full rudder, all stop
A cable on the starboard side, they had to stop the prop
All hearts stood still; no one spoke as they listened to it drag
And all on board just thanked the Lord, the cable didn't snag

They transited the La Pérouse eight boats of the nine
The Bonefish didn't make it through the salty brine
Four engines on the surface, the diesels loud and shrill
Went through at night prepared to fight; set course for Gooneyville

The welcome home at Royal H, Charles Lockwood in command
They had a very special card made for every man
Mighty Mine Dodgers; they helped to win the war
From east to west they were the best at sea and ashore.

This particular song came about in a very unusual manner. Besides the history *Mighty Mine Dodgers* represents, another set of circumstances had to occur before this song could exist.

In the late 1990s, the exact date escapes me, Marjorie Duke, the daughter of a submariner, purchased the *Take Her Deep* CD. This was a time when only that album existed as a collection of submarine music. The CD arrived in time for the final days in hospice of her Dad, James "Jeep" Shelden. The music brought Mr. Shelden much comfort. The CD was then played over and over at the funeral home wake for Jim.

Following the funeral Gladys and Marjorie contacted me with a note of thanks for the comfort the music had brought Jim and the family. I responded to their gracious notes, and that led to an Internet correspondence with Gladys. Initially, my intention was to comfort her for her loss and to praise her husband's memory for being a Navy submariner. With the ease of sending e-mails, Gladys and I began an ongoing contact that eventually developed into a friendship. She told me a lot about her life, and she was interested in my Navy career, the submarine music, and me. She is such a delightful personality that we soon became very comfortable in our discussions with each other. We were exchanging cards and letters during holidays. We now talk frequently on the phone, since she no longer has Internet access. Sandy and I consider Gladys a dear friend, and we look forward to the day when we can travel freely to Florida and the opportunity to meet her and Marjie. By that I mean there are responsibilities here in Maine that need constant tending, and we just can't take off the way we would like. We have many friends in Florida, and I'm sure we would love to visit the area.

Among our conversations, the subject of the possibility of more submarine music recordings came up. At the time, I was very disappointed in the singular lack of success of the *Take Her Deep* album. In the twenty years the collection had been available on record and CD, less than 10,000 copies had been obtained, with about half of them sold. In fact, I considered the album a hobby, not a business. This is also before I met Bobby Reed. My decision was not to go forward with such a losing venture, dismissing the whole idea as not being cost effective. At this news Gladys sounded so incredulous that I actually felt bad about sharing this perspective with her. She was so complimentary about the first album that, if I didn't know her better, I would have thought her comments were patronizing. She actually worked on me for a while to convince me to stay with it and continue to write submarine songs.

I actually began to give it more thought. With Gladys's urging, and Bobby Reed's gracious assistance, the final decision to go forward with more music, not for profit, but to support the history of our beloved Submarine Service and the memory of submariners became an avocation. The result is actually three more albums, *Brothers of the Dolphin* with Bobby, *In Honor of...* with Don Ward, and Bobby's *Proud to Be an American Veteran*. My *Spirituals* album contains religious standards, those with a submarine or seagoing theme, plus my song, *Sailor's Prayer*. Gladys has informed me she wants the spiritual album played at her funeral. I pray this will be many years from now.

Gladys met Jim Shelden in 1957 in Boston. Strangely, Jim, a submariner Fire Control Technician, got mistakenly assigned to the U.S.S. *Bigelow*, a Navy destroyer, home ported at the Boston Naval Shipyard. It seems a Personelman neglected to include the "SS" designator for "Submarine Service" behind his rate and rank designator, as in FT2(SS). So for a time, he was assigned as a "skimmer," the submarine sailor metaphor for a surface sailor. This turned out to be the will of God, as being in Boston allowed Jim to meet Gladys. In fact, like me, things happened in Jimmy's life that seemed to make no sense at the time. Besides being stationed on a skimmer in Boston, earlier in his career in WW II, he had orders to the U.S.S. *Tang*, O'Kane's boat, which was sunk by its own torpedo before Jim Shelden could report aboard. It happened again in 1963, when Jim got orders to the U.S.S. *Thresher*. These are just two more examples of the "luck" of some. But I firmly believe Jim's luckiest event was about to happen when he met the love of his life in Gladys.

It seems Gladys and Jimmy's sister, Rebecca, were friends, having served in the Air Force together. Gladys, who was then an Air Force First Lieutenant, was in Boston working at the Massachusetts Division of Library and also at the Arlington Library in Cambridge. She had been accepted at Rutgers University, where she intended to make a career change and to obtain a second degree in Library Science.

On a Saturday late in the year of '57, Jim Shelden received word from sister Becky that her close friend Gladys was in Boston and suggested he look her up. Jim was ashore at a bar doing what sailors do when they have the time and the money, having a few drinks. Jimmy was talking with one of the customers, advising that he had a girl's name and address, but he didn't have a phone number for her. It seems this fellow bar patron worked for the phone company, and he obtained Gladys's phone number from the address. Jimmy called and called and left messages. When Gladys came home from a tiresome day at work, she decided not to return Jim's call. But Jim was a persistent sailor, and he called again while she was home. They spoke for a while, and she agreed to meet with him. Jim got a taxi and gave the driver Gladys's address. The cab driver had a sense of humor and decided to do Jim a favor by suggesting that he not return to the neighborhood where he was picked up with a young lady from the address where they were going. The advice was that Jimmy was at a bar in a rather seedy part of town and on his way to a better part of town. Jim took the hint. Jim wanted to see Gladys the next day and asked her what she was doing. Gladys told him she was going to church. Jim asked if he could go with her. On Sunday they went to church together, and after a few short months, Jimmy asked Gladys to marry him on July 3, 1957, and they married just two weeks later on July 18th. Jim finally got back into submarines and continued what was a very distinguished career.

In our discussions, Gladys told me about Jim's World War II experiences in U.S.S. *Tinosa*, and she made me aware of the Mighty Mine Dodgers. When this fantastic mission occurred, Jim had just turned 19 years old. I started to ask Gladys about this. She told me what she knew, but she couldn't answer many of my questions. She gave me the name and e-mail address of Paul Wittmer, a submarine buddy of Jim. Paul suggested I read what had been written in the ship's newsletter, called the *Tinosa Blatt*, which was published by Paul on the Internet. You can access Paul's summaries of the war patrols of *Tinosa* at http://www.tinosa283.com.

Another source of information came from Pat Householder, a diesel boat sailor who served in the U.S.S. *Croaker*, who is now one of the national officers in the United States Submarine Veterans, Inc. Also, when I attended the *Lapon* reunion in Virginia Beach in September 2000, I had the honor of meeting Captain Bing Gillette, USN (Ret), who was the Executive Officer of the diesel boat *Lapon* in World War II. Captain Gillette was very helpful to me in understanding some of the terminology used in submarines in that era. It was also through Captain Gillette that I received a contact from Captain Edward L. Beach, USN (Ret). And Paul Wittmer put me in touch with Willie Z. "Dub" Noble, who served in the U.S.S. *Sea Dog*, the lead boat in this historic mission. Dub's version can be found at: http://www.submarinesailor.com/stories/SeaDogMineDodgers.asp. My knowledge of this operation is from these sources and allowed me to write the song.

Since the intention of my focus for this song was on Jim Shelden, Gladys's husband, I concentrated on the *Tinosa* (SS-283). As early as 1943, Admiral Charles Lockwood wanted to get submarines into the Sea of Japan to deny the Japanese the free use of this body of water to conduct commerce in support of the war. Some American submarines had already operated there, but the heavy interruption of commercial activities had not yet been achieved. In fact, Captain Gillette aboard the *Lapon*, was the first to operate in the Sea of Japan. Admiral Lockwood's intention was to convince the Japanese that continuation of the war was futile. It took quite awhile to get this mission underway.

American intelligence knew there were three separate minefields blocking the Tsushima Straits at the southern access into the Sea of Japan. Going through minefields is exceptionally hazardous for submarines. However, American technology had developed an FM (Frequency Modulated) sonar designed to detect the mines.

The operation was given to Commander Barney Sieglaff, and it was named "Operation Barney." The key to success in transiting the Tsushima Straits was this new FM sonar, affectionately called "Hell's Bells." Additionally, each of the boats was equipped with a 1¼ inch steel cable from the tip of the stern planes and bow planes to a point on the forward part of the boat designed to deflect mine cables to keep them from snagging on the planes. This was another Rube Goldberg rig that caused fouling in two of the boats when these cables broke loose and tangled on one of the screws. These were old contact mines, which were anchored to the bottom at a depth of about 50 feet. This would allow a surface ship to travel over the mines without problem, but a submarine following at periscope depth would very likely hit a mine. Occasionally, one of these mines would break its mooring and float to the surface, creating a real hazard to surface traffic.

Nine submarines were assigned to Operation Barney. The boats were formed into three groups of three submarines. All of them collectively were referred to as "Hydeman's Hellcats." Commander Earl Hydeman, Captain of the U.S.S. *Sea Dog*, was the senior officer present afloat in the group and was the at sea commander for Operation Barney. The "Hepcats" were *Sea Dog*, *Crevalle*, and *Spadefish*. The "Polecats" were *Tunny*, *Skate*, and *Bonefish*. And the "Bobcats" were *Flying Fish*, *Bowfin*, and *Tinosa*. This organization makes up the chorus of the song.

In May of 1945 these nine boats were in Apra Harbor, Guam, where the Hell's Bells FM sonars were installed, and a short period of training ensued. One thing that became quite obvious was the system was not totally reliable. In fact, the system installed in *Sea Dog* never did work correctly. By the end of May, all nine boats were underway for the Sea of Japan. During this period of time, the Sea of Japan was referred to as "Hirohito's Hot Tub." In my day we called the Sea of Japan the "S-O-J." To accommodate good rhyming, I exercised a bit of literary license to change Apra Harbor to Apra Bay, and I referred to the Sea of Japan as the S-O-J.

Tinosa was running with *Flying Fish* and *Bowfin*. While they were on their way to the Tsushima Straits, the Bobcat boats were diverted to attempt to recover an Army bomber crew that had to parachute. In the song I referred to this diversion as: "*Tinosa* got the draft." I guess this part was not too clear to the listener as several people did ask about this. Does the term "drafted" ring a bell? What I meant was *Tinosa* was drafted to go find the downed aviators. With the help of an aircraft, Captain Latham, Commanding Officer of *Tinosa*, found and rescued ten of the eleven airmen who had bailed out. The eleventh airman had the misfortune of a parachute malfunction, and he didn't make it. When the airmen were on board, they were informed of the destination of *Tinosa* and were given the option of remaining on board for the mission. When told *Tinosa* was headed for the Sea of Japan, and they would have to make their way through three minefields, the airmen literally pleaded to be transferred to another boat. That is how the U.S.S. *Scabbardfish* was directed to rendezvous with *Tinosa* to offload the Army airmen. They were pretty glad to get off considering the hazardous mission *Tinosa* was to fulfill.

On June 5th, 1945, the U.S.S. *Tinosa* began transiting the Tsushima Straits. Gladys's husband, Jim "Jeep" Shelden, was at his watch station at the helm. The Executive Officer's last name was Smith, and his nickname was Snuffy, after the cartoon character. The XO had the deck and the conn during the entry. All of a sudden the Hell's Bells rang, giving the alarm of the existence of mines ahead. The *Tinosa* had found the minefield. "Right Full Rudder" was ordered, and Sheldon spun the wheel to commence a radical right turn. The Hell's Bells rang again, and the XO ordered an immediate "Left Full Rudder." Shelden reversed the wheel. As *Tinosa* was in the left turn, the crew could hear a mine cable sliding along the clearance cable on the starboard side. Smith ordered "All Stop" and another "Right Rudder." As *Tinosa* slowed and began to drift with the current, the crew could hear the mine cable sliding for what seemed an eternity. Soon the cable slipped and *Tinosa* was free, and they proceeded into the Sea of Japan at dead slow speed, no pun intended. I know every submariner who reads this will feel the intensity of *Tinosa*'s experience and what those crewmen had to endure during these harrowing moments. The *Sea Dog* went through the minefields without hearing any Hell's Bells alarm. Captain Hydeman knew in his heart their Hell's Bells system never worked. They used up a great deal of their quota of luck during that transit. You can't help but admire the courage and skill of these intrepid submariners and marvel at the youth of most of them such as the 19-year-old Jim Shelden. God bless them all, and may they rest in peace.

Updated information indicates Hydeman's Hellcats sank 31 Japanese ships and 16 small craft for a total tonnage of 108,230 during their one month operation in the Sea of Japan. To egress the Sea of Japan, the Hellcats executed a rendezvous at midnight on Sunday, June 24th at a location west of La Pérouse Strait. Eight boats of the nine showed up. The *Bonefish* didn't make it.

Hydeman decided they would transit La Pérouse on the surface with all surface guns manned. He knew this Strait was also mined, so they could avoid that problem on the surface. Also, as mentioned in Chapter 8, the diesel boats were faster and more maneuverable on the surface. Eight boats working together could really raise a ruckus. There is a phrase used in the diesel submarine Navy regarding making a four-engine run. That is maximum power. I have no way of knowing that all eight boats were on four engines. In fact, some of the boats may have been limited to three diesel engines. But using the lyrics "four engines on the surface" makes it clear to submariners no barnacles were growing on the hulls during this run. And they were "prepared to fight."

The eight boats moved into a formation of two rows of four with about 2,000 feet between them. Of course, no lights were used, but the boats could see each other by watching the phosphorescence created by each boat as it passed through the water disturbing microorganisms. Sailors know these things. And you can imagine the sound of the diesel engines of eight submarines in close proximity to each other doing flank speed can make.

Half way through the Strait a Russian freighter illuminated its searchlights and shined them at the boats. After awhile they secured the lights, about a heart-beat before one or more of the boats would have opened fire on it to shut down the lights. Around 0235 on Monday morning, June 25, 1945, the boats had transited La Pérouse and were in the Sea of Okhotsk. They headed into the Pacific through the Kuril Chain and set course for Midway, affectionately known as "Gooneyville."

Back in Hawaii at the "Royal H," Royal Hawaiian Hotel, the rest and recuperation location for submariners, Admiral Lockwood had cards made up similar to shellback and bluenose cards that identified each submariner assigned to these boats as "Mighty Mine Dodgers." This was a unique honor among submariners. Bobby Reed has a song on his album *Proud to be an American Veteran* called *The Royal Hawaiian* about this locale. Bobby and Margie had a great experience there as the guest of Captain John Peters where Bobby got the background for his historic song.

In reminiscing about this song, I see it as a key crossroad in the future of the genre of submarine music as provided by Bobby Reed and Tommy Cox. Thanks to the influence of a lovely lady, Gladys Shelden, who will be eighty years young on May 3, 2006, the submarine music has continued. I certainly would not have continued to write, and it is likely none of us would have heard of or enjoyed the creativity of Bobby Reed and Don Ward. We are all grateful to James "Jeep" Shelden for his distinguished service in submarines. Thank you, Gladys for being you and sharing the history of you and Jimmy with me, which had the result of, continued music and especially this song, *Mighty Mine Dodgers.*

CHAPTER 19
SLADE CUTTER

Cutter's gonna get you, Nippon Maru
U.S.S. Seahorse in World War Two
McGrievy's gonna find you in the nighttime too
Hoffman's gonna hear you turning the screw
Message coded; warshot loaded
Cutter's gonna get you, Nippon Maru

He kicked his famous field goal in thirty-four
Football All American, Midshipman Corps
Heavyweight boxer, never hit the floor
XO of the Pompano, a Navy war
Hold her steady; battle ready
Lew Parks taught him how to raise the score

As C.O. of the Seahorse Cutter made four runs
Aggressive but not reckless, he got things done
Searching night and day for the Rising Sun
Forward tubes and after tubes and topside guns
Many losses; four Navy Crosses
Some say he sank a hundred thousand tons

The United States Congress has a mission to do
Award white stars on a field of blue

118

Promotion to Admiral is long overdue
Time is wasting, it's the right thing to do
Hear the requests from Navy SUBVETS
Honors for valor for cutter and crew

I became acquainted with Robert "Dex" Armstrong, first, through his writing which he posts on the internet or publishes in the *American Submariner*, second, through his many purchases of the *Take Her Deep* and *Brothers of the Dolphin* albums, third, through e-mail and phone correspondence, and, last, we finally met in person. My personal knowledge of Slade Cutter has more to do with Dex Armstrong than Captain Cutter himself. Dex wanted me to write a song about Captain Cutter.

Dex is one of the most generous individuals I have had the honor to meet. Out of high school he joined the Navy and became a diesel boat submarine sailor and served aboard the U.S.S. *Requin* out of Norfolk, Virginia. Dex never made it past Seaman (E-3). But he was a hard worker, full of mischief, and totally dedicated to his boat. Dex and his buddy, Adrienne Stuke, both the pride of *Requin*, terrorized the tender sailors, kept their boat in good working order and cleanliness, and kept barstools warm at Bell's. Slade Cutter was the first Commanding Officer of *Requin*, long before Dex's time.

Dex, as many submariners, was not average by any means and certainly no slouch. When he left the Navy, he attended college, married a gorgeous lady named Solveig from Norway, and took a job with government services. He will retire in 2007. He is presently the Deputy Director for GSA Services at the Pentagon as a GS-15. The man is a prolific writer who, in my opinion, has captured the essence of the U.S. Submarine Service better than most. He is equally at home with enlisted sailors as he is with politicians and high-ranking military officers. He is also a great historian, which is his hobby. Dex and Solveig have two beautiful daughters, one the wife of a Marine officer and the second an Army Major paratrooper, yes, paratrooper, with the 82 Airborne at Fort Bragg.

On 9/12/05 I couldn't take it anymore, I had to call the Armstrong household to hear that Dex was OK after the terrorist attacks. He answered the phone and we spoke for a few minutes. Then he said he had to go, as General Hugh Shelton was on the other line. That's the first time the Chairman of the Joint Chiefs of Staff ever waited for me. In 2002, after Slade Cutter had turned 90 years young, the Northern Virginia Base of the U.S. Submarine Veterans drafted a Resolution for Congress to award Captain Cutter the Medal of Honor and grant him what is called a "tombstone promotion" to Rear Admiral. Cutter had been awarded four Navy Crosses for his four war patrols as Captain of the U.S.S. *Seahorse*. Cutter's confirmed total enemy tonnage was second only to Dick O'Kane, who received the Medal of Honor (MOH) and did make Rear Admiral. Using the criterion of tonnage alone, several boat skippers with lesser totals received our nation's highest award. There can only be speculation about why Cutter did not receive the MOH or Rear Admiral. One possibility was one poor fitness report placed in Cutter's record by the first Commanding Officer of *Seahorse*, who was replaced for cause, and Cutter was made C.O. It seems the first Captain was ultra conservative when meeting the enemy and literally declined to engage. Cutter, the Executive Officer, it can only be speculated, would speak to the C.O. in private to encourage tactics that would result in sinking the enemy. Cutter had been XO of the *Pompano* under Captain Lew Parks, who was a real submarine warrior. Cutter, himself a tactical genius, had the self-confidence and courage required to get the job done. The first C.O. of *Seahorse* had an uncommon fear of Japanese sonar and would disengage whenever echo ranging was heard. Cutter understood and knew the limitations of sonar and conducted his own maneuvers accordingly and realistically. In short, the first war patrol of *Seahorse*, under the first commanding officer, considering the opportunities, did not qualify for the coveted war patrol insignia. This decision to deny the boat the war patrol pin, and loss of the command, was the ultimate insult to Seahorse and the Captain. Morale was terrible; Cutter took command.

Another possibility for not awarding Captain Cutter the MOH, or that eventual promotion to Admiral, could be due to a plague common to many of us: we can't keep our big mouth shut. I've always looked at it this way. If placed in a position of responsibility, my bosses are entitled to my opinion, and I would be remising by not sharing it. It could be critical in important issues. If I subscribe to a course of action, I should say so and support the issue. If I disagree, I must advise of the consequences and proffer alternatives. I believe this was Cutter's way.

The first political issue I chose to support with my music was the effort to *Bring the Nautilus Home* to Groton (See Chapter 14). While the efficacy of such a maneuver is questionable in my mind, it does assist in forming and supporting public opinion. This, I believe, is what Dex had in mind by suggesting a song about Cutter be created. Additionally, a published song about an individual is usually very complimentary.

In the late '90s, *Requin* had a reunion on Maryland's eastern shore of the Chesapeake. Captain Cutter and his lovely wife, Ruth, attended. Dex brought a CD player and had the *Take Her Deep* CD play over and over. Cutter liked the diving klaxon from *Seawolf*, and each time *Diesel Boats Forever* would play, Cutter would give Dex the thumbs up sign. Upon hearing this story, I was deeply pleased and flattered.

I decided to write the song, and then something happened. I phoned Captain Cutter to speak with him, to let him know what I wanted to do, and to interview him. I did not know at that time that he had Parkinson's. The phone call did not go well. He was very short with me, almost to the point of rudeness. Here was a man that I respected and admired greatly, that I wanted to honor in song, who was treating me like dirt. I'd had similar experiences while on active duty where "high class" officers treat "low class" enlisted like the scum of the earth. I greatly respected officers like Captains Mack and MacVean, who treated enlisted sailors with human dignity and abhorred those who didn't. I wasn't insulted by Captain Cutter. I was deeply hurt that the great Slade Cutter didn't fall neatly into my preconceived expectation of him.

I did obtain the empathetic perspective fairly early in this experience. How would I feel if some stranger called me on the phone out of the blue to say he wanted to write a song about me? What if I was 90 years old? But being put down created a tremendous writer's block. I just couldn't get it done. Did I want to get it done?

What I really wanted to do was comply with Dex's request. Dex had sent me two books about Captain Slade Cutter, plus I had downloaded articles from the Internet. I read the two books about Cutter, *Slade Cutter, Submarine Warrior* by Carl LaVO and *Maru Killer* by Dave Bouslog. The first time I read each book was for my own knowledge and entertainment. The second time I read the books was for research. I wrote two songs about Cutter and discarded them both. I asked another submariner, "Bodega" Bob Homme, of The Submarine Store to write a song about Cutter, which he did, and called it *Ridin' Herd on the Rising Sun*. This is a good song, but it didn't express some of the key elements to Cutter's service, and rather than change another songwriter's creation, I simply decided to continue with my own effort. And after learning of Captain Cutter's Parkinson's, I was able to overcome my perception of his antagonism towards me during my previous phone call. I wrote the song on the album in about one hour. It finally happened.

Slade Cutter was born on November 1, 1911. That's 11-1-11. He died on June 6, 2005, at age 93. When he decided to go to the Naval Academy, he borrowed money to put himself through a prep school to raise his scholastic ability. He was a tall, strapping lad who was a natural athlete. He was an academy All-American football player and an undefeated heavyweight boxer. In 1934, Cutter kicked a field goal in the annual Army-Navy game in inclement weather. Navy won by a score of three to nothing. This win ended a thirteen-year Army winning streak. This accomplishment immediately endeared him to the Naval Academy alumni and gave him a good career start. He was also offered the opportunity to become a professional boxer. Cutter declined the option for two reasons: (1) he felt the obligation to do his duty to his country for the education he received at the Academy, and (2) he knew in his heart he could not beat Joe Lewis. But he certainly would have been a contender.

By the time World War II broke out in the Pacific, Cutter was already a submariner. He made four war patrols as XO of the *Pompano* under the command of LCDR Lew Parks. Cutter and Parks were close friends and consummate professionals. Under Parks' command, Cutter was awarded one Bronze Star and two

Silver Stars for valor in combat. Parks and Cutter were a team. Cutter's ability had been proven.

After four war patrols in *Pompano*, Cutter was sent to Mare Island, where the U.S.S. *Seahorse* was under construction. Command of *Seahorse* was given to an individual who had been around a while and was not considered very aggressive. SUBPAC believed this officer could do well with Cutter as XO. The first war patrol of *Seahorse* did not go well. Admiral Charles Lockwood, who had fleeted up to SUBPAC, flew to Apra Harbor and relieved the CO of *Seahorse* and made Cutter its new Captain. Cutter, knowing of the morale problem in *Seahorse* and some speculation that he would be exceptionally aggressive, offered to transfer any crewman who did not want to remain in *Seahorse*. Thanks to the intervention and leadership of Chief Joe McGrievy, only one sailor opted to leave the boat. It turned out that Cutter was aggressive, but he wasn't reckless. Cutter understood tactics exceptionally well, and he knew the capability of his ship and crew. Cutter returned the pride and dignity to *Seahorse*.

American submarines, following the surprise attack on Pearl Harbor, conducted unrestricted warfare against Japan. That meant, under the rules of engagement, anything flying the rising sun flag could be attacked. On *Seahorse's* first war patrol with Cutter as C.O., he was encouraged to attack and sink two small fishing vessels that essentially were non-combatants. Cutter knew family units normally manned these fishing boats. He also understood that if the fishing vessel spotted U.S. assets, they would report to the Japanese Navy. They collected garbage at sea for intelligence purposes. If an American was found in the water, the fishing vessel would rescue the man, then either kill him or inter him as a prisoner of war. However, Cutter saw attacking fishing vessels as an impropriety and determined not to do so again. His decision was respected by SUBPAC.

Cutter had two outstanding chiefs aboard *Seahorse*. Jumpin' Joe McGrievy was one of those rare individuals who had exceptional night vision. McGrievy would either man the periscope or serve as lookout watch on the bridge at dark due to his excellent night vision. Additionally, Chief Radioman Roy Hoffman had outstanding hearing and manned the sonar stack when *Seahorse* was at battle stations. He could report to Cutter what the enemy was doing by listening to the sound their ship was generating. This accurate information allowed Cutter to outmaneuver the enemy frequently. It didn't hurt matters that *Seahorse* was a "thick-skinned" boat that had been built with exceptional care. The Superintendent of Ships at Mare Island had a nephew stationed in *Seahorse*. He saw to it everything was done with great care and perfection. McGrievy eventually became an officer and one of the Captains of *Requin*.

Dex told me Captain Cutter had little use for books that glorified individuals, so I concluded it would be the same for songs. Cutter always gave credit to his crew, and his song reflects that.

When I contacted Maine Senator Susan Collins, a member of the Senate

Armed Forces Committee, about the resolution in support of Cutter's promotion and Medal of Honor, she advised she was not aware of any such effort. This totally surprised me. After discussing this with Dex, I learned that Senator John Warner of Virginia, a former Secretary of the Navy, was the stumbling block. The Northern Virginia SUBVETS would have submitted their resolution through him. Warner was not in favor of the idea. He was the powerful Chair of the Senate Armed Forces Committee. I sent e-mails to Senator Warner and Senator John McCain, who is also on the Committee. Neither answered. John McCain is Slade Cutter's godson. I always admired John McCain's refusal to accept early repatriation as a prisoner of the Vietnam War. This opportunity to leave Hanoi early was offered because McCain's father was CINCPACFLT. It's easy to decide to do nothing, as John Warner was, doing instead of having to justify such an action. Ruth Cutter has advised Dex and the Northern Virginia SUBVETS that Captain Cutter is deeply honored that his shipmates suggested and supported this action. Warner need not further concern himself with Captain Slade Cutter now that Cutter is deceased.

I called Dex Armstrong. I had made a special tape of my two albums *In Honor of...* and the spirituals and sent it to the Cutters. I made the cassette because Dex advised me that the Cutters do not use compact discs. It was very important to me to know Captain Cutter had heard his song before his death. The day after speaking to Dex I received a nice card in the mail addressed to "Captain Cox" from Ruth Cutter thanking me for the nice tape of music. She said nothing of the song. She did say the good Captain was doing as well as could be expected with his Parkinson's at age 93. I was honored and pleased and deeply saddened that Slade Cutter passed away within a week of receiving Ruth Cutter's thank you card. I continue to admire and respect Captain Cutter greatly. I will always remember him as the submarine warrior and hero that he was. He made an impressive difference. God rest his soul and grant Ruth Cutter comfort in her sorrow.

Shortly after Cutter's death I received an e-mail from Ron "Warshot" Smith, author of the book *Torpedoman*, requesting I send a copy of the CD, *In Honor of...* with the song "Slade Cutter," to Cutter's son, Slade Cutter, Jr. Warshot offered to pay for the CD. I sent a courtesy copy with a nice inscription. Warshot is a World War II submarine veteran who served in U.S.S. *Seal*. He turned 80 years young in 2005. He is a submarine veteran icon.

Seahorse, Slade Cutter, and crew were the salt of the U.S. Submarine Service in World War II. When the U.S. fleet was seriously wounded during the sneak attack on Pearl Harbor, the submarines were not damaged. When the submarines were turned loose on the Japanese, they comprised 1.6% of the U.S. fleet. American submarines were responsible for 55% of Japanese shipping sunk. The Submarine Service paid a heavy price for the success. Fifty-two submarines were lost, and more than 3,000 men paid the supreme sacrifice. Captain Slade Cutter and *Seahorse* were survivors. They were great warriors, deeply respected and admired.

They survived due to a combination of skill, daring, and yes, luck.

CHAPTER 20
FRENCHIE

I met him at Birch Haven in May of '98
He saw my Seawolf ball cap, and said it was just great
To meet a fellow veteran here in Northern Maine
Someone who understood the war, who understood the pain

We'd sit around the campfire and never say a word
Our silence spoke in volumes the things that our hearts heard
I think about him often; he really touched me deep
Sometimes when I'm all alone, I break down and weep

Frenchie was a rifleman barely past his teens
He did his tour in Vietnam in the United States Marines
He saved the life of Ollie North, a man that he called "Blue"
Then Agent Orange took his life at only fifty-two

He dearly loved his family; sweet Beth was his wife
His children Mark and Cathy were so much of his life
His grandkids Jon and Braigan he did appreciate
Braigan was just three years old, and Jonathan was eight

His smile was so contagious, his face all shining bright
His fine sense of humor made everything seem right
His courtesy for others was never once constrained
Though he had troubles of his own, he never once complained

On Labor Day in Y-2-K they met him in Presque Isle
Ollie North and four Marines joined him for a while

All were combat veterans who made this last commute
To show him that they loved him and give one last salute

Always Semper Fidelis; he did answer the call
Though he stood only five feet four, his legend's ten feet tall
He was a true-life hero; he did his duty well
Frenchie's gone to heaven, 'cause he did his time in hell

In May of 1998, Sandy and I started summer camping at the Birch Haven Campground on Eagle Lake in northern Maine. We had decided to start buying the toys that we expected to enjoy in our retirement, like a boat and motor and a travel trailer. We'd set up our trailer on our campsite prior to the beginning of the season. The first weekend of camping would be Memorial Day. Our routine was to leave Caribou after I got home from work after 5:00 PM on Friday afternoon. Sandy would have our vehicle packed and ready to go, and, as soon as possible, we would drive the 50 miles north to the campground. We would travel north on Route 161 to within a few miles of Fort Kent, Maine, turn left toward a small town called Soldier Pond, then go south on Sly Brook Road for five miles to Birch Haven. We would spend our weekends there until some time on Sunday when we would return to Caribou to get ready to go back to work on Monday.

On our first arrival, we were met at the campground by Connie, Sandy's sister, her husband Roger Michaud (pronounced "me show"), and another short, wiry fellow who pitched in to help us unload our grub and duffle for the weekend. The first thing he spotted was the "Veteran" license plate on our Bronco and my blue *Seawolf* ball cap. At first opportunity, he inquired about my service to determine I was the real thing. He volunteered that he was a Vietnam combat Marine. I learned his name was Philip Sirois (pronounced "sear way"). This is a fairly common name within the Franco-American community in northern Maine. We determined he was not related to my Navy SEAL buddy, Rodney Sirois.

That evening around the campfire we got to know each other better. While we didn't determine relative ages at that time, Phil was 50 and I was 55. The bond between us had been established centuries ago as men of arms meet and interact. Phil had left the Marines as a Lance Corporal (E-3), and I'd retired from the Navy as a Senior Chief (E-8). Phil had learned to trust his NCOs in the Marines, and he could easily transfer that trust and blind faith to me whether I deserved it or not.

We also met Phil's wife, Beth, whose real name is Gilberte. She is a very attractive young lady who is a native Canadian. They'd met before Phil left for the Marines and married shortly after his return from the war. They have two grown children, a son named Mark and a daughter named Cathy. At the time Cathy had a son named Jonathan and a baby daughter named Braigan. Phil doted on them with great love and pride.

Phil and Beth were both bilingual. Most of the time they spoke French with each other. When they spoke English they both had a strong French accent. Of course, this led to Phil's nickname in the Marines as "Frenchie." In fact, LT Oliver North, Phil's Company Commander, often had Phil translate for him in Vietnam as French is a common language there, second only to Vietnamese.

Phil was comfortable with his campground friends. Many gatherings were on his campsite, where he would rush to get a chair for each person until there were no more available. He always had the ubiquitous cup of coffee and cigarette in his hands. Although we often retired around midnight, Phil would be the first one up around 6:00 AM to build a fire and enjoy his coffee and cigarette. You could only describe him as a man of nervous energy.

Each weekend, as we arrived at the campground, Phil was always there to assist with unloading. Over the summer we learned that he and Beth did not work. I never did get the whole story, but it seems that Phil had worked at Fraser Paper, a large mill in Madawaska, Maine. Fraser is Canadian based, with a mill in Madawaska, and a second mill in Edmondston, New Brunswick, across the Saint John River from Madawaska in Canada. Fraser Paper is the largest employer in both towns on both sides of the border.

When Phil returned from the war, he got his job back at Fraser. There were individuals there who were quite insensitive, and reveled in teasing Phil about his participation in an unpopular war. Then there were those who were downright vicious and called him such names as "baby killer" and others. Phil's small stature, about 125 pounds, encouraged the bullies to push him around. Some learned the hard way not to pick a fight with him. All Phil wanted was to be accepted by his coworkers and peer group. It was not to be. Eventually, Phil left Fraser, and, by the time we met him, he was retired on disability.

With me, accepting Phil for himself was automatic. It was clear to him that I respected his service and combat experience. I was also appropriately impressed that he had served with Oliver North. He'd showed me a variety of pictures of him, Beth, and Ollie. Of course, this was after the Iran-Contra hearings, which I'd watched with great interest. I had unilaterally come to respect LTC North for his service, his aplomb for keeping the promise of the United States government to support the Contras against communism alive under adverse conditions, and the fact that he was publicly taking the fall for President Reagan's administration for circumventing a Congress suffering from terminal cranial-rectal insertion on this specific issue. As a Navy spook, I could easily understand this event. Many of my contemporaries disagree with me. In LTC North I saw qualities of courage, ability, and honor. There is more to come that leads to my further respect of Ollie.

Later that summer in 1998 around August, Phil and Beth traveled to Washington, DC, to attend an annual Marine reunion. When I learned he was going and would be seeing Oliver North, I autographed a CD of *Take Her Deep* and asked Phil to present it to Col. North for me. When Phil returned, he had Oliver North's book, *One More Mission*, autographed to me by Ollie. I shall treasure that always.

Phil always seemed to have a smile on his face. Everything he did was done with enthusiasm. It wasn't long before our campground friends knew of the *Take Her Deep* album, and I was coaxed into bringing my guitar to do a little singing around the campfire. Phil loved the music, especially the songs about the military and submarines. I'm told some professional music acts hire shills to circulate in audiences to generate enthusiasm for performances. Phil unknowingly did this for me freely. His demeanor was contagious, and, with the support of others, the summer became "the 1998 Comeback Special" for Tommy Cox. I hadn't played music for 15 years, but my voice came back strong as ever, and my fingers calloused for guitar playing. In one instance my audience exceeded 100 listeners, as I sat on Phil and Beth's camper porch and belted out the songs I loved the most. Usually, the crowd numbered between 30 and 50 listeners. I especially appreciated those who really listened to the music.

Another thing happened that summer. Beth's brother Robert Cyr (pronounced "sear") came to visit at the campground from Saint Basil, Canada. Robert was a former professional musician who'd suffered a bad fall from a balcony that resulted in the loss of his legs. He suffered greatly from this loss, which led to a very understandable depression. Robert started getting into the music and brought an old guitar, and we'd play music together. Bob's specialty was singing songs in French. Soon, we learned that some of the songs he sang in French I could sing in English, so we'd do duets on those songs. Additionally, there is a song that he and Beth do together in French in beautiful harmony called *Partons la Mer est Belle* (Let's Go to the Beautiful Ocean). Bob's zest for life seemed to return, and I'm pleased our music together contributed to his overall recovery.

Bob's family, including Phil, were so pleased with developments that they wanted to surprise Bob by buying him a new guitar. Phil took up a collection, and a scheme was developed to get Bob to buy his own guitar, so he would get something he liked. At the time the exchange rate between Canadian and American currency was heavily in favor of U.S. money. One dollar American was worth about $1.50 Canadian. Phil gave the money to Bob to buy a flattop guitar in Canada, which was supposed to be a Christmas gift for my son Bill. Bob shopped diligently in Canada for a guitar within the price range of the amount collected to find an excellent guitar for Bill. Later that winter about 20 of us met at a motel in Saint Agatha, where we were allowed to take over the bar with our music, and presented Bob with that same guitar he bought, ostensibly for Bill. The group also surprised me by everybody wearing a special T-shirt that had my picture on the front with the caption "'98 Comeback Special." I waited for a moment during the evening when I had the attention of everybody and turned to the wife of one of the Michaud's, who was more easily embarrassed than others and said, "Gee,

Mary, I love what your tits do for my shoulders." Well, you had to be there, see the picture on the T-shirt, and the rest of it. Her crimson blush, and the laughter, were worth the indiscretion.

When the Birch Haven campground opened in May of 2000, it was clear Phil's enthusiasm for everything had significantly diminished. In time, we learned that Phil had been diagnosed with lung cancer, and, though we were never told, we conclude that radiation and chemo options had been declined. We learned later he had one chemo treatment and 10 days of radiation prior to the campground opening. He and his family were well aware that his cancer was too far advanced for these treatments to do any good, but doing "something" was better than nothing. He was no longer the persona of nervous energy. He was dying. His lung cancer was attributed to agent orange in Vietnam. He had described to me how they would see the aircraft spraying the defoliant over the jungle and over the Marines. It left a film on everything, and they, obviously, had to breath it. They were told it would not harm them. Since when is dioxin good for respiration? Would it surprise anyone to learn the Russians were doing the same thing in Vietnam? I strongly suspect the Soviet formula was not the same as Dow Chemical's. Who knows?

Phil had told me of an incident where LT North wanted Phil to check out a Viet Cong tunnel. Phil, being a small man, was the perfect choice for a "tunnel rat." But Phil knew the danger. He told the LT, "I don't want to go in that hole." But Ollie persisted and told Phil, "When I tell you to do something, you have to do it. You'll be alright." Phil did what he was told.

There was a local newspaper article here in Maine about Phil serving with Oliver North and how Phil had Ollie's two books (at the time) autographed to him. I saw the books myself and one said, "If it were not for you I would not be here." I asked Phil about that, and he told me that during a firefight, Ollie was on a berm "John Wayning it" when Phil and another Marine grabbed Ollie by the belt and pulled him to cover just as a mortar exploded near where Ollie was standing. Ollie was momentarily knocked unconscious, and Phil helped to defend the position while the enemy was pushed back. Additionally, Beth told me that Ollie himself told her that Phil had saved his life. This is why the song says, "He saved the life of Ollie North."

There's no doubt in my military mind that Oliver North was heroic in combat. I heard it from a first hand source, Phil. There's also no doubt that he is a man of principal and honor. How many O-5s would leave Virginia (or their home) and fly to remote northern Maine at his own expense on a holiday to spend a few hours with a dying former E-3 subordinate? Ollie and his four Marines did just that. No matter what anybody thinks of Oliver North, he and these four Marines must be respected for this act of kindness. May God bless each of you for what you have done for my friend. The combat experience establishes an exceptionally strong bond.

There was another time when the company had battled to the top of a hill where Phil had followed Oliver North to the top backing him up and executing his commands. At the top North's superior asked Ollie how it went, and Phil jumped in with his own answer, "My lieutenant was magnificent." Ollie mentioned this in one of his books where he was made to feel the camaraderie of the unit by this statement, because Phil referred to him as "my lieutenant." Now enlisted men usually don't describe anything by the term "magnificent," unless their primary language is French. *C'est magnifique!*

In one of those instances, Phil had been wounded in combat with shrapnel in his hand. He was given the option to be evacuated by helicopter with the rest of the wounded. Phil chose to stay with his buddies to help in the fighting. Phil was certainly a man of loyalty with a strong sense of duty. A couple years before he died, he was presented with a Purple Heart. He was very proud. Although I joked that the Purple Heart was the enemy's marksmanship medal, I also told Phil how I admired his courage for remaining in the battle and performing under fire. His face just beamed that he had my respect. I meant every word of it.

As the summer moved on, Phil's tolerance of others diminished as his personal pain increased. Although I am not fluent in French, I told Phil on one occasion that he was my brother and I loved him in that language. Harold Michaud overheard me, and I saw him nod his approval. Harold is an Army veteran. Phil beamed in appreciation. He and Beth did not spend as much time at Birch Haven in the summer of 2000.

They were gone from the campground on Labor Day of that year; we didn't know where. The campground was closing the following weekend, so when Sandy and I drove north to go to Birch Haven, we turned for Frenchville instead, where Phil and Beth lived near the Madawaska town line. It appeared nobody was home, but Phil was there in a wheelchair. Beth had gone to town. We visited for about an hour, and Phil showed me a video that had been taken over the Labor Day weekend.

On Labor Day Phil and Beth had gone to Keddy's Motor Inn in Presque Isle, Maine. Oliver North and four Marines, Wendell Thomas, Ernie Tuten, Everett Whipple, and James Lehnert, traveled to Presque Isle to visit with Phil for one last time. Phil's children Mark and Cathy were present. The four Marine enlisted men had arrived early. They joked about how Ollie would volunteer for every mission that became available, much to their chagrin. Remember, these were the survivors, literally. As the drinks and beers took effect, one of the men told Phil, they were calling him "Frenchie," that they were not there to give him sympathy; they were there to give him their support, and to let him know they were honored to have served with him. It was a poignant moment.

Soon after, Ollie North arrived with flowers for Beth. All hugged and the reminiscing began. They spoke of Vietnam and some of their experiences. Sometimes the conversation was graphic. Phil told me that some of the things that were said during that meeting he didn't like, because it brought back bad memories. He knew I would understand. But some very nice things were said that were intended to help Phil be comfortable with himself. Ollie told Phil he was going where none of them had been before; therefore, Ollie appointed Phil "point." This is a term applied to the first man in line on a combat patrol. The point man is responsible for the safety of the rest and is usually the first to get hit if a firefight ensues. Usually, it's an unpleasant position to be in, and each takes his turn. Frequently, the "best" man is assigned. Sometimes, when somebody is really good at it, he volunteers. Point is very important. Phil accepted the honor.

The video shifted to the Presque Isle Airport, where Ollie and two of the Marines were flying south after being in Presque Isle for only several hours. The other two Marines lived in Massachusetts and had driven. All were there at their own expense. Good byes were said in the terminal, and Ollie and the two others went out to the plane ramp. They then turned together, Ollie in the middle, and they saluted Phil. Then they waved and boarded the plane. By this time, my eyes were full of tears, as I comprehended the moment. I was glad the room was dark, so Phil wouldn't see me. I think he did anyway. We then said goodbye. We hugged each other, and he said in English, "I love you, brother." I said the same thing and hastened out the door, and the tears were becoming quite prolific. That was the last time we saw Phil alive.

The funeral was very sad. At 52, it's just too young to die. I took the day off from work. The funeral was in Madawaska, 60 miles from Caribou. The church was totally full. We were among the last to leave the churchyard, and the graveside ceremony was well underway by the time we reached the cemetery. We simply left for home.

I don't recall when the idea to write a song was born. I guess it's just the way I choose to express myself when I feel strongly about something. The only song that was more difficult to write was the song for my son after his death. I wrote the song in spurts, as I would continuously break down as I added more lyrics. Sometimes I'd get a whole verse written before I'd lose the bubble. It took all winter to finish the song. I thought I'd desensitized myself, through constant repetition, but when I sing a song, I renew and think about its meaning, which helps to include the emotion of the intent of the song, which contributes to what is called "feeling."

Maybe it was the summer of 2001 when I sang the song for the first audience at the campground. I was doing fine with it until I looked around and saw all the tears that were flowing and lost it myself. Most of those folks really loved Phil. Then Beth wanted me to sing the song for her daughter, Cathy, on the phone. I did so, and at the end of the song it was clear she was crying too. It's been six years now since Phil has passed away. I've done the song hundreds of times, so I can get through it now. But I still see the watery eyes of old warriors and even some police officer friends as these supposedly macho men hear this song. When others feel inside what I feel and they experience my sadness when I sing this song, I am deeply complimented. Just listen; applause is not necessary.

No, Phil Sirois did not kill women and children in Vietnam. But having grown up Catholic, in a religious family and community, there is a certain amount of consternation at having been successful in combat. There is survivor's guilt regarding the loss of buddies. And when the dust settles, there is concern for the enemy killed. I use the word "concern," because this feeling can take a variety of forms from hate to love. One way to look at it is the enemy who was dumb enough to take on my buddies and me committed suicide for being so stupid. As the saying goes, "The stupid shall be punished." The thought that we have deprived a parent of their son, a wife of a husband, or a child of a father is not pleasant. There is fear of the enemy, for if you did not kill him, he would have killed you. There is hate for the enemy for what he has done to your buddies. And there is hate for the circumstances that brought you to this place in time to experience these terrible things. Then there is pride in yourself for measuring up to your own expectations of courage under fire and pride in your buddies for an equally stellar performance. There is pride in your service and your country for doing the "right thing" under extreme circumstances. Of course, this is not all-inclusive, but it can give you the complexity of emotions a warrior must experience. No wonder there is combat fatigue, shell shock, and post-traumatic stress. Then, when some jerks like those at Fraser's, who made fun of Phil, are so stupidly unfeeling, disrespectful, and insulting, it just makes me sick. (I have expressed this much more graphically in language that is not suitable for children and clergy.) Philip Sirois was a patriot and a United States Marine. He was courageous and dependable. He was a family man, a husband, a father, and a grandfather. He was a human being. It was an honor to be his friend. I pray he will live forever in the song *Frenchie*.

CHAPTER 21
PAYBACKS

You kicked our tail on 9-1-1; three-thousand people died
The Twin Towers and Pentagon, so many loved ones cried
Killed Russian kids in grade school; it can't get worse than that
Paybacks are hell, coward, now it's our turn at bat

In Bali, Indonesia, and Jakarta too
Car bombs and IEDs are what you try to use
Our embassies in Africa and the U.S.S. Cole
Paybacks are hell, terrorist, as we cry, "Let's roll!"

You terrorize the innocent at will
Women, children, young men all get killed
Mr. Terrorist, that's all there is to tell
Get ready, Hoss, 'cause paybacks are hell

Navy SEALs and Recons and Army Green Beret
Have wasted many Taliban, hunting night and day
You can bet I'm confident Bin Laden will be found
Paybacks are hell, fool, al Qaeda's goin' down

Tomahawks from submarines, and the smart harpoon
Laser-guided ordnance and grenades all spell doom
You can run but you can't hide; here's what our warriors say:
"Paybacks are hell, punk, go ahead, make my day."

133

I hear your saber rattle at the unarmed in your land
Because we have respect for life you force the upper hand
You've burned one flag too many; it's no more other cheek
Paybacks are hell, coward, let's see your yellow streak

The series of terrorist acts of September 11, 2001, against the United States is one of the most tragic episodes in United States history. The impact these events have had on the American way of life is tremendous. From the terrorist perspective, the success was overwhelming. Even though they missed the White House, the cost and aftermath was magnanimous. The United States will never be the same.

Terrorism, like warfare, gears itself against the lessons learned from the last event. Every air traveler in the world knows the costs to pocketbook and freedom these acts have caused. The terrorists of the world are reveling in their glory.

The significance of the date of 9-11 is not lost on the American public. Our emergency number of 9-1-1 becomes an added insult to America. More people were killed on that date than were killed when the Japanese did the sneak attack on Pearl Harbor on December 7, 1941. That "day that will live in infamy" plunged the United States into war with Japan that lasted for more than three years. Thousands of lives were lost on both sides. The all out war lasted nearly four years.

Following 9-11, our president did what needed to be done and declared war on terrorism. He clearly stated this would be a protracted evolution that would take "as long as it takes" to put world terrorism down. The critics abound and seem to have neither tolerance nor patience to stay the course for the long run.

What's been done so far? The Taliban has been decimated and is without effect. Al Qaeda has taken its lumps and must exist in hiding. Afghanistan has new leadership and is fairly well stabilized. The problem with guerrillas is they can move around and not confine themselves to one specific country. So they move out of Afghanistan to other places like Pakistan, Iran, Syria, Jordan, Lebanon, Libya, Algeria, and a series of other countries. Those who insist on "martyrdom" suicide are appearing as insurgents in Iraq. The attitude of the true guerrilla is: "What can I mess with now?" The government tells us there are active cells in Canada and the United States. The world is infested with these vermin. World public opinion has us fighting terrorism with one arm tied behind our backs. This is my opinion, and, as I said before, you don't have to agree with me. But the vermin has to be exterminated. I do agree with "Thou shalt not kill," but the exception of "self defense" applies. If we do not kill them, they will kill us. These rats must be trapped and "terminated with extreme prejudice." The efficacy of this method is that death prevents recidivism.

If you are the typical American, who sits in an easy chair each evening to watch the news in your three-bedroom house, with your second or third spouse with your two and a half children and your two cars, two jobs, retirement programs, and your IRAs, you'd better get on your knees every Sunday morning and thank the God of your choice that there are those who will go into harm's way to protect the conditions that allow for all you hold dear in life and quit your sanctimonious complaining about perceived violations to your pseudo-moralistic semblance of a value system. Whew! Walk for once in the footsteps of our service-men and women, who get face down in the dirt with bullets zinging over their heads, who want to remove the buttons on their BDU's (Battle Dress Utilities), because the buttons keep them too far up off the ground. Be gracious enough to value and appreciate your freedom without fighting for it, but give credit where it is due. The 9-11 survivors and the families and loved ones of the deceased of that day have significantly been overcome by the events of what happened. Remember, it could have been you.

When I wrote "Paybacks Are Hell" (See Chapter 18) in 1979, terrorism was fairly well isolated, and the acts were quite random. After September 11, 2001, terrorism took on a whole new persona of significance and changed the world, as we know it, dramatically. The Twin Towers in New York, which came to be called "Ground Zero," represented free world commerce to Bin Laden and Al Qaeda and their followers. Remember, this was the second attack at the same location. Somebody is obviously a slow learner. Individuals from all walks of life represent-ing many countries and multiple labor strata plus the firemen and policemen who came to help were killed that day. Each individual victim had family, loved ones, and acquaintances who will suffer for the rest of their lives because of this event. How can the American public forget this?

Well, the media sure helped by declaring a moratorium on showing the dev-astating video footage collected on that day. The rationale was to restrict access to the images, because they incited violence. Of course they do, as they well should! Show it everyday. Americans have short memories. It's called homeostasis, all returns to "normal."

In rewriting the lyrics to this tune and retaining the same theme, I wanted to show that terrorism was a universal problem, not just an American issue. Russia has a terrorist problem. Originally, the song said "Killed Russian kids in Beslan…," but only those who follow the news or terrorism know about Beslan. I changed it to "grade school" to emphasize that young children were the victims. "In Bali, Indonesia, and Jakarta too" the victims were mostly Australians. "Car bombs and IEDs…" doesn't require much genius to create. Pack enough explo-sives and gasoline into a vehicle and devise a way to make it go "BOOM," and you have a weapon capable of killing. A lot of people are being killed by car and truck bombs, the Marine barracks in Beirut, the American Khobar Towers barracks in Dhahran, Saudi Arabia, and Oklahoma City are probably the most infamous. On 9-11 al Qaeda took it to a new level by using aircraft full of aviation gas and peo-ple. IEDs are "Improvised Explosive Devices." The possibilities are endless. These insurgents in Iraq have even gone to the extent of packing a child's rectum with

Semtex and a detonator and instructed the child to walk into a group of intended victims. (I know, "thank you for that image.") And we thought the kamikaze was bad! Of course, the U.S. Navy cannot forget the U.S.S. *Cole* in Yemen. The famous car bomb was turned into a boat bomb. And Americans should never forget the final statement of hero Todd Beamer, as the passengers on Flight 93 counterattacked the hijacking terrorists at the cost of their own lives and saved the White House. "Let's Roll!" The cruelty of man knows no limits. The only rule is there are no rules.

"You terrorize the innocent at will." What iota of logic supports the notion of combating the United States by killing and maiming innocent victims of any country including their own? I suspect it is because the U.S., as a nation, holds the value of human life precious and conducts itself (mostly) with appropriate moral turpitude. Our press has a role in this. "If it bleeds, it leads!" I doubt that will ever change. I don't blame the press. I blame the terrorists, who have no semblance of moral courage, respect, or dignity, who seek to shock the world by their cruelty and cowardly acts. Even the Japanese at Pearl Harbor in 1941 were targeting military assets, with some exceptions. The thing that would give me the most grief would be attacks on my family, killed or maimed. I can attest that losing a family member you love is absolutely devastating. My heart is deeply saddened for the families and loved ones of all victims of terrorism and the war against it, including the Muslims. It's all so senseless! How can any deity, including Allah, be pleased with that?

"Navy SEALs and Recons and Army Green Beret" is my favorite verse in the song. The biggest criticism of these lyrics is that it dates the song to the existence of the Taliban and al Qaeda. As soon as they cease to exist, this verse will not be applicable, but it expresses the history of the moment. Even with such a limitation, this verse is the heart of the rewrite. Afghanistan is a special warfare (SPECWAR) theater. The numbers of Americans involved are significantly low compared to Iraq. The Americans are actually participating in guerilla warfare. Our special forces are working with the supporters of Hamid Karzai to bring stability to the country and hunt down the remnants of the Taliban and al Qaeda. These various factions in the mid-East would be fighting each other whether the U.S. was involved or not. It has been so for centuries. Bin Laden invited the United States to participate when his cronies attacked us on 9-11. These are the consequences to his actions. It will be his ruin.

The next verse deals with the means to eradicate terrorism. The Karzai supporters were nothing short of flabbergasted to witness how laser guidance could make bombs so accurate. At least the United States was targeting the militants. Now if they would only group together out in the open, we could get this done a lot sooner and go home.

"Go ahead, make my day," the famous saying of Dirty Harry, seems appropriate in this song. It seems to bring a smile when I perform this song live and speak the words instead of singing them. Dirty Harry, Clint Eastwood's icon, is symbolic in American culture. "When the going gets rough, send for the sons-of-bitches." The rest of the time, keep them in cages and out of sight of society. This is what would happen to Dirty Harry, who was long on taking on the dirty jobs, but short on being appreciated. The same difference exists for the special warfare people, such as Navy SEALs, Marine Recons, and Army Green Berets. I'm told of an incident where a Marine Colonel was addressing a battalion of Marines with a small group of Navy SEALs present. When the Colonel talked about the SEALs, he described them as undisciplined, uncouth, sneaky, back-talking, back-stabbing, cutthroat murderers. The leading chief turned to his men and remarked, "Wow, I think they like us!" Go do your job and stay out of sight, out of mind. The solution is to beat the "bad guys" at their own game. When the "bad" vermin are eradicated, only the "good" vermin will remain.

The final verse was included verbatim from the original song, as these lyrics are universal and timeless. The expression "saber rattling" hasn't been used for quite some time. It's meaning has to do with one faction or country taking on the persona, and demonstrating the propensity for war, to strike fear in a potential adversary; to threaten, and to intimidate, the victim population or country to bow to the demands of the saber holders. It's not something to be done against the United States. The verse also identifies our weakness, "respect for life." Surprisingly, that respect for life even extends to our enemies. We are civilized people, who much prefer negotiation and the peaceful resolution of problems to combat. But when a Saddam Hussein attempts to murder an American president, and slaughters 500,000 of his own people, the latitude for negotiation is significantly limited.

Much has been said about Saddam's weapons of mass destruction (WMD). The two WMDs of greatest concern are poison gas and nuclear weaponry. Obviously, he had the poison gas. The dead Kurds in northern Iraq are pretty good evidence. And intelligence sources indicate Saddam was in the process of purchasing items that could be used to manufacture nuclear weapons. Any intelligence analyst would logically conclude this was Saddam's intent. Had Saddam been successful and obtained nuclear weaponry, there can be little doubt he would have used it. Then U.S. intelligence would have been raked over the coals for failure to act on such intelligence.

Now that our president has acted responsibly on the available intelligence, he is being raked over the coals, because massive WMDs have not yet been found or identified. In the court of public opinion, no matter what is done, it's wrong. Now it's postulated that U.S. intelligence was well aware that al Qaeda operatives were known to be taking flying lessons throughout the country. There are many legitimate reasons for taking flying lessons, including qualifying as commercial pilots. But the detractors suggest the "crystal ball" pointed directly to terrorism, and steps should have been taken to intervene to prevent the 9-11 tragedy. Hindsight is 20/20. Had anything been done, the administration would have been accused of racial profiling, violating the rights of these poor, middle-eastern men. Where is the common sense? Where is the patriotism and loyalty to our own nation? I remember the bumper stickers during the Vietnam War: "America, love it or leave it." There are no panaceas. Almost every choice and decision disenfranchises somebody.

"You've burned one flag too many; it's no more other cheek," is a statement of exasperation. We are openly insulted through a myriad of flag burnings and other actions, yet we continue to turn the other cheek and take it, and take it, and take it, etc. There has to be a limit. When it comes to warfare, terrorism is cowardice. That's my opinion. You don't have to agree with me.

The following is one of my tangents but perhaps the most important soapbox offerings in support of my country at this point in my life: I agree with those who state World War III began in November 1979, when Iranian "students" attacked the U.S. Embassy in Tehran and held Americans for 444 days. Anybody who believes this act occurred without the approval of the Iranian government is suffering from terminal cranial-rectal insertion. Ladies and gentlemen, this was an act of war. This was a blatant attack on U.S. sovereign soil. While I admire and respect President Carter greatly, as a submariner who "done good," a firm, effective, and immediate response was required ASAP. The Desert One debacle doesn't count, too late and too many bosses. Iran showed the Muslim world they could not only attack the United States, but they could get away with it. This set the tone for the future war against the free world in general and specifically the United States.

A listing of all terrorist incidents since 1979 has been widely disseminated. Clearly, I repeat, clearly these attacks have been executed by "Muslim male extremists mostly between the ages of 17 and 40." Yet our government, in the interest of political correctness, refuses to allow profiling in this war. We are going to "politically correct" ourselves into the grave. The politicians and fourth estate pundits, who openly and publicly criticize everything done to thwart terrorism, are sending the message to the enemy that we are divided and weak. We need unity to win this war.

One major perspective error and resulting response is the fact these acts are being treated as crimes and not as acts of war. More terminal cranial-rectal insertion! The free world in general, and the United States in particular, need to understand what the cost of this mistake continues to be.

Muslims make up one-quarter of the world's population. The religion is supposed to advocate peace. While I don't wish to criticize a religion, it is clear the Muslim religion has more than its share of fanatics. The goal of these fanatics is also clear: "Kill all infidels." Let me be clear about this: "If you ain't Muslim; you is an infidel." I can't be more emphatic or succinct. One Internet source identified the number of terrorist acts between 1981 to 2001 throughout the world as 7,581. Do you think these guys are kidding?

The terrorists dislike the freedoms, successes, and liberalism practiced and demonstrated by the free world. The liberties are "against their religion." What Muslim country allows freedom of speech, thought, expression, press, and religion? Ladies, focus on your future in a *burka*, sans lipstick and makeup. Like to have an occasional drink or go dancing? No way! That'll get you a public flogging. How about your IRAs, retirement programs, social security, personal investments, and bank accounts? How about your multiple vehicles, houses, boats, and personal collections? What about vacations, sports, affiliations, free travel, TV, computer access? How about a complete change of lifestyle? The communists referred to opulence as decadence. The Muslims find it "sinful."

The United States must take this bull by the horns and beat these terrorists down wherever they are found. Terminate with extreme prejudice. Support all the free world countries. Look at Spain and France to analyze the terrorist fallout. This is blackmail and intimidation at an international level. There are others more learned and eloquent than I who have made these arguments in a variety of media. At my age, I am tired of jousting windmills. However, I can still sing a song in support of what I firmly believe to be the right thing. It's Payback time and *Paybacks Are Hell!*

What I fear the most is the division in philosophies in our country. Congress is full of members who look for any opportunity to criticize, and oppose virtually any military action, for the sake of getting themselves in the media with the sole goal of publicity to get reelected. Some of these people don't stand for anything except themselves, through what the polls show. I guess this is how they stay in the mainstream? Well, I see the lack of support for our President for the big picture in combating terrorism as giving aid and comfort to the enemy. Remember Vietnam? That war was not lost in Vietnam, Cambodia, or Laos. It was lost in the media. Given time, the actions in Afghanistan and Iraq could go the same way. All the Muslim extremists have to do is continue to attack us, and every other free country in the world, and we will argue ourselves to death.

CHAPTER 22
THE DIVES WE'VE KNOWN

Groton has the biggest list of all the dives we've known
The submariners' hangouts where you never are alone
SUBVETS up on School Street keeps you in the zone
And Norm's Lounge down on Bridge Street, my home away from home

The Grotto and Oasis which is now the Golden Gate
DelMar's and El Rancho where you can stay out late
Dave's and Sportsmen's Cafes where you could find a date
Banana Boat, Shrimp Boat, Love Boat filled with jailbait

Rose's was the Mousetrap where we used to play
'Cross the river in New London, Lamporelli's was OK
Seven Brother's and Ernie's where the Skipjack crew did stay
And the Salty Dog is out there, that's all I'm going to say

The dives we've known in a submarine
And the dives we've known where the drinks are clean
And the dives we've known with a love machine
And the dives we've known in a submarine

Norfolk was the home base of the D & S piers
Bell's was the right place to have a couple beers
Where Dex and Stuke of Requin hoisted many cheers
And Thelma loved all SUBRON Six for many many years

The hot spot in Charleston, the Pink Pussy Cat
Where Bobby lost his glasses in a little tit for tat
Hogbody from the Carver got in a little spat
And threatened to burn down the Pink Pussy Cat

Out near Mare Island it was the Horse and Cow
Moved from San Diego; it's up in Bangor now
The H-boat, Wolf, and Parche were always there somehow
The Whinny and Moo was where we went when we crossed the brow

Well, there's no way we're ever gonna mention everybody's favorite watering hole
Like Pete's, Davy Jones' Locker, and the Dolphin Club in Honolulu
The White Hat and Starlight in Yokosuka, the Red Garter and Darby's in San Diego
The Pearl City Tavern and Monkey Bar in Pearl

The Four Aces, Hanlon's, and Western in Vallejo
The spooks hung out at the Parkway and Tack Room in Laurel, Maryland, where Bert and Betty will never be forgotten. There was the Argyle and P.J.'s in Dunoon, the Lucky Seven in San Juan and the Barrel and White Hat's clubs in Gitmo. Don't forget the Chiefs' Club in Norfolk, it was called the "Body Exchange."

Perhaps a subtitle to this book should be 25 ways to write a song. This particular creation is a rather unique approach in song writing methods. I believe it was in 2001 when George Dozier, a former U.S.S. *Pickerel* sailor from Alaska, suggested in an e-mail the title *The Dives We've Known*. That planted the seed, and a couple more correspondents, such as Ed Winner, hinted that a song needed to be written about the submarine bars of the world.

Well, I certainly had my personal list of the bars I've frequented, but I cannot even suggest that I've visited all the bars that fall into this category. And while I've visited most of the ports-of-call mentioned in this song, quite frankly, I didn't have the funds or the stamina to experience all the watering holes. On a whim, I posted a thread on Ron Martini's submarine bulletin board at www.rontini. com and asked submariners world wide to identify their favorite submarine bars. There were about 75 responses, and the song was developed from the postings and personal research. (Hic!!!)

It was to be expected that Groton and New London, Connecticut, would have the biggest list of submarine bars, being the "Submarine Capital of the World." Of course, bars change names from time to time, and during one period the crew of one submarine would chose one bar, while a later crew from the same submarine would chose a different pub. Like submarines, bars are evolutionary. They are also the rendezvous points for sailors to meet and a source of female companionship. These ladies were the bartenders and the waitresses who worked these bars, plus the patrons, such as Thelma at Bell's in Norfolk, well known to Dex Armstrong and Adrian Stuke of *Requin*. At the end of a deployment, the married guys would go home to their families, and the single guys would be welcomed back by the folks at these bars. Each venue had its own cast of characters.

Though I've never had the honor, I do recall the name "Snorkel Patty" from the days when the Horse and Cow was in San Francisco. I'll never forget Bert (lady) who was a bartender at the Parkway. Bert married Frenchie Perreault, the salty Chief mentioned in the Prologue. Then at the Tack Room there was Betty Douglas, who knew all the ACNSG sailors who hung out there. These two bars were on Route 198 in Laurel, Maryland. I do remember Sammy from the Horse and Cow in Vallejo. What a character! But my favorite barroom people were from Norm's Lounge, now Boomers, in Groton. There was Norm and Annie, the owners, and a dear friend who worked there was Cindy. In fact, Sandy worked for a while as a waitress as well as Veronica Corbett, Jim's wife.

In the few times this song has been performed in public, some of the listeners claim they've been in every one of these bars. Several have said this is the best submarine song ever. Well, I would disagree, but I know where their heart is.

In December of 1979 Gerry Rucker, Jim Corbett, and I began playing music in the Groton/New London area at a place called the "Mousetrap." We booked there for three weeks at a mercilessly low price to see if we could get our music act together. It was also the opportune time to take advantage of the free publicity that *Big Black Submarine* was generating by the air play given to the song by disc jockey Bob Edwards on WCTY radio out of Norwich. In the next year the Mousetrap owner expanded and opened a much larger bar called "Rose's Cantina," probably from Marty Robbins's song, *El Paso*. He also put in a mechanical bull, which was a real draw for the young sailors stationed in the area. This was shortly after the movie *Urban Cowboy* popularized the country-rock scene. This was exactly the type of music we were playing, new country hits, '50s rock and roll, and the unique submarine music. It was at the Mousetrap where our Caribou, Maine, buddy, Dick Anderson, brought Norm Brochu from Norm's Lounge to hear us play. I'm sure glad Norm showed up on the final night at the Mousetrap, after we got our act together, and Jim Corbett bought the electronic tuner. Norm hired us for New Year's Eve, and, after a very successful performance, he hired us for every Friday and Saturday night until April 1980.

When I first started thinking about this song and talking it over with Bobby Reed, he told me a "typical" submarine story that led to the *Pink Pussy Cat* verse in the song. Bobby served in the U.S.S. *George Washington Carver*, a ballistic missile submarine of the original *Forty-one for Freedom*. Bobby had two buddies on the boat who played guitars, while Bobby played the banjo. Bobby played guitar too, but with two other guitars, he mostly played banjo with the group. One guy was Joe Harris, an accomplished country singer from Connecticut. The other guy was Bob Devitt. The trio called themselves the "Beacon House Seekers" most of the time, but sometimes they called themselves "Bobby Joe Banjo and the Fantastic Few."

This particular night the boys headed for liberty in Charleston with their instruments. The first bar they hit was the "Slop Shoot." The boys were playing for drinks, and, as the blood-alcohol level increased, the unavoidable call of nature made its presence known to Joe Harris. He got lost on the way to the head and relieved himself in the barmaid's broom locker. Caught red handed, so to speak, one of the waitresses took after him with a broom. She was beating him mercilessly, and the group was invited to leave with great emphasis.

They went to a second watering hole, that remains unnamed, to rest from the first eviction. When the owner spotted their instruments, he invited them to get up on stage and go to work. They were quite amused to see the stage was protected by chicken wire like in the *Blues Brothers* movie or *Roadhouse*. As they approached the stage, Joe saw an electric guitar and amplifier on the stage and headed straight for it. He got it all hooked up, but when he turned it on he got repeatedly shocked until Bobby Reed had the wherewithal to pull the plug on the amp. They did a few numbers, which went over quite well, until Joe Harris decided to do the *Auctioneer*. Somehow that tune irritated the customers and they started throwing beer bottles at the stage. The boys were thankful for the chicken wire. For the second time that evening they were asked to vacate the premises.

Things had gone downhill fast when the group showed up at the "Pink Pussy Cat," where a lot of the *Carver* sailors were having a party. I guess this was quite an establishment. It was a bar, strip club, and house of some dispute or ill repute or something like that. Just about the time they arrived, one of the dancers made the announcement that because the crew was so rowdy, there would be no more show that night. This is when a sailor called "Hogbody" stepped to the microphone and announced that the *Carver* was going to sea in the morning, and, if there were to be no shows there that night, the place would be burned down before morning. The show went on. Hogbody made an impressive speech. Then he bought the entire bar a round of drinks.

Somehow, Bobby Reed got the front row, center seat right in front of the stage. As the next dancer started her act, some of the articles she was shedding were daintily placed on Bobby's head. Now in those days Bobby wore a pair of horn-rimmed glasses that were popular at the time. The first article on Bobby's head to impair his vision was a pair of panties. That didn't last long as a member of the crew grabbed them from Bobby's head and they were being passed around while the guys were playing bloodhound. The next article was a bra, then the dancer grabbed Bobby's horn-rimmed glasses and literally made them disappear. When he got them back he had to go to the restroom to try and wash the DNA off the glasses, so he could see with them. As soon as he returned to his seat, the guys grabbed his glasses again, and they followed the panties around the bar. Then for the next 80 days while on patrol, the guys would say to Bobby, "Hey, Reed, let me smell your glasses." No, I never went to Charleston.

When I started going to Mare Island to do missions in *Seawolf*, I was taken to the Horse and Cow in Vallejo. Bill Looby owned the bar; Jim Looby was a bartender. I never knew how they were related, but I think they were brothers. This was where I met many of the people with whom I would be working. This was the quintessential submarine bar. The walls, perhaps I should call them bulkheads, were covered with plaques from submarines old and new. There was enough memorabilia there to call it a submarine museum. All the submarine alarms were mounted behind the bar and were in working order. I asked for a Budweiser, and I was served an Olympia. That's when I found out the only beer they sold was Olympia. OK!

In 1978 when the *Take Her Deep* album was available only on vinyl, I'd had six separate songs from the LP album recorded on three special acetate 45 rpm records for the Horse and Cow juke box. Of course, the one played the most was "Seawolf," which mentioned the Horse and Cow. Three of the boats assigned to Mare Island were the *Halibut* (H-boat), *Seawolf* (Wolf), and *Parche*. Crews from these boats would often muster at the Horse and Cow following some function. I remember having a beer there one night with Commodore Chuck Larson, Captain Charles MacVean, and Captain Gus Hubble from the Pentagon, who we called "The Godfather." These were some pretty distinguished gentlemen who would have a drink or two with the troops at the Horse and Cow.

The story reported in the Prologue of the book *Blind Man's Bluff* about a *Seawolf* crewmember calling the White House from the Horse and Cow to let the President know that Charlie MacVean is a great commanding officer is true. Captain MacVean was truly a great leader of men.

While I only visited the Horse and Cow in Vallejo, California, the Horse and Cow actually began in San Francisco, moved to Vallejo, moved to San Diego, then moved to the vicinity of Bangor/Bremerton, Washington, where it is now located. While the H & C, also called the "Whinney and Moo," is probably the most famous submarine bar, the rest are equally loved by submariners in other parts of the world.

As stated in the final part of the song, "Well there's just no way we're gonna mention everyone's favorite watering hole." With the universe being every submarine sailor ever, this has to be a true statement. But with the help of Martini's BBS and those who responded to the post, getting a significant representation of submarine bars worldwide has been accomplished.

Lastly, I don't wish to imply the Submarine Service and the U.S. Navy is full of alcoholics, because that simply isn't true. My guess is the alcoholism rate in all the services is just slightly higher than the United States population in general. What is true for many sailors, the bar scene was a social environment where like minded folks could gather and feel at home away from home. These places were havens for sailors where, as they say at Cheers in Boston, "Everybody knows your name." Picture a sailor returning from patrol to his favorite bar and all the patrons shouting his name, "Norm." It's simply another place where sailors can share their opinions and great wisdom with shipmates.

CHAPTER 23
RUN SILENT RUN DEEP

Run Silent Run Deep
Captain Edward L. Beach
This tiger don't sleep
Run silent run deep

Ned Beach was a leader
Could mesmerize a reader
A humble man of courage, skill, and pride
He loved the Silent Service
Profession with a purpose
On December 1 oh 2 this hero died

He launched the nuke sub Nautilus
Set standards for all of us
And took the mighty Triton 'round the world
Fought the Battle of Midway
Navy Cross from Tirante
Made a dozen war patrols out of Pearl

He was naval aide for Ike
A job he really liked
For a man for whom he had so much respect
Steel boats and iron men

Long to take her deep again
Their mission to defend and to protect
In the footsteps of his father
He did become an author
And wrote about beloved submarines
Beach Hall is their honor
Two gentlemen of valor
They did their part to keep our country free

Captain Edward L. Beach, nicknamed Ned, was truly a legend in his own time. He had a brilliant and distinguished naval career. He graduated from the U.S. Naval Academy in Annapolis in 1939 second in his class. He was first in his class in Submarine School in 1941. He was a true World War II submarine warrior and hero. He conducted and survived twelve submarine war patrols in the Pacific, participating in some of the most intense actions in submarine history.

It was my honor to meet Captain Beach at the 38th Anniversary of the United States Submarine Veterans, Inc., in New London, Connecticut, in May of 2001. Captain Beach was the keynote speaker for that event.

At the *Lapon* reunion held at Virginia Beach in 2000, I met Captain Bing Gillette, USN (Ret). Captain Gillette had been the Executive Officer in the U.S.S. *Lapon* diesel boat in World War II. When Captain Gillette returned to his home in Washington, DC, with his courtesy copy of *Take Her Deep*, he played the collection for Captain Beach. The Captain then wrote me a letter asking how he could get a copy. I sent a courtesy copy to him with an autograph stating how much I admired him. I have a wonderful "thank you" letter from Captain Beach.

So when Captain Beach entered the banquet room of the Port and Starboard, I left my table to go meet him. I introduced myself as the fellow who had sent him the album of submarine music. I could see he wasn't recalling who I was or what I was saying, but we shook hands, and I returned to our table. I'd read four of Captain Beach's books, and he was nothing short of a hero for me.

I was totally captivated by Ned Beach's speech to the U.S. Submarine Veterans. It was clear he was in his element. He loved speaking to submariners. He was at home at the podium and in charge. Most of the material expressed in this song came from his own words on that day.

It was Captain Beach's death on December 1, 2002, that was the impetus for me to write the song. Like most submariners, I felt a personal loss at the death of Ned Beach. It was something like when John Wayne died. In this instance, the experience was very much like the night I wrote *Paybacks Are Hell* (See Chapter 18). I was touched by the death of Captain Beach. I wanted to honor him with a song.

Captain Beach's most famous book is, of course, *Run Silent, Run Deep*. He spoke about that book in his address to the SUBVETS. He suspected the movie people wanted the title when they bought the book rights, as the movie obviously didn't follow what he had written in the book. But the movie brought him a great deal of publicity and fame. He did a great service to the Navy and the Submarine Service with this book, as many of us readers were influenced to become submariners. When I sat down to write the song, its title could be none other than *Run Silent, Run Deep.*

In his speech Captain Beach told of his days as the White House Naval Aide for President Dwight D. Eisenhower. In fact, this was when he wrote *Run Silent, Run Deep.* Captain Beach deeply respected President Eisenhower as a great general and president. In Beach's capacity as Naval Aide, he accompanied Mamie Eisenhower to Electric Boat in Groton, Connecticut, to the launching of the U.S.S. *Nautilus,* the first nuclear submarine, on January 21, 1954. Captain Beach had explained to Mrs. Eisenhower that it was considered bad luck to fail to break the champagne bottle at the launching. He had also set up the sequence of events for the launching. There was an indicator installed below the staging where Captain Beach and Mrs. Eisenhower stood for the workers to know when to release the mechanism that held *Nautilus* on the ways until the proper moment. However, the indicator malfunctioned, and did not indicate properly. After Mrs. Eisenhower had smashed the champagne bottle, Captain Beach was trying, in a dignified manner, to get these workers to release the *Nautilus* for it to slide down the ways into the Thames River. However, the workers weren't really paying attention. The video shows Captain Beach literally pushing on a 4,092-ton submarine to commence the launch. Well, the workers were only about 30 seconds late, but it was the longest 30 seconds in Captain Beach's life.

Captain Beach also told us how "he personally won the war." He had made eleven war patrols in *Trigger* and *Tirante.* His twelfth war patrol was as commanding officer of his own submarine, *Piper.* While enroute to his patrol area, World War II ended. The Captain suggested the Japanese heard Beach was heading for Japan with his own submarine, and they decided they'd better surrender. Captain Beach was very proud that *Piper* rescued six Japanese sailors in the Sea of Japan, and his final act in the war was to save life, not take it.

A highlight in Captain Beach's career, following a distinguished war record, was the circumnavigation of the globe by the U.S.S. *Triton* under his command. This was a 41,000 mile voyage, completed in 84 days, submerged, in 1960 (the year I graduated from high school). In his speech, Captain Beach did not take personal credit for that. He stated this was an accomplishment of his submarine and crew. Captain Beach was among the small percentage of World War II era diesel boat officers who fleeted into nuclear submarines. The man was technically brilliant.

A rumor I heard in the boats was that Captain Beach wanted to remove all batteries from a nuclear submarine and roll it over completely to prove it could be done. I don't know if this is true, but the conversation centered around the daring of Captain Beach. He was such a warrior in World War II that his commanding officers in *Trigger* and *Tirante* had to hold him back as he continually suggested aggressive engagements. While serving in *Tirante*, the gallant performance of his boat in sinking a Japanese ammunition ship and two pursuing frigates during a surface attack on Quelpart Harbor was so significant that the commanding officer was awarded the Medal of Honor, and Captain Beach received the Navy Cross as the Executive Officer.

The rest of the song came from sources written about Captain Beach. The most influential person in Captain Beach's life was his father, who also retired as an O-6 Captain. They both had the same name, with his father being "Senior" and Ned Beach was "Junior." Both wrote thirteen books. The U.S. Naval Institute Building in Annapolis, Maryland, was named "Beach Hall" in honor of Captains Edward L. Beach, Senior and Junior.

The U.S. Submarine Service is what is today because of Captain Edward L. Beach and men like him.

CHAPTER 24
NAVY SEALS

We picked our teams from UDT back in '62
Aggressive men of confidence, the able and the few
Earned our stripes in Vietnam; teamwork was the key
Sea, air, land – a tight knit band – trust and unity

Hooyah! We're Navy SEALs
Hooyah! Fire in the hole
Hooyah! We'll never quit
Hooyah! We're good to go

Granada and Afghanistan and Panama's "Just Cause"
HALO jumps and SCUBA swims were missions for the frogs
Somalia, East Africa, Iraq, and Pakistan
Shoot and loot and sneak and peek and combat hand-to-hand

Naval Special Warfare Groups, SPECOPS, CQB
Locking out of submarines; go in by SDV
Terminating terrorists; we're nothing but the best
Standing tall in our dress blues with Tridents on our chest

This particular song needs to start with a glossary done in the order of the appearance in the song:

UDT   Underwater Demolition Team

SEAL   SEa Air Land
HALO   High Altitude Low Opening
SCUBA   Self Contained Underwater Breathing Apparatus
SPECOPS   SPECial OPerationS
CQB   Close Quarter Battle
SDV   Swimmer Delivery Vehicle

Prior to 1962 the Navy SEALs were known as UDT, Underwater Demolition Teams. Their primary missions were reconnaissance of beaches where amphibious landings were considered, blowing up obstacles that could impede such a landing, and measuring depths of the approaches to amphibious landing beaches. Of course, the UDT did basic diving jobs for the Navy plus other assignments as necessary including EOD, Explosive Ordnance Disposal. As time went on the UDT teams found themselves being assigned to missions generally assigned to special forces. Through evolution, it became apparent these UDT personnel needed special training for special operations. President John F. Kennedy, best known in the SPECWAR (Special Warfare) community for creating the Army Green Berets, likewise, created the opportunity for the Navy to take advantage of this emphasis and funding to create a cadre of special warriors circa 1961. In 1962 the first SEAL teams deployed to Vietnam.

One of the first SEAL Team officers was a fellow named Henry J. Rhinebolt, but, at the time, he was called "Jake." Now if you ask his name, he will tell you its "Jack." He is married to a delightful and energetic lady named Jean. They are both active in their 70s, and they swim almost every day. Sandy and I visited with them for about an hour in September, 2004. Since they appreciate their privacy I will not divulge where they live. Jake has declined every effort to encourage him to write or participate in writing a book about his Navy career. Others, such as Richard Marcinko, have mentioned Jake in their books. I can only share one story provided to me by Fred Miller who served with Jake in Nam.

Fred was in the Portsmouth Naval Hospital in Portsmouth, Virginia, in half a body cast after taking a sniper round. Fred was hospitalized for a year with this wound. He was on a ward with other wounded Navy SEALs. Jake was back from Southeast Asia and stopped to visit his teammates on Thanksgiving Day. During Jake's visit on this national holiday, he learned these wounded warriors had not been provided the typical Thanksgiving meal on this hospital ward. The turkey they received was pressed sandwich turkey, and there was no dressing or any extras. Fred says Jake was literally incensed at this neglect, and he stormed off the ward to correct the issue. Within an hour the hospital staff wheeled in roasted turkey, dressing, potatoes, corn, with gravy, rolls, and pumpkin pie and ice cream with all the usual trimmings. It seems Jake went to the duty officer and made him an offer he couldn't refuse to get this done. These guys loved Lieutenant Commander Jake Rhinebolt.

For many years I knew who Jake was, and I learned from my buddy Rodney Sirois, who I will introduce below, that Jake worked following his Navy years with the Maine Forest Service as a Forest Ranger. Since moving back to Maine in 1983, I did spend a lot of time in the North Maine Woods, and I looked forward to the opportunity to meet Jake on my sporting travels. I knew a few of the rangers, and, when meeting them, I would ask about Jake. Usually I was north of Jake's area. I learned by asking a few guarded questions that Jake did not share with his coworkers any knowledge of his service as a Navy SEAL. Most of his fellow rangers knew Jake had been in the Navy, but they had no clue as to what the nature of his service had been. I honored Jake's privacy by not sharing what I knew.

I met Fred Miller through my buddy Rodney Sirois. I had mentioned to Rod that I was going out to Moline, Illinois, in 2004 for my son's wedding, and I needed to find a place to shoot. Jim, my son, had bought a Beretta 9 MM, and he wanted my opinion on the piece. So I brought my Beretta with me, and, thanks to Rodney, Fred Miller provided us a place to shoot. Rodney and Fred Miller had trained together in the Caribbean back in their early UDT days in the early 1960s. Fred has his gunsmith shop in Moline, and, because of my friendship with Rodney, he invited my son and me to shoot at his indoor range. We spent an afternoon with Fred and came away knowing we had just met one of the world's finest gentlemen and an outstanding gunsmith. This is the most complete gunshop I've visited, with the exception of the Colt Firearms factory near Hartford, Connecticut. Fred serves as a full time consultant to Springfield Armory in nearby Geneseo, Illinois. Without divulging what programs Fred was involved with in Vietnam, suffice it to say he was a very active combatant. This man is one of the most educated and brilliant individuals I have had the honor to meet. He has earned a Master's in Business Administration. When Fred has something to say, I learned to listen, as his statements are well thought out and researched. Fred hunted black bear with us at Rodney's Northern Hideaway in September 2004 and 2005.

Rodney Sirois and I grew up together. His father and my father were buddies as youngsters. Both Dads were accomplished woodsmen and taught much to their sons. Rodney's birthday is October 8 and mine is October 9, one year earlier than Rod's. For the last eight years we have celebrated these birthdays together. I graduated high school in 1960, and Rod graduated in 1961. In high school in 1958 we became real good friends, when we were both members of the Caribou Bowmen, an archery club that met and shot at the local USO. We had a competition for Bowman of the Month, which I won on a regular basis until Rodney joined and started competing. Rod was an outstanding bow shot. We hunted both deer and dear together in high school.

When I decided to enlist in the Navy, I recall telling Rod of my interest in the Underwater Demolition Teams. I made it sound as interesting as possible, and I must have made an impression on him. He ended up in UDT, and I became a spook. To be accepted for UDT training, Rodney had to commit to five years of service instead of the standard four-year enlistment. While we were in the same Navy, we never came into contact with each other until Rodney left the Navy and became a Maine Game Warden. In fact, my Dad saw Rod more than I did in those years.

We hooked up again in the very early '70s, when Rod offered for us to visit him during deer season. Rod's first posting as a Warden was in Saint Pamphile on the northeast border of Maine with Quebec, Canada. My Dad, Gary Johnston, the Superintendent of Schools in Caribou, and I went up for a few days of hunting. The night before the season opened, Rod went out on patrol and invited me to accompany him. Besides driving all over the place without lights, we drove to the west side of the Saint John River, parked the truck, and hiked in about a quarter mile to the river's edge. He knew of a guiding outfit that would be camped across the river that had a reputation for bending the rules. It being the night before the season opened, it was likely they might try to take an early deer during the night.

We went in carefully, minimizing use of the flashlight and sneaking to the tree line on the river shore. Rod had a pair of binoculars that came from a German U-Boat, which were exceptional for use in the dark. I spoke not a word until Rod spoke. It was his operation, and I didn't want to compromise him in any way. Besides, he was the cop with the badge and the gun. It was a very cool evening with a temperature around 30 degrees Fahrenheit. When Rod spoke, he pointed to the sky where he could see lights. He said, "See those guys are shining their jacklights."

I looked at the lights to which he referred and answered, "Those are the Northern Lights." They were beautiful. I still don't know if he really thought those were jacklights or if he was playing a joke on me.

While we lay there in the dark scouting the opposite side of the river, I whispered to Rod, "If there's somebody over on the other side doing something you don't like, what are you going to do about it?"

Rod answered, "I'm going over after them."

I let that sink in for a moment or two, then I said, "You know what? You're going alone." That river was just about 100 yards wide, 35° water with a heavy current. But Rod had a wet suit with him and one of those waterproof bags to carry his pistol.

He told me a story of a report he received about gunshots in one particular area on the Saint John River. This was during the summertime, and the usual hunting season had not started. So Rod got up at oh-dark thirty, put on his cammies, and moved in on the area where he believed the shooters would be camped. He moved in at daybreak as the men in the camp began to stir. Rod also noticed these guys were also dressed in cammies and had what looked like automatic weapons. He remembers thinking these "poachers" are getting pretty sophisticated. Rod literally snuck right into their camp. Then at an appropriate moment, he stood up and introduced himself. He learned these guys were an Army Green Beret "A" Team conducting survival training. Yes, they had used weapons, but they had not been, and were not, hunting. They were appropriately embarrassed that Rod had broken their security, but they felt a little better about it when Rod let them know he was a Navy SEAL. Rod asked where they were going to be that evening, and he hiked in to meet them again with two cases of beer on ice in a cooler on his back. Rod just wanted to show them the Navy had its priorities straight.

Now I'm not sure if the next joke pulled on me was Rod's or his wife Judy's. Judy is an exceptionally attractive young lady who also has a great sense of humor. Well, we were all young then. Judy's Dad was a Brigadier General, and her twin sister had been married to a *Scorpion* sailor who lost his life when the boat was lost in May of 1968. The morning we were to drive back to Caribou from our hunting trip, I put on a clean pair of cammie trousers. I checked the cargo pockets and found a pair of lacy black panties. I knew what this was about. So before leaving, I found a short piece of rope and tied these panties to the front grille of Rod's State truck. When we got home I was bragging to everybody how I had turned the joke around on Rod. It's a good thing I did that, as Sandy found a second pair of frilly dillies somewhere else in my duffle. I should have known there would be a backup.

Rod Sirois is an exceptional individual. The Maine Warden Service would send their new guys to Saint Pamphile for a year. If they could hack it, they would be transferred to a more pleasant area. Rod took the toughest district in the State and made a home of it. Rod was the State's only law enforcement in 700 square miles. He operated alone. There was rarely anyone he could call for any backup. He was totally independent. True to his Navy SEAL ways, he kept himself in top physical condition. He earned a black belt in karate. So did Judy and their two sons, Clem and Guy. In fact, Rod and Judy taught karate for a number of years. He had an Associates Degree, which he obtained on the G.I. Bill after he left the Navy, and he burned the rest of his G.I. Bill on flying lessons and had his pilot's license. Of course, he was on the State Dive Team. He frequently taught defense and combat techniques at the Maine Police Academy. If he had one more ounce of self-confidence, he would have been arrogant (where have I heard that before?).

In one of his experiences Rod had to swim out to rescue a man and his son in the cold, spring waters of Two-Mile Pond in his district. While on patrol in the month of May, Rod came across vehicle tracks that headed toward the Two-Mile Pond. On a whim he decided to check out the fishermen. He drove in on the road as far as he could with the State truck, took his day pack, which contained survival equipment, and started walking the mile and a half to the pond. As he got closer he could hear what sounded like people hollering. He picked up the pace to make it to the pond as quickly as possible. When he arrived he saw an older man and a younger guy clinging to an overturned aluminum canoe. The water was so cold there were still areas of pack ice in the pond. The young guy had on a child's life jacket. Rod gave the young man direction to immediately swim toward him. The young fellow didn't want to leave the older man, who turned out to be the father. Rod repeated his instruction, telling them if they did what he told them, he would get them out of this mess. The young man did as he was told, but Rod had to strip down to his skivvies and entered the water to help. When the boy was ashore, Rod took the life jacket and swam out to the older gent. He got the life jacket on him, but it was really too small for the man. Rod did manage to get the man ashore with a considerable amount of difficulty. He told them they had to get out of there "right now" to survive. Rod had some dry clothes in his pack, which he gave to the victims. He had to literally push them to walk out to the vehicles, as he knew he couldn't carry them.

Rod didn't say anything about the incident except to a fellow warden, who passed the rescue details on to the District Supervisor. The supervisor interviewed the victims who told the whole story. The father told the Warden Supervisor that he was a devout Catholic who prayed to God for someone to come and help. As he finished his prayer, he was startled to see Rod standing on the shore shouting instructions to them. The Governor of the State of Maine honored Rodney with the Warden Meritorious Service Award. This rescue turned things around for Rod in that he began experiencing a heart arrhythmia after the event. He is still experiencing problems with his heart to this day.

Rod has a number of stories and unique experiences that went with his job. When I asked him about doing a book, he told me he'd already thought about it, and a cousin, a former submariner who is a published author, will be doing that in the future.

A thumbnail sketch of his guiding career follows: While a warden, Rod bought up what private property he could in the area and built camps. His goal was to establish a guiding business after retirement. His business is Northern Hideaway, and I've been fortunate to work for him for two seasons guiding bear hunters. Rod also joined the Naval Reserve and served as much active duty as he could, including a stint at the U.S. Embassy in Bulgaria. He obtained a private pilot license, and he was the first naval officer to attended the FBI Academy. He participated in the RED CELL Project with SEAL Team Six as a law enforcement resource. He retired from the Naval Reserve as a CWO-4 (SEAL).

With a couple exceptions, the rest of the SEALs I have met were at Rod's Northern Hideaway. Roy Maddocks and Dave Bixler (from Chapter 18) are two very capable individuals. I had the opportunity to meet with these guys on three different hunting trips. The year we first met, they were both E-8. The next time Dave had made Master Chief, and Roy was still E-8. The last time we met, Roy had made E-9. As much as us old fellers would have loved to hear of their experiences, they simply wouldn't talk about any of their ops. I asked Dave what his highest medal was, and he told me he had a Bronze Star. So that tells me he has had some "trigger time," as we say. Both SEALs had bird dogs that were champions. They loved hunting waterfowl and partridge (ruffed grouse). Rod told me he believed Roy had been deployed to Afghanistan. At our second meeting, Dave Bixler gave me a SEAL Team Two challenge coin. I considered this a real honor. So on the occasion of our last meeting, I returned the favor to Dave with a different challenge coin. (Nah, you gotta guess!)

Another SEAL I met at Rod's was Alan Archie. Rod knew Fred Miller was coming to hunt black bear in September 2004, and he knew Alan and Fred were good buddies, so he invited Alan to join them as a surprise to Fred. Alan's son brought him to Saint Pamphile. Alan was not in great shape, as he had cancer.

There were two other SEALs that I got to work with in *Seawolf.* The first guy was a tall, redheaded gent named John Hunt. John was married to this lady, and I use the term loosely, who shot John several times in the back with a .38. John was fed up with her antics and decided to leave, announcing he would be filing for divorce. As he was on his way out the door, she got his .38 and emptied the six rounds at his back. Unfortunately, one of the bullets hit his spine, and he has been a paraplegic ever since. That was back in 1977. Somebody from the community told me John is still working using his wheelchair. These guys never quit.

Another SEAL, that I got to know a little better, as we were both Senior Chiefs on *Seawolf* and lived in the Goat Locker, was a legend named Tom Holmes. Tom was a Hospital Corpsman who had served in Vietnam. His nickname is "Bác Si," which is Vietnamese for doctor. Later, after I retired, I read a lot of books about Vietnam operations. One of the books I read was about the team where Tom Holmes was assigned. He, too, was one heck of a warrior.

It was the adoption of my song *Paybacks Are Hell* by Roy Maddocks that led to a conversation that the Navy SEALs do not have a song of their own. Roy wanted the *Paybacks Are Hell* song on CD to play for his troops in Little Creek, SEAL Team Two. That conversation planted the seed for writing a song about Navy SEALs. I had a lot of conversations with Rodney, and he was a great help. The TV stuff about "Hooyah" wasn't used in the '60s. The Little Creek SEALs didn't use the term. The Coronado SEALs created the cheer, and it's been adopted and used for quite some time now.

If I thought introducing my music to submariners was difficult, introducing this song to Navy SEALs has been next to impossible. I haven't been able to get any interest in the song at the SEAL Museum near Panama City, Florida. The SOCOM Store out in Encinitas, California, has taken a dozen CD's to sell there. Sales are terrible in the last six months.

Every citizen in these great United States needs to understand just how fortunate we are that there are unique individuals who are willing to go into harm's way for the benefit of all of us. As stated in Chapter 22, most of us do not understand the critical seriousness of the terrorist threat to our way of life. We don't have to be a genius to have some concept of what life is like in the Mid-East.

When the hostages were taken in Iran, when Saddam gassed the Kurds, when the Taliban was summarily executing people in Afghanistan, we considered that "foreign" news that didn't affect us. Bad attitude! If not for the bravery, dedication, and effectiveness of these special warriors of all services, perhaps these tragedies will manifest themselves in our own hemisphere just as it did on September 11, 2001. Thank God for Navy SEALs.

CHAPTER 25
TANGO CHARLIE

There's a story about a friend of mine
Who made a patrol with us one time
We can't mention his name hardly
We'll just call him Tango Charlie
And nobody cared to ask him why
It's rumored he was a master spy

Now the Captain didn't brief the crew
'Till we were out at sea a day or two
He didn't tell us too much then
He just handed us a pen
And made us sign on the dotted line
So we wouldn't talk about old "Master Mind."

Now tell me if you have ever seen
A secret kept in a submarine
If you use the bathroom
The whole boat feels the vacuum
But if we've learned his secret we won't tell
We're such patriotic personnel

Now Tango Charlie was a friend of mine
Who made a patrol with us one time

We don't know where he went
And we haven't seen him since
We're hoping he won't be coming back
Another two-month cruise I just can't hack

"Tango Charlie" was my operator sign. It was no big secret. Operators identify themselves in official logs, and on tapes, with what is termed the "opsign." I always thought the purpose of the "opsign" was probably so the bureaucracy would know who to holler at if things went wrong, or didn't conform to operational or technical instructions. Well, they would also know who was responsible when things were done right, but I never ever heard of any compliments for any of our people for a job well done. Anyway, sometimes we would call each other by these phonetic alphabet names on telephones or radios. Of course, "Tango Charlie" stood for Tommy Cox. I also joked that it stood for "Task Completed."

This is a tongue-in-cheek song that points out a couple of things that are very obvious to submariners. The reference to "master spy" is a spin-off from the "spook" label, not any actual reality. The security briefing that occurs on every trip is mentioned. And the fact that everybody in the same boat on a submarine usually has a pretty good idea what is going on, where we are operating, and what the spooks are doing. If anybody hung out in Control while reports were communicated from the spooks to the OOD or our OIC, it was pretty obvious what was being done. But I'm not going to confirm or deny anything here. I suspect as time went by, the knowledge acquired by submariners by osmosis helped to establish a mutual respect between spooks and submariners. The Captains of naval vessels are also free to grant access to personnel who have a need to know under certain conditions. These realities drive the security weenies nuts. But submariners are used to security, and they know when to keep quiet. This is one of the reasons we are known as the Silent Service. I don't think there is a more patriotic organization.

The song was written as a spoof. Tower Productions thought enough of it to use it as the closing soundtrack for the History Channel *Blind Man's Bluff* Special. It's on the VHS tape and the DVD as the end credits are rolling, but you rarely hear it during the broadcasts.

As mentioned previously, much of the basic security standards changed over the years. In 1967, when I first started on the boats, crew members were cautioned to have absolutely nothing to do with us after the mission was over. I didn't realize this, and after my first trip in *Barbel*, I'd invited a few guys in the crew to my quarters in Yokohama, bought beer, hamburgers, and hot dogs, and offered a place to crash. The date and time had been set. Nobody showed. I saw a couple of the guys at the Enlisted Men's Club (Seaside Club) a day or so later, and they informed me of their direction to stay away from us for security reasons. I guess it would have been nice if these rules had been shared with our people, so we could follow them too. The song was written with this experience in mind.

After the first *Parche* run in special projects in 1978, a similar experience occurred. I had a singing job in Maryland near one of the sonar experimental facilities on Chesapeake Bay. There were several divers, including Dave LeJeune, back east for some training or post mortem, who accompanied me to the singing venue. Well, I was sure surprised to see some of the Sonar Technicians who had been on *Parche* at the bar at this club. It was good seeing these guys, but the security tension was ever present. It was just one of the realities of the job.

One of the divers was Gary Gorzoch who happened to be a really good singer along the style of Tom Jones. He was practicing with me at my quarters at the NSGA Maryland base before the gig, so we could do well with his songs at the club. During this practice session, Dave LeJeune tried a song or two. I made the tongue-in-cheek comment that he should stick to diving. Well, I suspect today that he would really have liked to have developed his own singing voice, as he has never let me live the remark down. Within the next few years Gary was promoted to a Limited Duty Officer. These divers are not only incredibly courageous, they are incredibly bright.

I would actually identify myself on occasion as "Tango Charlie." Sometimes ticklish subjects needed to be referenced on unclear telephone lines for the sake of expediency, using a double talk that would confuse anybody. In these instances I would identify myself as "Tango Charlie." LCDR Pira, to this day, calls me "Tango." This was fine until the new war on terrorism where the terrorists are now referred to as "Tangos." Do you suppose that could also stand for targets? As an aside, Pete Pira went to work for the California Department of Justice, and, on occasion, ran into the Russian mafia problem. On several occasions, remembering our service together in the Navy, he would send me Russian stuff that I would translate for him. It was quite interesting. Our faxes came to and from Tango Charlie. I hope we did some good. Remember my second career was in an area of law enforcement.

If you have read this far, by now I pray we have become friends. Thank you for the honor of spending your time with me to learn of this music. I hope you enjoyed the book, and I hope you enjoy the music with a new understanding and appreciation. I also thank the God of my choice and understanding that I am here to share this with you. This is operator Tango Charlie signing off after a lifetime of dedicated service to my country and to my State. Task Completed!

EPILOGUE

As an individual reaching the sunset years, I ask myself the following questions: Was it worth it? Did I matter? Did I make a difference? Have I been significant? Did I have a purpose on earth? Did I fulfill that purpose? Is my usefulness over?

Essentially, I have had three careers: Navy Submarine Spook, State of Maine Child Support Enforcement Supervisor, and musician/songwriter/vocalist. Sure, I did a few years in that defense industry company in Connecticut, and I worked four months for a General Motors dealership in Caribou, Maine. I even drove a taxi for two weeks, but the three careers were solid.

Navy

I was seventeen years old when I joined the Navy and 38 when I retired from active duty. I believed being in my late thirties made me an old man at the time. Well, I was older than a lot of the officers with whom I served and older than most of the white hats (E-3 through E-6) with whom I worked. Submarining is definitely a young man's profession. The older I got, the more I worried about lackadaisical attitudes in some of the boat sailors. This was something that was not consistent with submarine duty in my vision. I'm not sure if what I was witnessing represented a trend, or was I simply overly concerned. Perhaps it's more like an old warrior going on his last mission. Would I really survive it all?

An integral part of my duties as a spook aboard submarines was to be very knowledgeable about the inventory of potential military capability in our areas of operation. This includes warships, including submarines, and aircraft, which included their capabilities, weaponry, etc. We rarely concerned ourselves with assets normally associated with the Army, such as artillery and tanks. Naturally, we concentrated on units with an ASW (Antisubmarine Warfare) capability. I needed to know where these units were located and their response times and on-station times relative to our position. And I needed to have a good understanding of the tactics that would, or could, be employed against us in the event we were detected. I knew from the material I reviewed that, if detected, a potential adversary could attempt to destroy our submarine. It was as simple as that. This knowledge made me fully aware of how it could be done. The submarines of the world could have started to disappear during the Cold War. As long as the target submarine was kept deep, below periscope depth, that unit could not transmit any dire emergency, or report hostilities, by any radio circuits. Let's face it, these operations were very dangerous. If nobody else acknowledged it, at least some members of our spook teams were quite aware these could have been suicide missions. The kind of courage required to continue to do these missions was commensurate with the reality of this knowledge. Many of us sought the thrill of the danger. A term arose in the last several years that applied to many of us—"adrenaline junkie." Some of us had a dedication so deep that our devotion to duty could be described as fanaticism. And if nothing happened during one of these missions to get the sweat pumps going, then the boat wasn't aggressive enough and earned the reputation as a "Yellow Submarine" or a "Charlie Tuna" (as in Chicken of the Sea). But danger did not lurk only within the forces of a potential adversary. There was the tremendous power of the sea that will seek and find any weakness of all who go there. Any weakness or flaw in the construction of our submarine or interior components could result in our destruction. Weather was always a significant consideration. Simple accidents, without hostility, within our own submarine, or in mutual interference with other submarines or surface ships, could cause a fatal incident. Our intrepid submariners knew these risks and accepted the challenge.

Of course, the primary potential adversary during the Cold War was the Soviet Union, and it was a capable and worthy opponent. When the Soviet Union collapsed, our government and the media declared the end of the Cold War. The battle cry was: "The Cold War is over and we won." Well, the only thing that was won is called the peace dividend, and that is tenuous at best. It is very naïve to think the deeply set attitudes of Russians and Americans, which were developed during the Cold War, have disappeared mysteriously now that the fourth estate has declared the war over and the United States the winner. Thanks to prevailing wisdom on both sides, the Cold War never went hot. Now that the USSR is back to being Russia, the relations between our countries are much more cordial, and we have a common enemy—terrorism.

If the United States won anything, it was the arms race. The Soviet Union was spending a much greater percentage of its gross national product on military related expenses than the U.S. It eventually took a devastating toll on the Soviet economy. We didn't outfight, outsmart, or outgun them. It wasn't superior leadership or tactics. We certainly didn't outnumber them. The full credit for reaching the status quo goes to American industry. We simply out-manufactured them. The United States won the technology war.

I do know this: If we didn't do the things we did, we would not have forced the opposition to keep up with us. Weakness invites conquest. This is an historical fact! We couldn't be weak. I firmly believed both sides enjoyed the serendipity of the training we obtained through the constant challenge of each other's presence. No, we didn't win all the time. In fact, the motto on the insignia patch for the Fleet Support Division out of NSGA Maryland was: "*TU MODO URSOM EDIS—TE MODO URSUS EDIT.*" "Sometimes you eat the bear—sometimes the bear eats you." My personal view was we couldn't constantly tweak the bear without getting bit sooner or later. But the American fast-attack submarine presence, and the constant deployment of the American fleet-ballistic missile submarines in their deterrent role, contributed greatly to the results obtained by the United States throughout the Cold War. With all that was at stake, the investment in American submarines paid great dividends. So, YES, it was worth it to the United States.

Was it worth it to me? What about the deprivation to my family of my presence for what was an aggregate of the four years I spent under water? I was a part-time husband and a part-time dad. Last winter, I went to watch young children play basketball at Caribou Middle School with my wife. We watched three games that day, and between games some kids took the floor in the gym, and they were doing impromptu dancing and having a great time laughing and responding to the encouragement of the audience. Tears welled up in my eyes as it occurred to me what a great country we live in, with our freedoms and liberties. I thought to myself, "This is what it was all about. This makes it all worthwhile." I would have given my life to preserve this freedom.

Child Support Enforcement

My second career was not so spectacular, but it had its moments. You can't be taking money from people, even for such a noble cause as child support, without creating a lot of animosity. To those from whom we were taking money, we took too much. To those to whom we were sending the money, we were never taking enough. This is another of those government jobs that, like submarining, is not for everybody. I worked as an agent for a year and a half, and then I was promoted to district supervisor in Maine's most northern Aroostook County. We had the largest area in the State, with the smallest number of cases and staff. When I started this job on May 3, 1983, we collected $600,000 a year in child support in this district. When I retired on May 1, 2003, we collected five million dollars annually in Aroostook County. In those twenty years we went from a staff of three enforcement agents and one clerk to a staff of one supervisor, five enforcement agents, a fraud investigator, two technical assistants, and two clerks. In 1983 we had no attorneys from the Office of the Attorney General in Aroostook. When I retired we had two Assistant Attorneys General plus an administrative staff operating in this County. Of course, I did not accomplish this single-handedly, but it happened on my watch, under my aegis and leadership. Obviously, we did a lot of good for a lot of children.

Frequently, the child support effort required the first step of adjudicating paternity prior to establishment of a child support order. When my son Bill passed away in August of 2002, my personal tolerance for people who did not want to be parents took a nosedive. I lost my objectivity. I was old enough. I retired.

While some of these experiences may be interesting to some, this book is not about child support, so this limited summary will suffice.

Musician/songwriter/vocalist

I suppose calling myself a musician is stretching it. I know enough about music to identify written notes on music scores, but I certainly cannot sight read. Over the years I've learned a lot of chords on a guitar, all by ear. I went through a stage in my writing where chord complexity seemed to be synonymous with sophistication. And as much as I would like to be an accomplished guitar picker, and as much as I admire those who can do this, I never had the personal talent nor the ability to be a lead guitar player. But I could chord a guitar with the best of them, with enough skill to accompany myself when I sang.

I was told of a Submarine Ball in Hawaii where *Big Black Submarine* was played and the attendees all stood with hands over their hearts, some on chairs. If I'd been there, I would probably have cried like a baby in the honor of the moment.

I've been advised of too many times the song *Sailor's Prayer* was used at shipmates' funerals, including the time in 1979 when I sang the song at the funeral of Master Chief Bobby Kays in Maryland. A request to sing at the funeral for this great sailor was not something I could refuse. In my mind, I believed it would simply be another few minutes of singing a song. I wrote a new verse for the song, more appropriate for funerals. But when I rose to sing, it was the most difficult song I ever sang in my life with my heart in my throat. The whole congregation was in tears and so was I. That was the last funeral I ever sang at, with one exception. I sang *Amazing Grace* at the burial for Ella Malm, in New Sweden, Maine. My mother and Ella shared a hospital room in October 1942. Ella's daughter, Bonnie, preceded me into this world by four hours, and we are the closest of friends ever since. I loved and admired Ella deeply, and my recording of *Amazing Grace* on the Spiritual album is in her memory. She loved that song.

One of my favorite stories of this nature involved an elderly, terminally ill, submarine sailor who had the *Take Her Deep* album on record. He loved the diving klaxon on that album, from the U.S.S. *Seawolf* (SSN-575). He loved to turn the volume on his record player as loud as he dared and let the sound of that klaxon blare. The nurses on the ward were sick of it, but it raised the spirits of this old submariner. Of course, it was the klaxon he liked the most, not my vocal quality. Robert "Dex" Armstrong, whose friend has since passed away, related this story to me. Here is Dex's Internet post untouched:

"Posted by DEX Armstrong (159.142.xxx.xx) on December 04, 2002 at 06:25:04:

You can make out the words in your songs... Your lyrics make sense... They contain sentiments incomprehensible to the majority of semi-literates comprising the Music Buying Public of today. There is nothing in ANY of your songs about hating Law Enforcement Officers...abusing women or setting small animals on fire. Your music is easy on the ear and doesn't lend itself to the over amplified eardrum-buster systems found in many cars today. The folks responsible for these wonderful recordings were remarkable selfless career dues payers.... None of the above will get you a Grammy or a headline in ROLLING STONE...but what it will get you...is what it has already gotten you both.... The sincere thanks of every sonuvabitch who drew breath through a snorkel headvalve. You two old coots are Sub Force treasures. I know, I'll bet I've purchased fifty or sixty of your CDs....and actually learned about Tommy's first album from an old shipmate and friend laying flat on his back in Norfolk Naval Hospital playing Tommy's TAKE HER DEEP and driving the nursing staff completely nuts. He had an old 33 ⅓ scratchy record in a taped up album cover.... The *Diesel Boats Forever* track was so shot to hell that it sounded like Tommy recorded it in a Maytag washer during the rinse cycle. I think anyone who listened to Tommy's recordings that came in a cardboard cover should be able to call themselves PLANKOWNERS... Just joking,Warshot...don't set fire to my house and stake me out over an ant hill. Seriously, if you don't have BOTH of these albums...you are robbing yourself of a pair of productions that will keep giving... They are one of those presents that provide repeated good moments and there's not a whole lot of music that can make that claim these days. I personally think a lot of it is recorded by terrorists in Yassir Arafat's basement...it has to be. DEX"

If what Dex says is true, and submarine sailors appreciate this music specifically and military people in general, then I am satisfied with my contributions. Perhaps someday a real musician will put this music on paper for the sake of posterity. It is my intense desire this music will live on as part of the legacy of our Submarine Service and the United States military. Thank you to every submarine, every submarine sailor, every person who has served our great country in the military, and thank you for sharing the stories with me that are reflected in the music. I believe in the mission as much as I believe in the music. God bless American from sea to shining sea.

Many of us wonder who we were and who we are. I'm not sure I'm any closer to the answer at this stage of my life. I do know there were several times in my life when I reached crossroads and had to select one path or another. Sometimes it was fate, other times it was consciously selected. I think it was in high school where I first learned of the poet Robert Frost. There is a poem he wrote that always held a significance for me called *The Road Not Taken*. I added a couple verses, certainly not in the caliber of Robert Frost, which seemed to bring it home for me. I can only suggest you read Frost's poem. These two verses I wrote in the same meter as Frost's.

> The Road Not Taken has been for me
> A source of much frustration
> When I think of all that I should be
> And the many things I'd come to see
> In my over-expectation
>
> But my faith could not be shaken
> In my country, my duty, my oath
> To the double life I was awaken
> And when it came to The Road Not Taken
> I tried to take 'em both

This is a parable (remember them?):

A frog and a scorpion faced a brook, and they both wanted to cross to the other side. Of course, the frog could make it, because he was a frog and that's what frogs do. But the scorpion couldn't cross on his own. He pleaded with the frog to take him across, but the frog declined in fear of the scorpion. The scorpion pleaded further saying he couldn't kill the frog, because if he did that he would drown. The frog relented and agreed to ferry the scorpion across the brook. The scorpion crawled on the frog's back and they started across. Half way across the brook the scorpion stung the frog. With his dying breath the frog asked, "Why?" As the scorpion was drowning, he gasped, "I can't help it; I'm a scorpion." (by anonymous)

To quote the most famous sailor of all, Popeye: "I yam what I yam."

A wise man once said something to the effect that you can look at a picture, an image, or what you see before you, and see the person. But if that person is an artist, any kind of an artist, when you see the art, you see that person's soul. And if that artist is a submariner, then part of him will always be with the shipmates lost in the wars, the *Thresher* and *Scorpion*, all on Eternal Patrol.

Appendix A

In order to experience the essence of this book, it is suggested that the reader listen to the CDs that are the spirit, inspiration, and motivation behind its creation.

Tommy Cox has produced and released 3 solo CDs:

1. *Take Her Deep*
2. *In Honor of...*
3. *Spirituals*

To order any of the above CDs check his website for current pricing:

http://donmac.org/submarinesongs.htm

Or contact him at:

Tommy Cox
3 Farrell Street
Caribou, ME 04736-2105

Or E-mail him at:

tommycox@maine.rr.com

Send Check or Money Order to the above address.

Tommy has also co-produced and released another CD with Bobby Reed called

Brothers of the Dolphin

To order this CD check Bobby's website for current pricing -

http://donmac.org/bobbyreed.htm

Or contact him at:

Robert Reed
10817 Buckboard Street, N.W.
Albuquerque, NM 87114

Or E-mail Bobby at:
    BobReed_656@msn.com
Send Check or Money Order to the above address.
Related Submarine Music—a solo CD by Bobby Reed called
    Proud to Be an American Veteran
To order this CD use Bobby's contact info noted above.
SUBVETS Bases and submarine related fund raising organizations can receive quantity discounts. Contact Tommy or Bobby at the above addresses for details.
Album Song Lists:

Take Her Deep – By Tommy Cox
1. *Big Black Submarine*
2. *Scorpion*
3. *Ballad of Whitey Mack*
4. *The Sacrifice*
5. *Boomer Patrol*
6. *Gitmo Blues*
7. *Seawolf*
8. *Diesel Boats Forever*
9. *Long Separation*
10. *Freedom Patrol*
11. *Tango Charlie*
12. *Torpedo in the Water*
13. *Sailor's Prayer*

In Honor of... – By Tommy Cox
1. *Star Spangled Banner* (Instrumental by Don Ward)
2. *Slade Cutter*
3. *Frenchie*
4. *Ballad of Whitey Mack*
5. *Paybacks*
6. *The Dives We've Known*
7. *Run Silent, Run Deep*
8. *Navy SEALs*
9. *Safely Home (Billy's Song)*
10. *Blind Man's Bluff* (New Verse)
11. *Kursk*
12. *Seawolf*
13. *Diesel Boats Forever*
14. *Trilogy (Dixie/Battle Hymn/America)*

Spirituals – By Tommy Cox
1. *Peace in the Valley*
2. *Old Rugged Cross*
3. *How Great Thou Art*
4. *Amazing Grace*
5. *Just a Closer Walk with Thee*
6. *I saw the Light*
7. *He*
8. *Navy Hymn*
9. *Lord's Prayer*
10. *Crying in the Chapel*
11. *Ship from King's Harbor Shore*
12. *Sailor's Prayer* (Funeral Verse)

Brothers of the Dolphin – Tommy Cox and Bobby Reed
1. *Brothers of the Dolphin*
2. *Bring the Nautilus Home*
3. *Kursk*
4. *Lady of the Water*
5. *Blind Man's Bluff*
6. *I Can Hear Her Softly Calling*
7. *Still on Patrol*
8. *If I Could Only Change One Thing*
9. *State of Maine*
10. *Sorrow Mixed with Joy*
11. *Wishin'*
12. *Paybacks Are Hell*
13. *Someone Haunting Me*
14. *If You Didn't Get Enough While in Navy Blue*
15. *Mighty Mine Dodgers*
16. *Every Now and Then*
17. *These Eyes*

Proud to Be an American Veteran – By Bobby Reed
1. *Proud to Be an American Veteran*
2. *My First Dive*
3. *Forty-One for Freedom*
4. *Hey, COB*
5. *Five Tough Questions*
6. *We Just Call Him Gumba*
7. *Hop on the Back of my Harley*

Printed in the United States
104429LV00004B/220/A

9 781932 606164